Explorations in Stylistics

Functional Linguistics
Series Editor: Robin Fawcett, Cardiff University

This series publishes monographs that seek to understand the nature of language by exploring one or other of various cognitive models or in terms of the communicative use of language. It concentrates on studies that are in, or on the borders of, various functional theories of language.

Published
Functional Dimensions of Ape-Human Discourse
Edited by James D. Benson and William S. Greaves

System and Corpus: Exploring Connections
Edited by Geoff Thompson and Susan Hunston

Meaningful Arrangement: Exploring the Syntactic Description of Texts
Edward McDonald

Systemic Functional Perspectives of Japanese: Descriptions and Applications
Edited by Elizabeth Thomson and William Armour

Text Type and Texture
Edited by Geoff Thompson and Gail Forey

From Language to Multimodality: New Developments in the Study of Ideational Meaning
Edited by Carys Jones and Eija Ventola

An Introduction to the Grammar of Old English: A Systemic Functional Approach
Michael Cummings

Forthcoming
The Texture of Casual Conversation: A Multidimensional Interpretation
Diana Slade

A Multimodal Approach to Classroom Discourse
Kay O'Halloran

Reading Visual Narratives: Inter-image Analysis of Children's Picture Books
Clare Painter

Morphosyntactic Alternations in English: Functional and Cognitive Perspectives
Edited by Pilar Guerrero Medina

Explorations in Stylistics

Andrew Goatly

Published by
UK: 1 Chelsea Manor Studios, Flood Street, London SW3 5SR
USA: DBBC, 28 Main Street, Oakville, CT 06779
www.equinoxpub.com

First published 2008

British Library Cataloguing-in-Publication Data
A catalogue record for this book is available from the British Library.

ISBN-13   978 1 84553 908 5   (paperback)

Library of Congress Cataloging-in-Publication Data

Goatly, Andrew, 1950-
   Explorations in stylistics / Andrew Goatly.
      p. cm. -- (Functional linguistics)
   Includes bibliographical references and index.
   ISBN 978-1-84553-296-3 (hb)
   1. Language and languages--Style. 2. Style, Literary. I. Title.
   P301.G575 2008
   410--dc22

                              2007038492

Typeset by Catchline, Milton Keynes (www.catchline.com)
Printed and bound in Great Britain and the USA

Contents

List of tables

List of figures

Acknowledgements

I would like to acknowledge the help of the following in making this book possible. Joe Foley for his helpful suggestions on chapter 2, Anneliese Krämer-Dahl for her useful feedback on chapter 5, and Barry Asker for his insightful comments on chapter 7. Connor Ferris and Barnard Turner for being good enough to read aloud for me Jennings' poem 'One Flesh', chapter 5, without which my analysis would have been less objective.

Pinter Publishers for permission to use material for chapter 2 which I first published in Mohsen Ghadessy's *Thematic Developments in English Texts* (1995), pp. 164–197 in chapter 4. Mouton de Gruyter for permission to use material first published with them in the *Journal of Literary Semantics* (2005) 34: 139–163, in chapter 5. And Vivian Heberle and J. L. Maurer for permission to use material first published in *Ilha Do Desterro* (2004) 46: 115–154, in chapter 3.

The following publishers allowed me, at great expense, permissions to quote from the literary texts under consideration. Faber and Faber Ltd. and New Directions Publishing Corp. for the poem 'In a Station of the Metro' by Ezra Pound from *Personae* copyright © 1926, in chapter 1. Faber and Faber Ltd., Harcourt, Inc. and the estate of William Golding for extracts from *Pincher Martin, The Two Deaths of Christopher Martin* copyright © 1956, in chapter 2. Carcanet/David Higham Associates Ltd. and the estate of Elizabeth Jennings for the poem 'One Flesh' from *New Collected Poems* copyright © 2002, in chapter 5. Faber and Faber Ltd., Grove Atlantic Inc. and Harold Pinter for extracts from *The Birthday Party* copyright © 1968, in chapter 6. Faber and Faber Ltd. and Alfred A. Knopf a division of Random House, Inc. for extracts from *Remains of the Day* by Kazuo Ishiguro, copyright © 1989 in chapter 7.

Sadly the agent of J. K Rowling denied me permission to quote concordance lines from *Harry Potter and the Philosopher's Stone*.

Typographical conventions

Words as types are indicated by *italics*

Quotations and scare quotes are indicated by single inverted commas ' '

Meanings and propositions are indicated by double inverted commas " "

Metaphor themes/conceptual metaphors/root analogies are indicated by CAPS

1   Developments in stylistics

In this book I attempt to trace a journey – a personal journey which represents my own various and developing approaches to stylistics; and a roughly parallel theoretical journey which traces some developments in stylistics from the 1960s onwards. In this introductory chapter I sketch these theoretical developments and indicate how they are exemplified by the essays in stylistic analysis in the other chapters of the book.

A case can be made for saying that modern stylistic theory begins with Roman Jakobson. Jakobson (1960: 353) advanced a model in which an act of communication has to involve six elements: Addresser; Addressee; Context (topic and setting); Message; Contact (medium and channel); and Code (see Figure 1.1). Briefly, an addresser (for example, a speaker), who has some channel for physical sense contact (air through which sound waves can travel) linking her/him with the addressee (the hearer), and a productive medium for creating a physical sign (the articulatory apparatus of mouth, lips, tongue, vocal cords etc.), selects items from the code (the language system), and combines them into a message about a particular topic in a specific social and physical setting – the context. The addressee, who has a receptive medium (the auditory apparatus) and knowledge of the code, receives the message and decodes it.

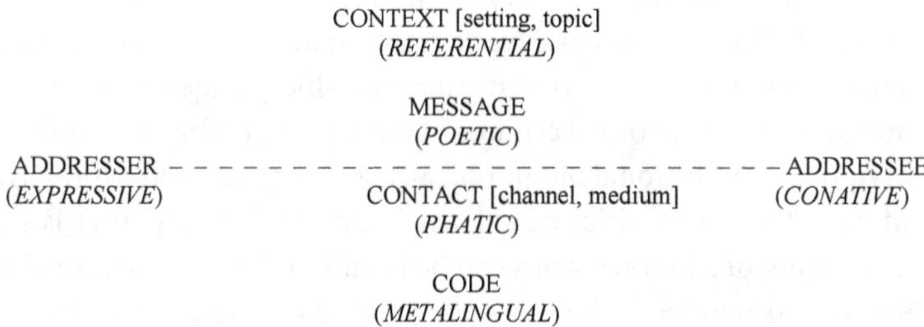

Figure 1.1. Jakobson's model of communication

Jakobson's model is powerful because it also incorporates the different functions of language (given in parentheses below in Figure 1.1). Although, according to him, all these six elements are necessary for communication, different elements receive different emphasis according to the function of the communication. Emphasis on the addresser gives us the Expressive function. Emphasis on the addressee gives us the Conative function – an attempt to affect the actions of the addressee. Emphasis on the context gives us the Referential function, where what is most important is the description of the world. Emphasis on the contact gives us the Phatic function – which is either physical or psychological. Examples would be saying '1, 2, 3, 4, testing' when checking whether a physical channel of a microphone and sound system is working, or saying apparently meaningless greetings such as 'How do you do?' or 'Hallo!' to keep open psychological contact. Emphasis on the code gives us the Metalingual function, in which language is used reflexively to talk about language. Emphasis on the message would give us the Poetic function, where the artful patterning of the text is an important issue. For Jakobson it is this extra patterning in text created by the poetic function which is the main concern of stylistics. His famous example is 'I like Ike', the slogan in General Eisenhower's election campaign (Jakobson 1960: 357).

Emphasising these respective elements according to these functions means de-emphasising others. For example, when, with expressive purpose, one says 'bloody hell', reference to context is de-emphasised, since there is no blood around, and there might not even be an addressee present. When phatically saying '1, 2, 3, 4', one is not counting anything in the context, and 'how do you do' does not even seem to be a meaningful message in keeping with the rules of the code, where 'do' is a transitive verb.

Jakobson's theories grew up out of formalism and in most respects reflected the dominant mode of literary criticism of the 1950s and 60s, known as the New Criticism. In these theories the text's message itself was emphasised at the expense of the other elements. Context was de-emphasised, by formalists at least, if not by the New Critics for whom the author's vision of the world was important. This de-emphasis was a reaction to mimetic/representational criticism, for example Marxist-realist criticism, which suggested that literature holds a mirror up to nature or is a critique of society. The addresser was de-emphasised as a riposte to traditional biographical, psychological, and expressive criticism, and what the New Critics called 'the intentional fallacy', that is the idea that the meaning of a literary work can be found in the emotions and intentions of the author prompted by his/her state of mind during a particular period of his/her life. The addressee was de-emphasised to confute the 'affective fallacy', the theory that the meaning of the text was the structure of feeling that it creates in the reader. In step with this, Jakobson regards everything but the message as being de-emphasised in poetry. For example, the addresser is probably only an 'implied' author, whose intentions are irrelevant, and the context, for instance, the world described in a novel, is not a real one, and is therefore bracketed.

Jakobson's model is problematic for a number of reasons. Firstly, some of the elements are dependent on each other. For example, according to Whorf (1956), code determines context: the languages we speak create a reality rather than just describing it. While according to Bhaktin (1981) meaning (message and code) can only be produced in the interaction of addressers and addressees. And others see code as a theoretical idealisation from message. Secondly, some discourse analysts have seen the need for more fine distinctions in the elements. For instance, addresser might be split into principal, author, and animator, and addressee into ratified listener, bystander and eavesdropper (Goffman 1981: chapter 3). Lastly, some have questioned whether all these elements are necessary or sufficient, for example, pragmaticians, highlighting inference from mental context, have even questioned the need for a code in communication (Sperber and Wilson 1995).

Problematic as some aspects of Jakobson's model are, it does provide a useful framework for discussing the course of stylistics over the past 40 years. This is because developments in linguistics – cognitive linguistics, (critical) discourse analysis and pragmatics – seem to have systematically challenged Jakobson's model, and stylistics is parasitic on these linguistic developments.

For Jakobson and the formalists the question for literary theory to address was the nature of literariness. Poetic language was supposed to be different from ordinary language, in order to 'defamiliarise' our experience of linguistic messages. This was achieved as follows: 'The poetic function projects the principle of equivalence from the axis of selection into the axis of combination' (Jakobson 1960: 370, 372). That is to say, selection on the paradigmatic axis (similarity and difference) is projected into combination on the syntagmatic axis (similarity and difference).

To make this clearer let's have a look at a concrete example of a poem and see how it might be approached using a Jakobsonian approach to stylistics. This three line poem, by Ezra Pound, is probably familiar to the reader:

In a Station of the Metro
The apparition of those faces in the crowd;
Petals on a wet, black bough.

The patterning in the text of this poem caused by the projection from the paradigmatic to syntagmatic axis is quite obvious on three levels – grammar, phonology and semantics.

Grammatically, one might look at the determiners: we begin with the indefinite 'a', proceed to the definite 'the', 'the', 'those' and 'the', and finally the zero/indefinite before 'petals' followed by the indefinite 'a'. One might also consider the pattern of adjectives. All the noun phrases are simple without adjectival premodifiers, until we reach the final noun phrase where we have the two adjectives 'wet' and 'black'. This breaking with internally-established patterns is one kind of foregrounding. Of the seven noun phrases in the poem five are complements of prepositional phrases – the only exceptions being 'apparition' and 'petals'. In the title the postmodifying prepositional phrases are recursive, with 'of the Metro' postmodifying 'Station'. There is no recursivity in the last line since there is only one prepositional phrase. In the second line whether 'in the crowd' postmodifies 'faces' recursively or postmodifies 'apparition' is ambiguous.

The grammatical structures also affect the rhythm and sound of the poem. (I mark stressed syllables /, unstressed -)

    - - / - - - / -
    In a Station of the Metro

    -   -   - / - -   -   / - -   -   /
    The apparition of those faces in the crowd;

    / - - - /   /   /
    Petals on a wet, black bough.

The last half of line 3 is clearly foregrounded, different from the patterns set up in the remainder of the text, because of its concentration of stressed syllables. One might notice more subtle sound patterns: 'crowd' and 'bough', 'station' and 'faces' and 'metro' and 'petals' not only share the same rhythmical pattern but similar sounds on the first syllable – assonance in the first two pairs, rhyme in the third. 'Pet-' also rhymes with 'wet'. 'Black' and 'bough' alliterate, which is part of a general increase in (bi-labial) plosives as the poem progresses.

Semantically, it is interesting to note that the nouns in the first line (title) refer to man-made objects, those in the second line to humans (or ghosts of humans), and those in the final line to vegetation.

Developments in stylistics since Jakobson have shifted the emphasis onto the other elements in his model. Developing from Jakobson and the Prague school we have structuralism, which puts emphasis on the code, the underlying system of oppositions, the 'grammar' of which the text is a realisation. The speaker doesn't impart meaning to utterances, but the linguistic system, the code produces it. 'Literature had been regarded as a message without a code for such a long time, that it became necessary to regard it momentarily as a code without a message' (Genette 1966: 150, quoted in Jefferson and Robey 1987). Here the text becomes not just a pattern of forms and meanings but data from which underlying patterns of rules and systems can be hypothesised. For example Vladimir Propp in the *Morphology of the Russian Folktale* (1968) uncovers the systematic rules for the interactions of characters underlying a large corpus of data. He identifies seven roles: the villain, the helper, the donor (provider of magic), sought for person/her father, the dispatcher (who sends the hero), the hero, the false hero, and 31 functions or interactions between the characters. Because the Pound poem is only one short text we cannot use it to illustrate the structuralist enterprise of discovering systems of underlying rules from a collection of texts. But Northrop Frye (1957) has identified a particular grammatical structure, apposition, as the favourite device for loosely linking images in poets, like Pound, of the imagist school. So we might regard this apposition as part of the 'grammar' of short imagist poems, a pattern which each individual text realises. Perhaps a clearer example would be the rules by which we generate poems in a particular genre. For instance, a well-formed haiku is a realisation of an underlying rule. It has 17 syllables in a pattern of: line 1 – 5 syllables; line 2 – 7 syllables; and line 3 – 5 syllables.

Structuralism claimed that the structures in texts and social practices were a reflection of the structure or structuring principles of the mind (Hawkes 1977). We can therefore see a link between structuralism and cognition. Emerging from cognitive linguistics, the theory of metaphor associated with Lakoff, Johnson, Turner, Gibbs, Steen, Kövecses, Sweetser, etc. has shown that metaphorical items in the dictionary – part of the vocabulary code of the linguistic system – occur in groups or patterns, variously known as conceptual metaphors, root analogies or metaphor themes (Goatly 1997, 2007). Lakoff and his followers claim that much, if not all, of our conceptualisation of abstract categories is dependent on this metaphorical structuring. From a stylistic point of view, they also claim that much of the 'originality' of poetic texts is actually highly dependent on this metaphorical structuring of abstract entities (Lakoff and Turner (1989), Gibbs (1994)). Though the Pound poem is imagist and therefore not abstract, we might think of the potential metaphors within it – 'faces are petals', 'the crowd in the metro is a bough' – as realisations of the underlying metaphor theme HUMAN IS PLANT. More obviously in Elizabeth Jennings' poem 'One Flesh' (see chapter 5) the rather original 'tossed up like flotsam from a former passion how cool they lie', which describes the emotional relationship between an old couple, is highly dependent on the metaphor themes EMOTION IS WEATHER (where strong passions are storms) and LOVE/PASSION IS HEAT.

Deconstruction within stylistics can be seen as focussing on undermining the code, as well as the message. Barthes emphasised the radical ambiguity or the play of signifiers. Whereas the New Critics strove to find a unity in a literary text, Barthes (1984) rejected the concept of a unified meaning or consistent purpose. Developing the notion of defamiliarisation, he suggested that the greatest literature was *scriptible* (writable) but less than *lisible* (readable). The value of the *scriptible* was that it undermined the stability of the code. 'Code' items in the *scriptible* text are echoic, intertextual, fragments of voices from other texts, from other codes. Derrida also developed, and challenged two formalist ideas: with his notion of *différance* (difference/deferring) he conflated the distinction between the paradigmatic and the syntagmatic, as distinguished by Jakobson, and also between diachrony (the change of language code through time) and synchrony (the state of the language code at any one point in time). Meanings, dependent as they are on difference, are deferred and never complete (Derrida 1973). Secondly he stated most strongly the lack of context independent of message. For him there was nothing outside the text, no meaning or truth independent of language (Derrida 1978). All we have is a play of signifiers without any pre-existing signifieds or referents.

With reader response theory, associated with Riffaterre, Spitzer and Fish, we move radically to a focus on the addressee. Within this theory the meaning of a poem is the experience produced in the reader, with the poem itself an action produced on a reader rather than a container from which a reader extracts a message. Spitzer (1948) and Riffaterre (1966) could be seen as a bridge between formalism, structuralism and reader response: reader's response must be taken as the starting point for analysis: 'No grammatical analysis of a poem can give us more than the grammar of the poem' (1966: 213). Spitzer, with his philological circle (Figure 1.2), started with the literary interpretation (the response of the reader) and moved on to grammatical or linguistic analysis.

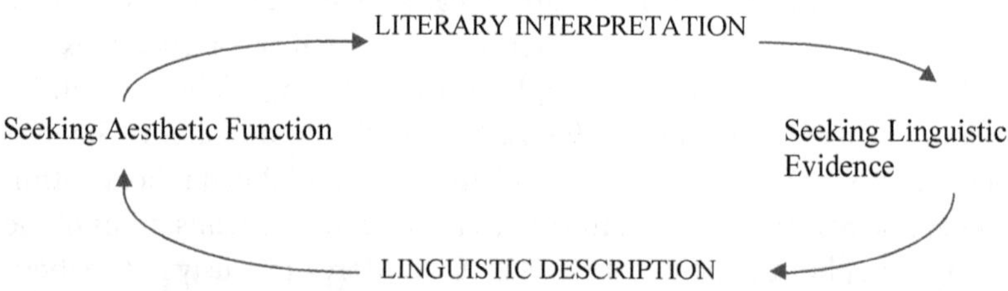

Figure 1.2. Spitzer's philological circle

Fish was more radical, with his contention that meaning is an experience in the reader, the effect of a process within the addressee. He demonstrated this with his famous analysis of the sentence 'That Judas punished by hanging himself there is no certainty' (Fish 1980: 23ff.), which iconically generates its own uncertainty in the process of reading. Returning to the Pound poem we can illustrate how reader response theory might apply. In the second line, when we read the phrase 'the apparition' the first meaning that comes to mind is "ghost". But as we proceed with the rest of the phrase 'of those faces' we reassess the meaning and the grammar: the whole noun phrase will probably be re-processed as a nominalisation of 'the faces appeared'. This second take on the meaning recreates the experience of the poet – initially the white faces looked like ghosts, only later were they correctly perceived as faces in a crowd.

Discoursal and pragmatic approaches to stylistics go beyond the addressee and place emphasis upon the addresser/addressee relationship, and the alternation or fragmentation of voices in the text. Here we can locate Bhaktin/Volosinov (1963, 1965) with his emphasis on the dialogic or polyphonic nature of the best novels: '*Word* is a two-sided act. It is determined by whose word it is and for whom it is meant' (Jefferson and Robey 1982: 161). We also find here those working within the pragmatic tradition (Grice 1975, Leech 1983, Sperber and Wilson 1995, Goatly 1997) who maintain that the principles in operation in other kinds of communication apply equally to literature or poetry: meaning is generated by the attempt of the hearer/reader to hypothesise the intentions of the speaker/writer, according to principles such as co-operation, politeness or relevance. If we look again at the Pound poem, we see that a great deal of inferencing has to take place if we are to make sense of it. We simply have three lines, made up of three unconnected noun phrases. We infer, I suppose, that the first line sets the scene for the experience in the second line, so that the crowd with its faces is in the metro station. But what is the relationship between the second and third lines? Through the pragmatics of reference we might infer that this noun phrase apposition places one literal description next to a metaphorical description. We hypothesise petals as a likely metaphor for faces, and boughs as a likely metaphor for the crowd, partly guided by the grammatical parallelism. How do we work out the grounds of comparison? These are by no means certain: faces, especially if they at first are mistaken for ghosts, might be white, and white is a common colour of petals. What are the grounds of comparison between wet, black boughs and the crowd? Do the passengers crowded together create a long homogenous solid structure like the bough of a tree? Are the winter clothes of the passengers uniformly black? Have they just come down from the street where it is raining? As with most inferences, these are less than certain, especially so in literature. The strength of a pragmatic approach is precisely the potential for a formal exploration of how different knowledges brought to a literary text may result in different inferred meanings, none of them certain.

Finally, we can detect in stylistics a move to reinstate context as a stylistic focus. Quite probably the characters, the heroes, the representations of behaviour and attitudes expressed towards that behaviour, though fictional, can serve as a value-laden model for human behaviour in the real world. Maybe Don Quixote, in his imitation of fictive texts in his own life, is more typical than we dare admit. Stylistics within a critical discourse analysis (CDA) tradition might therefore wish to question the ideological representations within literature: this could be, for example, from a feminist standpoint (Mills 1995), a postcolonial standpoint (Talib 2001), an ecolinguistic standpoint (Goatly 2000: chapter 10). Using our poem as an example, perhaps, and it is a big perhaps, it could be seen as dehumanising the crowd of commuters, or reflecting their dehumanisation, by reducing them either to insubstantial ghosts or to plants.

How do the chapters in this book exemplify the different approaches to stylistics outlined above? In chapters 2 and 3 on Golding's *Pincher Martin* and Rowling's *Harry Potter and the Philosopher's Stone* I adopt an approach which looks at semantico-grammatical patterning in the message or text, which might be seen as based on a Jakobsonian approach to stylistics. Such analyses of patterns have been much enhanced by the computer concordancing techniques which I employ. However, especially in the *Pincher Martin* analysis, since the patterns are over large sections of the text, and different parts of the text are seen to have different likelihoods of grammatical patterning – intransitive verbs predominating in the early part of the novel, transitive verbs in the later passage – one could almost say that the text establishes its own sub-grammars, or sub-codes, which moves us towards a focus on code, in the Proppian structuralist mode. In a sense code is an abstraction from message in any case. In addition, the *Pincher* chapter to some extent is a critical discoursal reinstatement of the context, since is discusses process philosophies and ideologies. However, the *Harry Potter* chapter is the clearest example of such reinstatement in the book, suggesting as it does that the speciesism, sexism, celebration of the ideology of competition and collective punishment, bureaucratic imposition of time and so on, are potentially dangerous representations of the world for young minds. However, I end this by raising questions about the validity of the naive CDA/Jakobsonian approach, and suggest the need to consider propositional attitude, irony, and other pragmatic factors, especially in literary texts with their multiple levels of addresser and addressee.

Chapter 4 on marked theme in Housman's *A Shropshire Lad* looks at the message, but from an informational distribution point of view, which involves elements of reader response theory. The chapter discusses the effect on the reader of, for example, the piling up of prepositional phrases as adverbials before the subject of a clause. But, as with chapter 2 on *Pincher Martin*, there is an attempt to see overall patterns or sub-codes in the different genres of lyric, ballad, dialogue and in the different stages of the poem sequence, as well as in the ways in which Housman loosely applies classical rhetorical schemes. This latter perspective moves back, perhaps, in the direction of a message-oriented stylistics.

Chapter 5 on Elizabeth Jennings' 'One Flesh' is a pivotal chapter in the book. In the first half I try to use a Jakobsonian approach, regarding the poem as a product, looking for grammatical and phonetic patterns in the poem, and detecting multiple foregrounding of the final sentence. But the main thrust of the chapter is that the poem has to be analysed in terms of the processes going on in the reader's head if this foregrounding is to be fully understood. This necessitates a pragmatic approach, and an exploration of how expectations are set up and defeated in the course of reading. Therefore one might locate this quite firmly in the reader response tradition of Fish, emphasising the addressee, with an important contribution from pragmatic theory, stressing the addresser-addresseee interaction.

Chapters 6 and 7 on Pinter's *The Birthday Party* and Ishiguro's *The Remains of the Day* make heavy use of pragmatic theory, the principles guiding the inferential processes by which an addressee hypothesises the intentions of the addresser. This places them in a stylistic model with a focus on the addresser-addressee relationship. Chapter 6 tries to apply Gricean pragmatics and theories of politeness, silence, face and territoriality to two short sections of the play, and uses these to account for communication breakdown, menace and absurdity. Chapter 7 is a detailed analysis of how Leech's (1983) principles of politeness can help us to understand the character of the butler Stevens. The politeness principle indicates that rational efficiency in the exchange of information, which is assumed by Grice, Sperber and Wilson to be the overriding imperative in communication, needs supplementing with a principle which allows for face and dignity as equally powerful factors. The analysis attempts to show how much more interesting the novel is if the social values of self-restraint and human dignity are given equal weight to the principles of efficient rationality and truth.

The eighth and final chapter of the book, on the treatment of metaphor themes in the poems of John Donne, focuses on the importance to Donne's poetry of the underlying 'code' – the patterns of conventional metaphors in the dictionary, and a deconstructionist attempt to undermine this code through paradox and conceit. The chapter takes a number of prevalent metaphor themes (conceptual metaphors) found in *Metalude*, my on-line database of conventional metaphors, and shows how Donne exploits them and conceptually undermines them. For example there is a tension between RELIABILITY IS STABILITY and EMOTION IS MOVEMENT; or between RELATIONSHIP IS BINDING/TYING/UNITY/COHESION/PROXIMITY and FREEDOM IS SPACE TO MOVE. And between permanence of a relationship in general and destructive metaphors like SEX IS VIOLENCE, FEELING/EMOTION IS BEING EATEN, and LOVE/PASSION IS HEAT or FIRE. Donne deals with these oppositions, more or less successfully through paradox, conceits and 'capitalist' themes such as RELATIONSHIP IS TRANSACTION, which I analyse with a minor gesture towards CDA and Jakobson's representative function.

2 Lexico-grammar and process in Golding's *Pincher Martin*

2.1   Introduction

Pincher Martin tells the story of Christopher Hadley (Pincher) Martin, a Second World War naval officer, who drowns in the sea after his cruiser is torpedoed. He drowns somewhere between pages 8 and 10 of the novel (Golding 1956). The next 190 pages constitute Pincher's imagination of his own six-days survival, in which he kicks off his sea-boots (p.10), swims to an isolated rocky island, builds a rescue beacon out of boulders and stripes the island with seaweed as a signal to any passing ships or aircraft, lives off mussels, limpets and anemones, which poison him, self-administers an enema, and pretends madness as he is attacked by black lightning, which finally reduces him to a pair of self-clutching lobster claws, while around him his imaginary island disintegrates like torn shreds of paper. This fabricated narrative is punctuated with flashbacks, memories of his life before being torpedoed, which centre on his relationships with his friend Nathaniel, whom he was attempting to murder in the instant before the torpedo struck, Mary Lovell, whom he tried to rape and who finally married Nat, other sexual conquests, childhood nightmares, and his ruthlessly competitive career as an actor. In the last chapter, beginning on page 202, his body, with feet still in sea-boots, is picked up from a Hebridean island where it has been washed ashore.

In the main part of this paper, sections 1 and 2, I shall be using Hallidayan Systemic Functional Grammar for the textual analysis of passages and of patterns of lexical development. The grammatical patterns analysed are probabilities of occurrence of certain grammatical sub-codes, applied in different stages of the novel, and this kind of stylistic analysis can be thought of as interrogating the message in order to discover the code beneath.

But before starting the analysis I wish to raise some questions about the world depicted by what Halliday (1985a) calls *congruent grammar*. By this phrase Halliday means, to put it succinctly, the unmarked ways of wording semantics: namely Processes as Verbs, Things as Nouns, Qualities of Things as Adjectives, and Qualities of Processes as Adverbs. My question is to what extent the congruent construction of the world is actually consonant with the theoretical descriptions of matter found in modern science (Goatly 1995, 2007).

Modern theories of the physical nature of matter and ecological theories such as Lovelock's *Gaia* hypothesis (Lovelock 1988) set themselves in opposition to traditional Newtonian concepts of matter and change. Relativity theory, for example, undermined the Newtonian belief that physical laws operated on permanent rigid bodies:

> Indeed it is not possible in relativity to obtain a consistent definition of an extended rigid body, because this would imply signals faster than light. In order to try to accommodate this new feature of relativity theory within the older notions of structure, physicists were driven to the notion of a particle that is an extensionless point … Actually, relativity implies that neither the point particles nor the quasi-rigid body can be taken as primary concepts. Rather these have to be expressed in terms of events and processes (Bohm 1980: 123–124).

The following metaphor, derived, one might notice, from the phenomena of fluid dynamics which physicists have lately investigated, emphasises the primacy of process:

> The best image of process is perhaps that of the flowing stream whose substance is never the same. On this stream one may see an ever-changing pattern of vortices, ripples, waves, splashes etc., which evidently have no independent existence as such. Rather they are abstracted from the flowing movement, arising and vanishing in the total process of the flow (Bohm 1980: 48).

The problem is that this emphasis on matter as process clearly conflicts with the congruent grammatical division of phenomena into processes and things, represented by Verbs and Nouns respectively.

A further difference between modern science and traditional Newtonian concepts concerns the controllability of natural 'objects'. In the Newtonian system of dynamics change was seen in terms of an external force imposing movement from outside, a conception very much suited to the development of technology and man's domination of his 'environment' (Goatly 2007: chapter 7). This myth of the controllability of natural objects was undermined by the study of thermodynamics and the theory of entropy, which allows for the dissipation of energy:

> Thus the 'negative' property of dissipation shows that, unlike dynamic objects, thermodynamic objects can only be partially controlled. Occasionally they 'break loose' into spontaneous change (Prigogine and Stengers 1985: 120).

By contrast, the semantics of congruent grammar often divides the participants in processes into agent and affected. Typically, transitive material process clauses construct a simplified Newtonian world-view in which a (human) Actor imposes change on an inert and passive (non-human) Goal. Most seriously this construction reinforces the myth that humans can dominate nature, and represents a false unidirectionality of cause and effect.

Thirdly, modern physics has lain to rest the assumption that humankind is outside the world which it observes and acts on. Scientific experimentation and observation depend on an experimenter/observer who is alive, and they are always time oriented. But life is the manifestation of a far-from-equilibrium system, and time depends on entropy within this system. Therefore the living observer and his/her time-based measurements are inescapably part of the system being observed and not external to it (Prigogine and Stengers 1985: 300). The observer and the observed object are inextricably interdependent. However, the grammar of the mental process clause (see 2.1.1. below) tends to insist on the duality of observer (Senser) and external reality (Phenomenon), construed as independent of each other. This fails to acknowledge the mutual conditioning between the construction of external reality, and the supposition of an observing coherent and permanent self.

Besides modern physics one should mention James Lovelock's radical theory of biological development called *Gaia*, especially since William Golding supplied Lovelock with the name for the theory (Lovelock 1988: 3). The gist of the Gaia hypothesis is that the world, including the atmosphere, the oceans, the biota, the rocks and minerals of the crust, functions as one large self-regulating organism. The world resembles a giant redwood tree, which, although made up of a core of 99% dead wood with only a thin layer of living cells on its surface, nevertheless functions as one living entity. Specifically the Gaia hypothesis says that the temperature, oxidation state, acidity, and certain aspects of the rocks and waters are at any time kept constant, and that this homeostasis is maintained by active feedback processes operated automatically and unconsciously by the biota. Life and its environment are so closely coupled that evolution concerns Gaia, not the organisms or the environment taken separately (Lovelock 1988: 19). Gaia theory, with its emphasis on wholeness, conflicts with the grammatical separation of participants from processes and processes from circumstances (cf. the word *environment*). And it also insists on the importance of feedback: nature is never simply a passive Goal but always and simultaneously an Actor.

In opposition to the label *congruent* I shall from now on use the word *consonant* to label the resources in the grammar which can be exploited to represent the aspects of modern scientific thinking discussed above (see also Goatly 2007: chapter 7). In particular the consonant use of middle voice and of incongruent structures like nominalisation will be explored.

2.1.1   Halliday's transitivity system

Before starting analysis, for the benefit of readers who may be unfamiliar with it I will sketch in quickly a summary of Halliday's transitivity framework (Halliday 1994). Systems of transitivity encode the representational or ideational/experiential meanings of the clause, as follows. Any clause can be divided into:

- A lexical Verb – which refers to one of 5 Process types.
- Subject and Object(s)/Complement(s) realised by Noun Phrases – which, in active voice, represent the Participants corresponding to the Process referred to in the Verb.
- Adverbials or Adjuncts representing Circumstances.

The five process types are:

Existential	representing what exists in the world.
Relational	representing the state of the things which exist and what relations they have to each other.
Material	representing what is happening in the world, what actions and events are going on.
Mental	representing how people are perceiving, feeling and thinking.
Behavioural	representing behaving as a result of an inner process or state.
Verbal	representing how people are communicating or expressing their perceptions, feelings and thoughts.

Different Processes will have correspondingly different participants, those of which are relevant to the anlayses in this book are given in Table 2.1.

Table 2.1. Process types in Hallidayan transitivity analysis

Existential:		Existent			
	There are	*six moons of Uranus*			
Relational:		Token		Value	
		(Carrier)		(Attribute)	
		John	*is*	*a stupid politician*	
		(Possessor)		(Possession)	
		John	*has*	*a guitar*	
Material	Actor			Goal	Circumstance
	John	*killed*		*an elephant*	*[yesterday]*
	Actor			Beneficiary	Goal
	John	*gave*		*Mary*	*the tusks*
	Actor			Range	
	John	*climbed*		*the mountain*	
Behavioural	Behaver				
	John	*shouted*			
Mental	Sensor			Phenomenon	
	John	*noticed*		*the bird*	
Verbal	Sayer			Verbiage	
	John	*said*		*'Go away'*	

2.2   Transitivity, nominalisation and process in two contrasting passages

2.2.1   Introduction: a sample of the passages analysed

Following Halliday (1973), who analysed three contrasting passages from Golding's *The Inheritors*, I undertook a linguistic analysis of transitivity and nominalisation in two passages from *Pincher Martin*. Passage A is from p.13: 'His voice died and his face untwisted' to p.23: 'He lay still' (2,957 words). Passage B is from p.58: 'As in the sea at a moment of desperate crisis' to p.67: 'A gull moved a little then settled down' (3,063 words).

In Passage A Pincher is still in the sea supposedly fighting for breath. By Passage B he has succeeded in creating the illusion that he has swum to an island, clambered on to it and is piling up rocks to make a rescue beacon as a signal to any passing ships. I show that Passage A uses the resources of lexico-grammar to represent a world of flux and process, relatively consonant with modern science and process philosophy. But that by Passage B Pincher has constructed a concrete world of things which is distressingly familiar: one in which humans impose their will on nature, act on nature unidirectionally, as though they were separate from it, where transitive effective clauses with Pincher as agent predominate. The contrast suggests that the more firmly established our illusions of the permanence of matter, the more we speak in congruent transitive effective grammar. The use of nominalisation in the first passage is, on the one hand, Golding's recognition of the primacy of process, and, on the other, a strategy employed by the protagonist as a first stage in reifying the flux of sensations and processes.

To give a flavour of the two passages, and to provide examples of different transitivity options I give two representative samples from Passage A and Passage B.

A Sample of Passage A

(1) There were hands to be sure and two forearms of black oilskin and there was the noise of breathing, gasping. (2) There was also the noise of the idiot stuff, whispering, folding on itself, tripped ripples running tinkling by the ear like miniatures of surf on a flat beach; (3) there were sudden hisses and spats, roars and incompleted syllables and the soft friction of wind. (4) The hands were important under the bright side of the circle but they had nothing to seize on. (5) There was an infinite drop of the soft, cold stuff below them and under the labouring, dying, body.

(6) The sense of depth caught him and he drew his dead feet up to his belly as if to detach them from the whole ocean. (7) He arched and gaped, he rose over the chasm of deep sea on a swell and his mouth opened to scream against the brightness.

(8) It stayed open. (9) Then it shut with a snap of teeth and his arms began to heave water out of the way. (10) He fought his way forward.

(11) 'Ahoy–for Christ's sake! Survivor! Survivor! Fine on your starboard bow!'

(12) He threshed with his arms and legs into a clumsy crawl.

(13) A crest overtook him and he jerked himself to the chest out of water.

A sample of Passage B

(14) There was a broken rock below his hands, leaning against the wall from which the clean fracture had fallen. (15) He climbed down and wrestled with a great weight. (16) He made the stone rise on an angle; he quivered and the stone fell over. (17) He collapsed and lay for a while. (18) He left the stone and scrambled heavily down to the little cliff and the scattered rocks where he had bathed his eye. (19) He found an encrusted boulder lying in a rock pool and pulled it up. (20) He got the stone against his stomach, staggered for a few steps, dropped the stone, lifted and carried again. (21) He dumped the stone on the high point above the funnel and came back. (22) There was a stone like a suitcase balanced on the wall of a trench and he pondered what he should do. (23) He put his back against the suitcase and his feet against the other side of the trench. (24) The suitcase grated, moved. (25) He got a shoulder under one end and heaved. (26) The suitcase tumbled in the next trench and broke. (27) He grinned without humour and lugged the larger part up into his lap. (28) He raised the broken suitcase to the wall, turned it end over end, engineered it up slopes of fallen but unmanageable rock, pulled and hauled.
(29) Then there were two rocks on the high part, one with a trace of blood. (30) He looked once round the horizon and climbed down the slope again. (31) He stopped, put a hand to his forehead, then examined the palm. (32) But there was no blood.

(Numbers in parentheses below refer to sentences in the sample passages above.)

2.2.2   Transitivity options in Passages A and B

In order to examine the grammatical options within Material process clauses for a more process-oriented ontology I used Kristin Davidse's model (1992) (see Figure 2.1) which gives a fairly comprehensive account of the choices in the linguistic system for construing phenomena into Processes, Actors, Instigators, Mediums, and Goals.

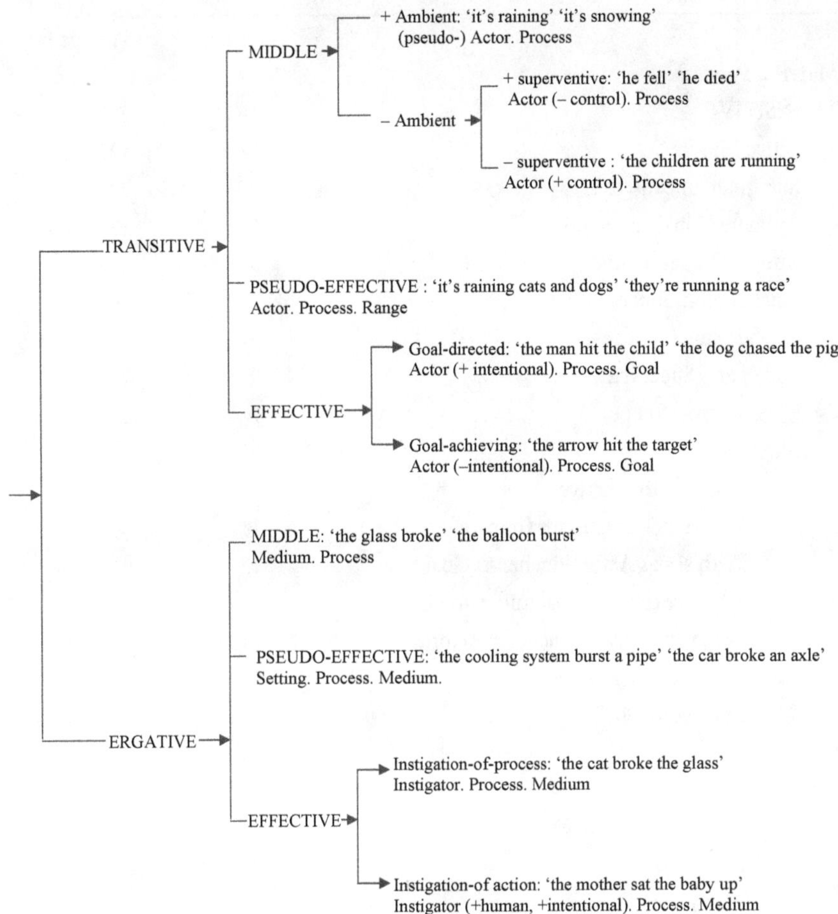

Figure 2.1. System choices for Material processes (after Davidse 1992)

I analysed the finite and non-finite clauses in the two passages focusing on the Existential and Material processes, where differences between the two passages are most significant both statistically and thematically. I also selected various potentially significant categories of participant in each of these process types. When analysing Material process clauses I distinguished Transitive clauses from Ergative clauses, and Effective from Middle clauses. In addition I counted and sub-categorised, in a number of ways, the nominalisations in each passage. The results of my calculations are given in Tables 2.2 and 2.4.

Table 2.2. Tokens of transitivity

	Passage A	Passage B
Material Processes		
TRANSITIVE	183	277
<u>Transitive Middle</u>	79	127
Inanimate unconscious	25	24
Animate Non-Superventive	0	12
Animate Superventive	0	9
Pincher Non-Superventive	21	66
Pincher Superventive	24	10
Body parts Superventive	9	7
<u>Pseudo-Effective</u> (Range)	7	2
<u>Transitive Effective</u>	97	148
Transitive Effective Active	72	125
With Pincher as Actor (non-reflexive)	11	80
With sea as Actor, Pincher as Goal	12	0
Effective clauses, Goal understood	2	13
Reflexive clauses, Pincher = Actor & Goal	21 (14)	33
Transitive Effective Passive	25	23
Pincher as Goal	17	4
ERGATIVE	34	49
<u>Ergative Middle</u>	26	30
Medium		
Body parts	9	7
Inanimate	10	23
Indeterminate (shape/thing)	6 (4)	0
<u>Ergative Effective</u>	7	19
Instigator		
Pincher	2	16
Medium		
Inanimate (rock)	0	15
Animate	0	3
PINCHER AS ACTOR/INSTIGATOR in Effective Clauses	13	96
BODY PARTS (BODY) AS ACTOR/INSTIGATOR	20	19
NOMINALISATIONS AS SUBJECT	24	11
<u>Middle</u>	7	9
<u>Effective</u>	17	2

In the following subsections I shall both comment on the relevant right-hand outputs on Davidse's model (Figure 2.1), and discuss the corresponding statistics emerging from my analysis of the passages (Table 2.2).

Transitive Middle

Near the top of Davidse's Figure is the Transitive, Middle, –Ambient category, with the important non-superventive/superventive distinction, involving control or the lack of it respectively[1]. In the case of Animate Actors we ask whether the action is deliberate as in 'He climbed down' (15) or not as in 'He collapsed' (17) (see Davidse 1992: 111). Though this distinction cannot always be determined, in Passage A the use of present-in-present tense often signals that the action is involuntary, e.g. 'then he was blubbering'; 'his teeth were chattering again'. It is as though he suddenly found these things happening to him without any conscious willing of them.

Transitive Middle clauses are more frequent in Passage B: 127 to 79. Despite this fact there are almost twice as many with Pincher as Actor that can be interpreted as involuntary, i.e. Superventive, in Passage A: 24 to 10.

> (7) He **arched** and **gaped**, he **rose** over the chasm of deep sea on a swell and his mouth opened to scream against the brightness.

Conversely, three times as many are probably Non-Superventive in B compared to A, 66 to 21 ('climbed down' (15), 'scrambled' (18)).

Pseudo-effective

The Pseudo-effective structure occurs in my analysis when a nominalised Range or its equivalent is used as the Object (Complement) e.g. 'He began to make swimming motions' or (10) 'He fought his way forward'.

Pseudo-effective material process clauses are noticeably more frequent in Passage A, 7 as against 2. 4 of these 7 repeat the formula: *make swimming movements/motions*. And out of these, two admit that the movements are made, or made up, by the mind:

> His mind inside the dark skull **made** swimming movements long after the body lay motionless in the water. (p. 16)

> His mind **made** swimming movements. (p. 16)

However, Pincher soon finds it more convenient to ignore the mental origins of his swimming:

> He **made** swimming movements again without thought. (p. 18)

It is worth comparing these Ranges with similar Cognitive Process Ranges:

> He thought movements that did not happen. The sea came back and he thought the movements again and this time they happened because the sea took most of his weight. (p. 22)

It is telling little sequences such as the above that, along with the general patterns I have outlined, give credence to a process philosophy interpretation of the novel. For this somewhat deviant construction, *to think* + Direct Object, suggests that the experiences of processes are themselves a mental construction, that we are inevitably caught up in the cognitive creation of what the congruent material, existential and relational clauses represent as external to us.

Transitive Effective

The Transitive Effective structures (most of which are goal-directed) are, it is worth reminding ourselves, symptomatic of a Newtonian world-view in which an outside force acts on the environment in a unidirectional fashion. They symbolise domination of rather than respect for the environment.

Under Transitive Effective structures we must also include those in which the Goal is understood, generally through ellipsis of a previously occurring noun phrase. e.g. 'He got the stone against his stomach, staggered for a few steps, dropped the stone, **lifted** and **carried** again' (20). Another sub-category of Transitive Effective is the reflexives. In this category I include both those where the Object is *himself* and those where he is acting on part of his body e.g. 'he drew his dead feet up to his belly' (6).

The number of Transitive Effective clauses with Pincher as Actor which are not reflexive is much higher in Passage B than in A: 80 to 11, cf. sentences (18)-(21). Pincher is a great deal more passive in A, often at the mercy of the sea, hence the 12 clauses with sea as Actor and Pincher as Goal. This is also evident from the Passive voice clauses: in Passage A Pincher is the Subject-Goal in nearly three quarters of these, 17 out of 25, but in Passage B in only about 15%, 4 out of 23. By the second passage Pincher has established the norms of dominant purposeful human action on the environment, hence taking the role of Actor. In both passages however, there is the tendency for the verbs to be reflexive, with Pincher acting on himself, e.g. (13), (31).

Ergatives

The Ergative paradigm centres on pairs of clauses like those in Table 2.3, where the introduction of a second participant extends the clause to the left (Halliday 1985: 146).

Table 2.3. Ergative verbs and processes

MEDIUM	PROCESS		INSTIGATOR	PROCESS	MEDIUM
The boat	sailed	v.	Mary	sailed	the boat
The cloth	tore	v.	The nail	tore	the cloth
The rice	cooked	v.	Pat	cooked	the rice
<u>MIDDLE</u>			<u>EFFECTIVE</u>		

Davidse draws attention to the fundamental difference between the Transitive and Ergative systems:

> In 2) ['John opened the door' (ergative)] Instigator *John* 'affects' the door by instigating its opening, but the door co-participates in the process of opening … In the transitive model there is 'energy input' only at the level of the Actor, while in the ergative model there is 'energy input' at two levels: that of the Instigator in the outer ring, and that of the Medium within the inner ring (Davidse 1992: 118) [my insertion in brackets].

The use of the Ergative Effective clause type can construe a reality in which energy is not simply imposed on an inert nature from the outside to produce change, as in the Transitive model, but in which nature provides its own energy, and its own propensity for spontaneous change, rather as is the case in fluid dynamic systems.

The use of the Middle Ergative option is actually even more consonant. Since no agent/instigator is specifically mentioned, then the causal element must reside either in the Subject referent, or perhaps even be ascribed to the process itself, e.g. (26) 'The suitcase tumbled in the next trench and broke'. This seems more in step with the notion of reality as process, the idea that any state or succession of states we find ourselves in are abstractions from a process.

Turning to our statistics under the Ergative paradigm, we note again the higher proportion of Material Processes in B than in A, 49 to 34. Significantly, most of this difference arises in the case of Effective clauses, 19 as against 7. We further notice that Pincher is himself the Instigator in 16 out of the 19 Effective clauses, and this confirms the pattern of Effectiveness in Passage B that we noted within the Transitive paradigm. Looking at the Ergative Effectives in Passage B it is not surprising that prototypically Pincher is the Instigator and Inanimates are the Medium, since, after all, Pincher is for the most part moving rocks to build his rescue beacon, e.g. 'He raised the broken suitcase to the wall, **turned** it end over end…' (28).

As far as the Ergative Middle breakdown is concerned the fact that the Body-part category reverses the normal frequency pattern may be significant. Body-parts have a life of their own and a spontaneity in Passage A that is diminished slightly in Passage B. (Note that the following boldened clauses were interpreted as Ergative Middle):

> **His mouth opened** to scream against the brightness. It stayed open. **Then it shut with a snap of teeth** and *his arms began to heave water out of the way.* (7–9)

However, such is the frequency of Body-parts as Actors in the early chapters of *Pincher Martin*, e.g. in the italicised clause of (9), and so important is the establishment of a controlling consciousness to co-ordinate and use them, that it is tempting to accord these boldened examples the status of Transitive, Middle, –Ambient (even, perhaps, Superventive). Then the Effective equivalent 'he opened his mouth, he shut it with a snap of teeth' could be interpreted as Ergative, Effective, Instigation of Action, with the mouth as an Enforced Actor.

The number of Ergative, Pseudo-effective clauses is negligible. And I only analysed Ergative Effective clauses to the primary level of delicacy in this study. An example of an Ergative Effective clause would be 'He … dropped the stone' (20).

Pincher as Actor/Instigator

So far I have analysed the contrastive participant patterns separately in the Transitive and Ergative paradigms. But three important overall patterns emerge if we combine our analyses. Firstly and most significantly we can comment on the combined statistics of Pincher as Actor/Instigator. There are more than seven times as many of these in Passage B as in Passage A, 96 to 13. This sums up his transformation from passivity to dominance in relation to the environment.

Body Parts as Actor/Instigator

A second point of interest is the frequency of body parts as Subject in Material Process clauses. This suggests that in neither passage has the controlling consciousness fully established itself as a unifying and co-ordinating principle, that Pincher is no more than a fragmentary assembly of body parts. Within Passage A, however, there seems to be a significant shift: there are 9 occurrences in the first two of the ten pages, which is before Pincher's eyes open. This reinforces the overt statement that sight is crucial in establishing his sense of a unified personality:

What had seemed an eternal rhythm, had been hours of darkness and now there was a faint light that consolidated his personality, gave it bounds and sanity. (p.56)

Nominalisations as Subjects

Thirdlly, if we include other process types besides the Material, we note a significant pattern in Passage A. Pincher often acts on himself at one remove: he will make an action, experience a feeling or a thought, and subsequently this action or experience will act on him:

… [the snarl] worked on the wooden face
… and his movements broke up the stony weight of his legs
… and the thought drove him to foam in the water–
The first, fierce excitement of sighting had burned up the fuel
The force of his return sent him under
The little warmth of anger flushed blood back into the tops of the cheeks
… they [the movements] moved him forward over the hard things

There are a high number of Nominalisations as Subjects of Transitive clauses in Passage A, 17 out of 24. This construes processes as producing other processes, a comparatively consonant way of representing experience. By contrast, in Passage B most Nominalisations are Mediums, 9 out of 11.

Table 2.4. Tokens of Existential clauses

	Passage A	Passage B
Existential Processes		
With *there*	26	21
Nominalisation as Existent	17	5
General Word/Shape as Existent	14	5
Specific thing as Existent	12	20

We return now to the topmost category in Figure 2.1, Transitive, Middle +Ambient. Though strictly speaking this category is of marginal occurrence, and not included in my calculations, it is worth a passing comment since it stands on the boundary between existential and material processes. Slightly further to the Existential side would be structures in which the 'dummy subject' is *there* and in which the Existent is a nominalised process, e.g.

> *Existents…*
> There were   sudden hisses and spats, roars and incompleted syllables and
> the soft friction of wind. (3)

These do figure extensively in my calculations (Table 2.4). Incidentally this is a structure recommended as consonant with the process emphasis of Buddhist ontology by Malalasekera, though the example is of a cognitive rather than material process: 'There's thinking' (Malalasekera 1951). Note too that the gerundive *thinking* seems to give slightly more emphasis to the process than the conversion *hisses*. In fact *there* + nominalisation by conversion tends to predominate over suffixed nominalisations.

There is little difference between the two passages in the overall number of Existential process clauses introduced by *there* (Table 2.4). What is significant is that in Passage A there are much higher numbers of nominalisations and general/shape words as Existents, 17 and 14 compared with 5 and 5 in B. Conversely there are more specific things as Existent in Passage B, 20 as against 12 in A. In section 2.3 I explore in more detail the stages by which Pincher constructs the world of Process into the world of things, and in its use of general/shape words Passage A seems to represent the third stage.

2.2.3   Nominalisation, congruence and consonance

Nominalisation is one kind of incongruent wording of experiential semantics which has been called 'grammatical metaphor' (Halliday 1985b, Martin 1985, 1986, 1992, Eggins, Wignell and Martin 1983a, 1993a, Goatly 1995, 2007). In the case of Nominalisation, the incongruent wording represents Processes and Qualities as Nominal Groups.

There are three kinds of nominalisation, corresponding to three different orders of entities. First-order entities/things have existence in space, second-order entities/processes have existence in time, and third-order entities/ abstractions have existence in neither. In 'proper' nominalisation the process or quality is 'abstracted' from things and time respectively, as a third-order entity e.g. '**Cooking** food involves irreversible chemical **changes**', '**Gurgling** is an infant's natural **expression** of **pleasure**'. A second type of nominalisation of process verbs refers to second-order entities, countable tokens of processes occurring at different times or a specific time, e.g. '**The gurglings** continued', '**The cooking** took three hours'. The final kind of nominalisation, which has been called 'improper' (Vendler 1968), refers to first-order entities, with physical substance and, prototypically, dimensions in space, e.g. 'I like John's **cooking**', which means the food which results from the cooking.

In analysing these texts I have made a distinction between lexicalised first-order nominalisations, which will be found in the dictionary, and nominalisations that are construed as first-order because of their collocations. In 'he rose over the chasm of deep sea on **a swell** and his mouth opened to scream against **the brightness**' (7), we have lexicalised first-order nominalisation in 'a swell'; and collocational first-order nominalisation in 'the brightness', because the preposition *against* implies spatial dimensions for its complement.

The distinction between improper first-order nominalisations and others is relatively easy to draw in the case of material process verbs. Improper nominalisations often refer to the thing which is the physical result of the process e.g. 'John's cooking' (above), or *secretions*. And with mental processes of visual perception verbs, improper nominalisations often refer to the thing sensed or Phenomenon e.g. *sight*. It is however rather difficult to draw in the case of other mental processes, so that most of these have to be classified as either proper or improper collocational.

What relation does nominalisation have to consonance? It would seem that nominalisation is neither congruent nor consonant. After all, it realises and re-codes types of processes as nouns and therefore suggests that they have a kind of permanence, a reified existence outside time. This is especially true of first-order nominalisation; it is hard to see how the now lexicalised *secretions*, for example, can do anything more than make some marginal gesture in the direction of consonance by associating the physical thing/substance with the process from which it results. In fact, in its improper first-order form nominalisation seems more thoroughly inconsonant than in its second and third-order forms.

However, since nominalisation has been called *grammatical metaphor*, we are justified in suggesting that, like many other metaphors, it is 'interactive'. In his interaction theory of metaphor Black claimed that transfer of features operates simultaneously in opposite directions (Black 1962). He pointed out that in the utterance 'man is a wolf' not only does the interpretation involve making men seem more like wolves, but also the reverse, wolves come to resemble men. Interaction would mean, in the case of nominalisation, that the Topic (process) is made to resemble the Vehicle (thing), but that simultaneously the Vehicle (thing) is made to seem more like the Topic (process). Thus nominalisation can give rise to the following reasoning: if in the case of nominalisations nouns can realise processes, may it not be the case that all nouns really refer to processes?

Furthermore, proper nominalisation displays a crucial feature that tends towards consonance. Even more than is the case with Ergative Middle clauses, nominalisations can exclude any reference to an agent or external cause, so that the same effect of suggesting a self-generated process can be achieved.

By way of illustration, we can consider a passage cited by Eggins, Wignell, and Martin (1993b: 159) from a Geography textbook. Instead of the congruent *water condenses* we have the nominalisation *condensation*, which is later re-coded as a process with a dummy process verb: 'condensation occurs'. What is of interest in this sequence is its graphic demonstration of the 'absorption' of the Medium into the Process. Such is the extent of this absorption that, when the discourse demands a clause rather than a nominal group, the possibility of 'squeezing' the Medium out again is resisted.

The possibilities for a more consonant grammar opened up by nominalisation should not be underestimated, especially since it can be used as one kind of 'conjuring trick' making our permanent selves as Actors, and permanent Things in general, disappear. Indeed the following listed choices of wordings (Table 2.5) give progressively higher profile to process in the options which they allow for ignoring 'Things'. (Optional reference to participant Things is indicated in parentheses.)

Table 2.5. Transitivity options for eliminating participants

Participant Thing Profile	Transitivity choice	Participants	Process Profile
HIGH	TRANSITIVE EFFECTIVE: PASSIVE:	ACTOR + GOAL GOAL (+ ACTOR)	LOW
	ERGATIVE MIDDLE:	MEDIUM	
LOW	NOMINALISATION:	(+ ACTOR/GOAL)	HIGH

In summary, nominalisation is ambiguous in relation to consonance. We shall see, particularly in section 2, that Pincher uses it inconsonantly, on behalf of permanence and reification of process. Golding, however, sometimes seems to be using it consonantly as a gesture towards a process philosophy.

When we look at the figures for nominalisation in the two passages (Table 2.6), we notice that this is more than twice as frequent in Passage A: 140 to B's 64; e.g. 'there were sudden **hisses** and **spats**, **roars** and incompleted syllables and the soft friction of wind' (3). In Passage B the nominalisations are likely to be improper ones like 'traces' (29) which are permanent with spatial dimensions and also lexicalised, whereas in A there are more proper ones like 'snap' (9).

Table 2.6. Tokens of nominalisation

	Passage A	Passage B
Nominalisations	140	64
First-order: lexicalised	29	37
First-order: collocational	46	12
Second/third-order	65	15
De-adjectival	40	13
De-verbal	100	52
Conversion	59	47
de-adjectival	5	8
de-verbal	54	39 (20 I)
Suffixation/Form change	81	17
de-adjectival	35	5
de-verbal	46	12

There is also a much higher frequency in A of nominalisations whose lexicalised meaning is basically second/third-order, but which, by collocation seem pushed towards acquiring the status of things, as with 'brightness' (7). This is a particularly significant finding, suggesting the first stage in a semantic sleight of hand which creates things with spatial dimensions out of processes.

De-adjectival nominalisation is three times as frequent in A as in B, 40 to 13. This is in keeping with our findings in section 2.3, where we will note the strategies of abstracting and nominalising remembered Qualities which are later fabricated into Things. Passage A is prototypical of the 2nd/3rd Stage, and Passage B of the 4th.

De-verbal nominalisation is also extremely important in Passage A, and confirms the hypothesis that Golding is describing a world of processes. The most significant difference between the two passages is the preponderance of suffixed deverbal nominalisations in Passage A, 46 to B's 12, e.g. 'There were hands to be sure and two forearms of black oilskin and there was the noise of **breathing, gasping**' (1). Whereas conversions (nominalisation without change of form) can slip easily into lexicalised improper nominalisations – there are 20 such improper de-verbal conversions in B – the suffixation of verbs, especially the -*ing* gerunds, reminds us that, though nouns, they are nevertheless referring to processes.

The use of nominalisation in Passage B tends to be a confirmation of solidity, the existence of first-order entities with spatial dimensions and permanence. The use in Passage A is more equivocal, however. We have a kind of double vision: from the authorial narrator's point of view nominalisation seems a gesture towards consonance, especially when nominalisations become Actors/ Instigators, or when Pincher initiates a process which comes back as a nominalisation to affect him. But from Pincher's fictional point of view, we can see the beginnings of an attempt to fabricate a substantial world.

2.2.4   Conclusion

The conclusions about the transition from Passage A to Passage B seem quite clear. A dying passive man, at the mercy of the fluxes and processes that surround him, reifies his sensations and memories to construct an illusory stable world where he has the power and the ability to dominate his physical environment. In Passage A Pseudo-effective clauses and Existential *there* + Nominalisation are witness to this. The change is illustrated graphically in the increase in frequency of Effective Material Process clauses, with Pincher as Agent (Actor/Instigator) only 13 times in Passage A, but 96 times in Passage B. He inhabits, by the second passage, our normal experiential world confirmed by a more congruent and effective grammar. In Passage A, however, he is more aware of the processes, impermanence and flux recognised by modern physics. His defence against this frightening world of no-thingness is to use nominalisation, incongruently and inconsonantly, and improperly in B, to disguise fluid processes as solid things. By doing this he turns away from true seeing and insight which for Golding must move onto 'the revelation of a field of force and design in the universe, to which our normal experience is a concealing screen' (Kinkead-Weekes and Gregor 2002: 371). Ironically the abnormal experience of Passage A brought him close to this revelation, but as Eliot said 'humankind cannot bear too much reality'.

I think the above analysis of transitivity contributes important evidence to counter the argument by Simpson (1993), who is sceptical about the stylistic value of such analyses. Simpson claimed that although Halliday's anlaysis of transitivity in Golding's *The Inheritors* was valid enough in showing the different behaviour of Neanderthal man and homo sapiens towards their environment, such easy equations between transitive and intransitive Material processes, and power or lack of it over the environment, could not be transferred to *Pincher Martin*. My analysis, in the context of Golding's novel would tend to show, on the contrary, that Pincher in his person precisely represents an evolution from the relatively passive (cf. Neanderthal man) to the relatively active (cf. Homo sapiens). If *The Inheritors* is about The Fall, then *Pincher Martin* seems to be about Creation, The Fall and Final Judgement.

2.3   General patterns of nominalisation

Now that we have looked in detail at two short passages from the novel, it is worth considering various wider patterns of nominalisation and the use to which they are put. I shall concentrate mainly on Golding's/Pincher's use of de-adjectival nominalisation.

2.3.1   Non-congruent and non-consonant uses of nominalisation

By far the most common nominalisation has to be the word *darkness* [48 times]. Against the background of a darkness he is unwilling to face, Pincher goes about the business of creating whiteness, brightness and colour. And to construct an illusion of existence he uses remembered feelings of hardness and coldness. The senses of both touch and sight become crucial to his project of personal survival. To show in some detail the general patterns of nominalisation I will trace the adjectives *white* (sight) and *hard* (touch), and their nominalised forms throughout the novel.

The formula for their use seems to follow four stages:

(1) Take a remembered object or substance that is white or hard.

(2) Nominalise these qualities so they float free of the remembered 'thing'.

(3) Re-apply these qualities firstly to some general shape or substance word.

(4) Complete the transfer by secondly applying them as premodifiers or predicates of a specific identified imaginary object.

While this is the general method of development, sometimes stages 2, 3 and 4 may take place in a different order, or simultaneously.

Stage 1: The remembered object

Whiteness has its origins in a number of memories:

• A toy Christopher had as a child, a Cartesian diver:

  The top of the jar was covered with a thin membrane – **white** rubber. (p.8)

• The white bodies of his sexual conquests:

  The pictures that came and went inside his head did not disturb him because they were so small and remote. There was a woman's body, **white** and detailed, there was a boy's body; (pp.25–6)

- These merge with the image of white maggots. This is taken from the story Pincher hears of an exotically grotesque Chinese culinary practice: burying a fish in a tin box, waiting for the maggots to emerge and gradually devour one another until only one remains, and finally opening and eating the triumphant maggot.

  > She's the producer's wife, old man. Fat. **White**. Like a maggot with tiny black eyes. I should like to eat you. I should love to play Danny. I should love to eat you. (p.95)

- The explosion when the cruiser is torpedoed, where *white* is already nominalised:

  > A destroying concussion that had no part in the play. **Whiteness** rising like a cloud, universe spinning. The shock of a fall somewhere, shattering, mouth filled–and he was fighting in all directions with black impervious water.

  > His mouth screamed in rage at the **whiteness** that rose out of the funnel. 'And it was the right bloody order!' Eaten. (p.186)

We notice here that this whiteness seems to spread its symbolic significance to encompass being eaten, recalling the white maggot.

The references to hard objects from the life before he drowns are much sparser but include the following:

> When the air had gone with the shriek, water came in to fill its place–burning water, **hard** in the throat and mouth as stones that hurt. (p.7)

Stage 2: Nominalisation

The next stage is to abstract this quality of whiteness and hardness from the remembered object by nominalisation:

> He pulled with both arms, thrust with both legs. He saw a trench of rock beyond the edge, glimpsed sea, saw **whiteness** on the rocks and jumble. He fell forward. (p.39)

> The **hardnesses** under his cheek began to insist. They passed through pressure to a burning without heat, to a localized pain. (p.24)

> Some of these were inside the skull, behind the arch of the brow and the shadowy nose. They were right in the indeterminate darkness above the fire of **hardnesses.** If you looked out idly, you saw round them. (p.26)

Stage 3: Application of quality to a general shape or substance word

Simultaneously one may apply the adjective to a general shape or substance word or to the inexplicit *thing* (I underline these general words in the quotes that follow):

> There came a new noise among the others. It was connected with the motionless <u>blobs</u> of **white** out there. (pp.55–6)

> His legs before him were covered with **white** <u>blotches</u>. (p.159)

> The <u>lumps</u> of **hard** water jerked in the gullet, the lips came together and parted, the tongue arched, the brain lit a neon track. (p.8)

> The **hard** <u>lumps</u> of water no longer hurt. The was a kind of truce, observation of the body. There was no face but there was a snarl. (p.9)

The use of general substance or object nouns like *stuff* or *thing* is very common throughout the novel [162 tokens]. For example, as he is washed up onto the beach of the imagined island, hardness is transformed into unidentifiable *hard things*:

> **Hard** <u>things</u> touched him about the feet and knees. The sea laid him down gently and retreated. There were **hard** <u>things</u> touching his face and chest, the side of his forehead. The sea came back and fawned round his face, licked him. He thought movements that did not happen. The sea came back and he thought the movements again and this time they happened because the sea took most of his weight. They moved him forward over the **hard** <u>things.</u> (p.22)

This next example illustrates the transition from a general object word to a specific white object, a hand:

> There was a **whiter** <u>thing</u> beyond them. He examined it without curiosity, noting the bleached wrinkles, the blue roots of nails, the corrugations at the finger-tips. (p.24)

Stage 4: Application of the original adjective to an imagined object

As the last example anticipated, the adjectives *white* and *hard* can now be re-applied to the objects of Pincher's imagination, or the nominalisation may be transformed into an object. *Whiteness* is now transferred to:

- Hands

> Inside his head it seemed that the pebbles were shaking because the movement of his **white** hand forward and back was matched by the movement of his body. (p.24)

> That whiter **white** under the water along there is my hand, hidden. (p.41)

- Pebbles, sometimes metaphorically referred to as potatoes

  The **white** pebbles led up into a dark angle. (p.28)

  Their [the pebbles'] **whiteness** was qualified by yellow stains and flecks of darker material. (p.25)

- Guano (erroneously imagined as dissolved)

  When he was below the level of the **white** bird-droppings he stopped and began to examine the rock foot by foot. (p.59)

  He scrabbled in the **white** water with both hands and heaved himself up. He felt the too-smooth wetness running on his face and the brilliant jab of pain at the corner of his right eye. (p.42)

- Seagulls

  A sea-gull was drifting over the water a stone's throw from the rock, and now the bird was rounded, **white** and harmless. (p.62)

  There was a **white** <u>dot</u> sitting between the sun and safety Rock. He watched closely and saw that the dot was a gull sitting in the water, letting itself drift. (pp.114–5)

Let's now turn to *hard*. Initially when Pincher is drowning sounds are very important since presumably the drowning man can actually hear them. But by synaesthesia they are transformed into visual and tactile stimuli which seem more important props for permanence, because less evanescent:

> Words and sounds were sometimes visible as shapes like the shouted order. They did not vibrate and disappear. When they were created they remained as **hard** enduring <u>things</u> like the pebbles. (p.26)

As Kinkead-Weekes and Gregor point out 'the pebbles are first felt, then seen: "solidity … dulled and rounded … potato-shapes … whiteness … qualified by yellow stains and flecks of darker material"' (2002: 101). The quality of hardness realising itself as pebbles, also realises itself as the rock itself.

> Under the weed the rock was furry with coloured growths or **hard** and decorative with stuff that looked like uncooked batter. (p.112)

The ironic consequence of the 4 stages

In keeping with karma, that ultimate feedback mechanism, Pincher's self-delusions, achieved in this four-stage manipulation of lexico-grammar, inflict pain and threaten destruction. The tragic irony of his delusions becomes more seriously apparent towards the end when he realises that the hardness is a property not of the rock but of the remembered tooth:

> There is something venomous about the hardness of this rock. It is **harder** than rock should be. And–familiar.'
> The ponderous weight squeezed down. (p.129)

> The centre attended to the rock between its claws. The rock was **harder** than rock, brighter, firmer. (p.201)

The logical consequence of this is that Pincher becomes food to be eaten by the surviving white maggot:

> 'My flesh aches inside as though it were bruised. The **hardness** of the rock is wearing out my flesh. I will think about water.' (p.126)

> Panic. Black eyes in a **white** face with no more expression than **hard,** black stones.
> Eaten. (pp.154–5)

Or if not devoured by the white maggot, he will be torn to shreds by the white lightning:

> 'Hoé, hoé! Thor's lightning challenges me! Flash after flash, rippling spurts of **white** fire, bolts flung at Prometheus, blinding **white, white, white,** searing, the aim of the sky at the man on the rock.' (pp.188–9)

> Black centre, trying to stir itself like a pudding.
> The darkness was shredded by **white**. (p.192)

> Then the sky above the old woman jumped. It went **white**. An instant later the light was switched off and the sky fell on him. (p.192)

> 'Ajax! Prometheus!'
> The old woman was looking down at him as he struggled through bouts of **white** and dark. Then her head with its silver mask was taken by a **whiteness** and she hunched against the sky with her headless shoulders. He fell in the **white** trench over the book with his face against the engraving and the insoluble muck filled his mouth. (p.192)

Sensation, perception and feeling are, consequently, doubled-edged, initially co-operating in the creation of illusion, in the end recognised as a source of suffering, and imminent destruction. Pain is the condition of existence [2].

Summary

I hope these copious illustrations have made the thrust of my argument clear. Nominalisation for the most part is used by the character Pincher Martin as an accessory in weaving an illusion of reality. He abstracts physical qualities of visual and tactile sensation from memories into the substance of a new reincarnated life. It is a crucial linguistic strategy in making a transition to a congruent world, the world of Newtonian dynamics, from the world of process and flux, symbolised by fluid dynamics and dissipative structures; from the fluid sea to the solid rock. But it is ultimately and ironically self-defeating. As Kinkead-Weekes and Gregor incisively comment, drawing attention to the linguistic deceptions in Golding's novels

> Or we may say that sight is nothing without insight, and may deceive like words; that it is only when the physical eye is 'made quiet' by some deeper kind of perception that we can for a moment 'see into the life of things', wordlessly. (2002: 364)

Less helpfully, Kinkead-Weekes and Gregor draw a contrast between Crusoe's imginative vision and Pincher's. They claim that Crusoe 'sees the world as objects for people to act on, objects dangerous, or useful, or not useful' (2002: 100). That 'the novel will be a loose, widely ranging, rapid account of actions which gradually impose a man's organisation on the world. Golding, on the contrary, will do everything to cut down distance, to maximise detail, to build up the narrative in the detail itself' (2002: 102). However, this contrast is too simple. We have seen how Pincher moves away from the world of sensory detail to construct a world, to 'impose a man's organization on the world'. He does this both by inconsonant uses of nominalisation as well as through the increasing use of transitive material process clauses with Pincher as Actor.

2.3.2   Incongruent but consonant uses of nominalisation

But I also suggested earlier that nominalisation can be used as a means of highlighting certain aspects of consonance. And Golding does so as I show below, particularly when using nominalisation to refer to psychological processes. The kind of analogical reasoning I hinted at before works here, so that the personification of attention and consciousness, for example, and the reification of sensation and intersection, begin to suggest that being is no more than an intersection of processes, personality no more than attentive consciousness, and so-called reality no more than a projection of the mind via remembered sensation.

Attention, conciousness, sensation

These are both given the status of things, reified by nominalisation, and also felt to be first-order entities, because of their collocation with *fasten, into* and *among*:

> The centre felt the gulping of its throat, sent eyesight on ahead to cling desperately to the next light and then the next – anything to fasten the **attention** away from the interior blackness. (p.182)

> Water washed into his mouth and he jerked into **consciousness** with a sound that was half a snore and half a choke. (pp.16–17)

> The darkness was shredded by white. He tumbled over among the **sensations** of the crevice. (p.192)

A further stage goes from reification to personification of the state of consciousness:

> But inside, where the snores were external, the **consciousness** was moving and poking about among the pictures and revelations, among the shape-sounds and the disregarded feelings like an animal ceaselessly examining its cage. (pp.31–2)

For the centre of being is nothing other than man's dark consciousness:

> **Consciousness** in a world asleep. The dark, invulnerable centre that was certain of its own sufficiency. (p.163)

These examples suggest that, instead of interpreting this nominalisation as personification, the metaphorical tension can be resolved by a transfer in the opposite direction, de-personification, so that what we call a person is 'reduced' to consciousness. Existence simply means being conscious.

Intersection

This rather consonant nominalisation suggests that we are constituted by interacting processes, a 'concrescence' in Whitehead's terms (see Sherburne 1981). Looked at mathematically, of course, an intersection, in the improper nominalisation meaning a place where two things intersect, has no more of a spatial dimension than does a point or an elementary particle. It is therefore somewhat ironic that Pincher invokes intersection as a token of the rock's and his own spatial location, extension and identity:

> The solid rock was coherent as an object, with layered guano, with fresh water
> and shell-fish. It was a position in a finite sea at the **intersection** of two lines,
> there were real ships passing under the horizon. (pp.76–7)

Pincher seems willing to describe the personality of Mary Lovell, the girl-friend
who refuses his sexual advances, in terms of an intersection of processes:

> There was the individual, Mary, who was nothing but the **intersection**
> of influences from the cradle up … This **intersection** was so inevitably
> constructed that its every word and action could be predicted. The
> **intersection** would choose the ordinary rather than the exceptional; would
> fly to what was respectable as to a magnet. (p.148)

However, Pincher never really admits that his own personality and being could
be so constructed, or so determinedly predictable. Towards the end of the novel
he takes his last refuge against the destruction of his illusion by pretending to
become mad. In this case the madness inside the madness of illusion works
like a double negative, so that only in this mad speech does he come close to
admitting the ultimate reality:

> 'Mad,' said the mouth, 'raving mad. I can account for everything, lobsters,
> maggots, hardness, brilliant reality, the laws of nature, film-trailers, snapshots
> of sight and sound, flying lizards, enmity – how should a man not be mad?…
>
> All your lobsters and film-trailers are nothing but the random **intersections** of
> instant bushes of lightning …
>
> 'You are the **intersections** of all the currents. You do not exist apart from me.
> If I have gone mad then you have gone mad. You are speaking, in there, you
> and I are one and mad.' (pp.191–92)

2.4   Summary and conclusion: *Pincher Martin* and *The Inheritors*, process and Buddhist philosophy

It is some 35 years since Michael Halliday published his pioneering work in
the stylistics of transitivity in relation to William Golding's *The Inheritors*
(Halliday 1973). He discovered much the same pattern of contrast in the
grammatical sub-codes between the intransitive clause world of Lok, the
Neanderthaler, and the transitive world of agentive homo sapiens, as has been
shown between the Pincher Martin of Passage A, and the Pincher Martin of
Passage B. (This difference in the two tribes in *The Inheritors* was confirmed by
Black (1993: 47), who, incidentally, takes a more positive view of agency than
I do.) A further similarity is that, in Lok's normal mode of existence his body
parts have an autonomous life, rather like that of the autonomous nervous

system, and are seldom brought under the control of an organising purposeful volitional consciousness (Goatly 1987). As Tiger comments, 'Pincher believes that – like the New People in *The Inheritors* – he can survive by the linguistic appropriation of the world' (2003: 100). The contrast between Lok and Pincher is, of course, that Pincher, who inherits his own karma in a second life, goes on to develop into a thorough post Reagan-Thatcher man, who insists on living alone as though there were 'no such thing as society', to coin a phrase. Lok, by contrast, learning of the death of all other members of his tribe, lies down and surrenders his existence, gives up the ghost (*The Inheritors*: 221). Without society life for him is impossible.

The Pincher of Passage B is prototypically naïvely Newtonian in world-view. He dominates the environment and makes changes to it by moving objects (rocks), imposing a force from outside the material universe to effect change in the tradition of Newtonian dynamics. Lok is unable to do this effectively, except when under pressure of survival, and therefore is happier to respond to the environment and accord it the right to remain relatively undisturbed. By contrast, the new people who invade Lok's world, homo sapiens, have begun the long journey of technological development which, in their descendants' time, our time, threatens both the environment and, through negative feedback, or karma, the quality of life, perhaps the life itself, of the human species.

Pincher uses nominalisation, at the discourse level of character, as an inter-mediate strategy in creating this illusory Newtonian world of solid permanent objects subject to his domination and agency. Golding uses nominalisation at the author-reader discourse level[3] to point out the process-based nature of matter. Nominalisation stands Janus-like facing both in the direction of inconsonance and in the direction of consonance.

Finally, we might take a philosophical perspective on the interpretation of *Pincher Martin*. We can interpret the results of our linguistic analysis in relation to process philosophies of the nature of matter and life, philosophies more consonant with the findings of modern science that we discussed briefly in the Introduction, such as those of Whitehead and Peirce. Whitehead (Sherburne 1981) explores how reality is created from one moment to the next and inherited in its interrelatedness in memory and perception. Peirce (1958: Vol. 1 paragraph. 357), in his category of Firstness, conceives the world as it was to Adam 'before he had drawn any distinctions, or had become conscious of his own existence – that is first, present, immediate, fresh, new, initiative, original, spontaneous, free, vivid, conscious, evanescent'. This interpretation contests Kinkead-Weekes and Gregor's claim that Golding is concerned with Being not Becoming and that there is 'no chain of causality between Pincher's past life (cellar) and present (the rock)' (2002: 133–4).

Wishing to adopt a post-post-colonial perspective on the text, I would point out that the religious philosophy of Buddhism is entirely compatible with this philosophical and scientific emphasis on process:

> Until our own time, the West has been unable to free itself from non-process perspectives – philosophies of consciousness – which turn their backs on the immediately experienced, aesthetically breathtaking, rich and intense momentary nows. Non-Buddhist orientations of this kind generate the subject-object duality of thought and thing, mind and body, self and world, spirit and matter, man and nature, time and eternity, fact and value, that no amount of dialectic has ever been able to heal. This is another reason why, as Whitehead told Northrop when the latter was a graduate student in London, 'we cannot be too suspicious of ordinary language, whether in philosophy or everyday life'. (Jacobson 1988: 74)

However, most culturally-imperialist critics of *Pincher Martin*, with the exception of Lee Whitehead (1988), have never entertained the possibility of a non-Western, non-Christian perspective on the novel. Dick (1967) draws parallels between *Pincher Martin* and Dante's *Divine Comedy*, a parallel taken up by Redpath (1986). Boyd (1988) insists even more strongly on a Christian interpretation, drawing explicit comparisons with the Christian significance of *Robinson Crusoe*. Names are used as evidence for this Christian interpretation with Christopher 'the Christ-bearer become Pincher' (Kinkead-Weekes and Gregor 1967: 132) and Dickson (1990) even sees Christopher's suffering as a simulation of Christ's passion. Nathaniel, through allusion to his namesake in the gospels, represents the guileless, innocent saint (Kinkead-Weekes and Gregor 1967: 127–8). Most of the critics cited above emphasise that Pincher is an embodiment of Greed, Virginia Tiger (1974) viewing the fable as a morality play with Pincher playing this particular deadly sin, and his imagined existence on the rock as Purgatory/Hell.

Nor is it surprising that critics sympathetic to Pincher should have interpreted his struggle for survival as a heroic one. The Western ideological obsession with the preservation of life, with its cultural reflection in the genre of shipwreck survival stories (e.g. *Robinson Crusoe*, *A Coral Island*, *Swiss Family Robinson*, *The Poseidon Adventure* etc. and more specifically *Lord of the Flies* and *Pincher Martin O.D.*) is one factor behind such an interpretation. Another is Pincher's own self-comparison with Atlas, Ajax and Prometheus which invites the reader to view him as a tragic hero, punished by the gods but to be pitied and admired (Babb 1970: 95). Kinkead-Weekes and Gregor at one point view it as 'an epic of human endurance' (2002: 103), though they come closer to my evaluation when they admit alternative interpretations 'either heroic or a damnable folly' (2002: 131).

Though the interpretations based on Western religion and myth have a number of textual allusions to back them up, I think the grammar and the patterns of nominalisation which I have analysed demonstrate that the novel can support a process philosophy/Buddhist interpretation just as well as a Christian/heroic tragic one. The following quote from a Buddhist scholar might sum up the gist of this moral fable:

> By ignorance the being fails to view the true impermanent and substanceless nature of existence. He relishes the things of the world, taking them to be real and lasting and creates a craving for them. Due to his cravings, he grasps to attain one and avoid the other. This leads to the continuity of his life process, a chain of struggle for living. His cravings and graspings do not end with the destruction of his physical frame, but they keep the struggle on in another birth. (Kashyap 1954: 212)

Golding in an interview with Campbell talks succinctly about Pincher's 'thirst for separate individual life' (Tiger 2003: 96).

Jacobson, in an introductory book on Buddhism, gives a clear enough picture of Pincher's personality and behaviour, as we glean it from the flashbacks in the novel:

> Or we use people as rungs on the ladder to prestige and social power. However it expresses itself in different people, the unconscious and rigid drives we call *tanha* [craving] become a style of life. They make every affection for another person a crutch for those who cannot stand alone, a friend for those who are afraid of the dark, a source from which to derive the security that is missing in them by nature. We are driven to make into objects for some special need or hunger wonderful people in whose company … there might otherwise be the free play of pure quality that is the food of the human spirit. … *Tanha* is manifested as insatiability … Its function is not to release. (Jacobson 1966: 78)

This chimes with Kinkead-Weekes & Gregor's observation on Golding's moral vision: 'What is before the eyes is converted to an image for the ego's urgency, is a potent source of evil' (2002: 365).

A Buddhist/process interpretation invites us to dissolve the boundaries between the real world outside the fiction, and the 'non-hallucinatory' parts of the fiction (up to p.9 and the final chapter), just as we have been tricked on a first reading into dissolving the 'non-hallucinatory' parts and the 'hallucinatory' parts – from the kicking off of his sea-boots up to the end of chapter 13. From this perspective our life too is not only a fiction but a hallucination.

Notes

1   There are procedural problems in the superventive/non-superventive distinction, especially with verbs which convey manner in their semantics, e.g. *scramble*: The semantic feature of /movement/ is clearly willed, but the manner of moving is not.

2   'Whatever the nature of the sexual impulse in whatever direction it is pointed, it seems, in Golding's works, to be as much pain as pleasure' (Kulkarni 2003: 67).

3   What I have in mind are the levels of discourse in the novel identified by Leech and Short (1981: chapter 8).

3 Corpus linguistics, Systemic Functional Grammar and literary meaning: a critical analysis of *Harry Potter and the Philosopher's Stone*

3.1 Introduction

The enterprise of Critical Discourse Analysis is an attempt to discover the ideology in and behind texts. Some of the ideological representations may be semantically encoded in the text, and analysis which takes this approach I call Critical Linguistics (Fowler, Hodge, Kress and Trew 1979, Fowler 1991 etc.). A stylistic approach which follows Critical Linguistics would attempt to analyse messages to discover sub-codes or patterns of representation which construct or represent the world (Jakobson's Context in Figure 1.1) in ways which reflect or reinforce the power structures of society. However, ideology may be just as prevalent pragmatically, behind the text in the gaps between the lines, as for example when ideologically-fraught assumptions are invoked in the process of implicature, or when the speaker/writer has a complex propositional attitude to what is expressed. Critical Discourse Analysis, it seems to me, has to embrace both semantic encoding and pragmatic inference/propositional attitude (Fairclough 1989). This pragmatic side of CDA has been curiously neglected, a fact pointed out and to some small extent remedied by O'Halloran (2003).

Corpus linguistic analysis obviously aligns itself with the former of these approaches, since it uses techniques such as the calculation of word frequencies and concordancing to investigate the surface forms of the text, and manipulates these forms in a relatively de-contextualised way, thereby precluding inferencing based on supplying information from elsewhere in the text or co-text. The enormous computational power of corpus linguistic techniques has the potential to skew Critical Discourse Analysis in the direction of Critical Linguistics. And this will tend to give an impetus towards a stylistics that remains wedded to the message or the code.

This paper falls into two halves. In Part 1 I use a Critical Linguistic approach, based on Systemic Functional lexico-grammatical (SFG) analysis, to investigate how word frequency data and concordancing can help reveal the ideologies represented in the text. In Part 2 I briefly argue that such an analysis gives only a partial view, and that, especially in the case of literature, the straightforward move from forms to meanings inherent in the semantic Critical Linguistics approach is problematised by factors such as propositional attitude.

In critical analysis of this kind the ideological perspectives that one takes may be of three kinds. First, one can take a deductive approach based on external ideologies, for example interrogating the text for sexist or speciesist ideologies. Second, one could look at the internal ideological preoccupations that are apparent from a reading of the text, for example the ideology of educational competitiveness. Thirdly, one could take a more inductive approach, and keeping 'an open mind' look carefully at concordance and word frequency data to attempt to find hidden ideologies that may not be apparent from reading the text, for example the power of time and the obsession with periods of time.

In Part 1 I demonstrate these three approaches in my analysis of *Harry Potter and the Philosopher's Stone*. This text was chosen because its phenomenal popularity is bound to have ideological effects on its young readers, through cultural reproduction or construction. Just exactly what kind of a world is constructed, validated and celebrated by this novel would seem to be a vital enterprise of cultural analysis.

3.2   Part 1. Applying SFG to the corpus

I shall be using Systemic Functional Linguistics in Part 1. Systemic Functional Grammar is especially useful as a tool for Critical Linguistics and the analysis of representational functions of discourse because, unlike formalist approaches to syntax, it attempts a more or less successful fusion of semantics with syntax (somewhat similar to Case Grammar). Michael Halliday, the prime mover behind this grammar, has always put an emphasis on semiotics, the code of language, and has distanced himself from approaches that make pragmatics a separate field of linguistics divorced from grammar (Halliday 1994). I gave a sketch of Halliday's system of transitivity analysis in chapter 2 (2.1.1), which readers unfamiliar with this kind of grammatical analysis should consult before reading further.

3.2.1   A deductive approach using external ideologies

The first external ideological perspective that I have taken is that of environmentalism or anti-speciesism. Following research into the way in which nature is represented in other texts (Goatly 2000, 2002), I am interested in such representation and the latent effect it might have on the young minds that read it.

In the transitivity analysis in this chapter I adopted the following methodology. I used the Wordsmith software to compile a word frequency list; I then selected the word categories, in this case types of animals and plants, which were mentioned four times or more. I then accessed concordance lines for these categories and investigated the most common patterns in which the words (e.g. *owls*, *trees*) featured as participants or circumstances. (In the following analysis the number of token of the types in italics appears in square brackets.)

Animals

Owls feature as one of the three animals that students are allowed to keep and as the postal service. They are consciously used, if not exploited, by the witches/wizards. Concordance lines for owls and Hedwig (Harry Potter's owl) do represent them as flying: they *swoop* [4], *flutter* [4], *fly*, *speed*, *stream*, *soar* and *battle their way*. Here, as Actors of these intransitive material process clauses, that is without Goals, they are not powerful enough to affect another participant.

However in transitive clauses they are Actors with Goals, which confers more power on them. The main purpose of all this flying is delivering post (the Goal), their major contribution to the action of the book. They *drop* [3] parcels, letters and newspapers, *bring* [5] packages, notes and dead mice, and *carry* packages.

However, the force activating the owls' flight and delivery of messages are the human characters. Owls are the Goals that human Actors *send* [10] and when they arrive at their destinations *get* [2] and *receive*. They are also Goals (of a particular kind called 'Beneficiaries') when humans *pay* or *give* them money for their work. In other cases owls figure as Goals because they have become commodified – bought, kept and treated as the students' possessions: students might not be able to *afford* them but if they can *get* [2] them they can *carry*, *shut* or *hold* them in a cage *bring* them to school or *pull* them from under their overcoat. Their treatment as a commodity also accounts for owls' representation as Possessions in Relational clauses, or Phenomena of affective Mental process: the pupils *have* or *want* them.

To summarise, the representation of owls seems to conform to a similar anthropocentric pattern I noticed in the BBC World Service (Goatly 2002), where animals are most mentioned or significant when they are of use to humans.

Cats are significant because early on in the novel Professor McGonegall is disguised as one. The cat has not entirely lost its human characteristics, 'reading a map' or 'looking at the sign'. It therefore becomes the object of attention for Mr Dursley (and later Dumbledore), that is a Phenomenon with him as Sensor. The former *spots*, *looks at* [2], *watches*, *stares at* it, and the sight of the cat seems to *amuse* him so that he cannot *put it out of his mind*. But the cat can conversely be a Senser/Behaver, who *stares* [2], *watches* [2], and *reads* [2] maps and signs.

Apart from these mental processes the 'cat' is an Actor in intransitive clauses, not having much effect on the other characters or the world around it: *move* [2], *stand*, *sit*, *twitch* and *slink*. The cat would be an effective disguise, this analysis suggests, were it not for the fact that it continues to read maps. The implication is that animals are less significant than humans/witches and therefore more likely to be ignored. Nor, when acting in character, do they make much significant difference to the world.

Apart from this disguise, cats and rats, especially the caretaker's cat Mrs Norris, and Ron's rat Scabbers, tend to be viewed negatively. As Actors in transitive material process clauses they are: destructive, '"He's chewing my sheets." '; violent, 'they were going to get caught by Filch or Mrs Norris', 'Scabbers the rat was hanging off his finger'; or a threat to health '"I don' like cats, they make me sneeze." ' As Actors in intransitive clauses they are sinister: 'they spotted Mrs Norris skulking near the top', 'there were more rats lurking among the sweets'. So, as far as being Goals is concerned, they are viewed as justifiable potential victims: '"An' as fer that cat, Mrs Norris, I'd like ter introduce her to Fang some time"'; 'It was the dearest ambition of many to give Mrs Norris a good kick'; '"Turn this stupid, fat rat yellow." ' The adjectives associated with them are also negative: *scrawny*, *useless* and *old*.

Dogs are viewed not only negatively, but also as a threat, especially the three-headed dog Fluffy who has the participant role of Actor in transitive clauses to *guard* [4] the philosopher's stone, and *bite* anyone trying to get past him. He fulfills his role as a guard dog by being a threatening Actor in intransitive material process clauses, or nominalisations of them: *growl* [3] and *bark*. As a Phenomenon he is repulsive: 'They could feel the dog's hot, smelly breaths'.

Less threatening is, occasionally, Fang, Hagrid's pet boarhound: 'Fang was clearly not as fierce as he looked', even protective: '"There's nothing in the Forest that'll hurt yeh if yer with me or Fang."'

Moreover, being turned into an animal is seen as a punishment. The best example is when Dudley Dursley is turned into a pig by Hagrid: '"Meant ter turn him into a pig, but I suppose he was so much like a pig anyway there wasn't much left ter do …"'

To sum up, the general pattern of representation has non-magical animals as used and exploited (owls), regarded as insignificant relative to humans (cats) or, negatively, as a destructive or violent threat (rats, dogs), and as inferior (pigs).

The one exception is the Brazilian boa constrictor that Harry meets at the zoo. Harry has a special gift of communication with snakes, and this snake is humanised, thereby achieving significance. Even here animals are not significant in their own right, only when having qualities of humans. The communication makes this snake a Sayer in Verbal processes: by way of communication it 'shook its head', 'jabbed its tail at a little sign', 'nodded vigorously' and 'jerked its head towards Uncle Vernon'.

Plants

Plants generally function as marginalised, that is as referred to by the noun phrases in Circumstantial Adjuncts. This is particularly true of grass: *on the grass* [2]; *on to the grass* [2]; 'over the grass'; 'out of the grass'. And it is also true to some extent of trees: 'out of the tree'; 'in a towering beech tree'; 'in the trees'; 'over the branches of the new tree'; 'into the trees'; 'past a mossy tree-stump'; 'up a tree'; 'past the tree'; 'under a tree'; *through the trees* [2]; *behind the/that tree* [2].

Trees, however, are also exploited and used for human cultural purposes, as with Christmas trees, which are Goals: 'they found a large fir tree': ' "the last tree – put it in the far corner" '; 'Hermione followed Hagrid and his tree', or intransitive Actors: 'twelve towering Christmas trees stood around the room'.

Nevertheless, trees in their natural state are, like animals, regarded negatively, mainly as impediments to vision, and therefore threats: as parts of Circumstances, or Tokens when they are typically *dense, dark, thick* and *black*; 'the trees were so thick he couldn't see'; or when they function as Actors, 'the trees blocked their view', 'the Forbidden Forest, whose trees were swaying darkly'. The tendency for trees to collocate with *dark* and *thick*, create sinister overtones of evil in line with the metaphor theme EVIL IS DARK.

In fact the trees in question are those in the Forbidden Forest, almost always seen as a dangerous sinister place, whether as Token where its Values are 'black and silent', 'not safe', 'full of dangerous beasts', or Actor where it 'hides many secrets', or Goal as a place to avoid 'the forest in the grounds is forbidden to all', ' "the quicker he leaves this Forest, the better." ' Similarly as a Circumstance of location the Forbidden Forest is where evil lurks, a place where he 'met vampires', where 'Voldemort's waiting', or where something unknown 'is lurking' or where there's ' "summat bad loose" ', the last two examples suggesting that the reason EVIL IS DARK is that UNKNOWN IS DARK.

Finally, on their way to find the philosopher's stone, Harry, Hermione and Ron encounter a particularly hostile plant, though they are slow to recognise its hostility: ' "Lucky this plant thing's here, really," said Ron'. As an Actor it is particularly powerful and nasty: 'the plant got a firm grip on her', 'trying to stop the plant curling around his neck', 'the plant had started to twist snake-like tendrils around', and the more they fight against it as Actors with plant as Goal, the less successful they are: 'the two boys fought to pull the plant off them, but the more they strained the tighter and faster the plant wound around them'.

On the basis of these most frequent lexical items referring to plants we might generalise that, as with animals, they are depicted as either insignificant (a Circumstance as part of the environment in which things happen), or sinister and hostile.

There are a couple of objections to these generalisations about plants and animals, in that I have omitted discussion of magical creatures, like Hippogriffs, and the herbs used in herbology classes. The reason for the first omission was that I do not regard magical creatures as naturally occurring objects in the real world as we know it. And in the second case herbs were not mentioned four or more times in the word frequency list, which was my criterion for analysis. But let's discuss them here, anyway.

Magical creatures tend to be, like owls, less sinister and less threatening. Their magical character makes them objects of great attention and fascination. Animals are represented as doing something significant, only if they are magical. So the existence of magical animals does nothing to undermine the pattern that, unless exploitable like owls or behaving like humans, ordinary animals are not worth much attention and have negative effects. Plants are treasured and used for magic purposes in herbology classes. But, like animals, they are only valued if they can have magic results and are exploitable. Photosynthesis would not be an interesting object of study in Hogwarts.

Women and men

This is a very male children's book. Two of the three main student characters are male, Ron and Harry, and the student villain Malfoy and his mates, Goyle and Crabbe are all male. *He* occurs 1525 times, and *she* only 229 times!

Only scratching the surface of the question of the representation of males and females, for which there is too much data to analyse, I simply looked at the degree to which women are stereotypically associated with the expression of emotion. The lexical items *cry*, *tears*, *scream* and *shriek*, referring to Behavioural processes, occur disproportionately more with females than with males, bearing in mind that 6 to 7 times as many clauses feature males as females. Look at the instances of *crying* (meaning "weeping" not "shouting") where all but the last are associated with females: 'Gran was crying, she was so happy'; 'their sister, half laughing, half crying'; 'Hermione was crying in the girls' toilets'; 'then he noticed that she was crying; smiling, but crying at the same time'; and 'Hagrid was so shocked, he stopped crying'. Harry himself has learnt not to cry: 'In fact, he wasn't really crying, it had been years since he'd really cried'.

In a similar way notice that 50% of tears are female, and the others belong to Hagrid, as in these three examples: 'Hagrid took one look at him and burst into tears: "It's-all-my-ruddy-fault!" he sobbed'; 'Hagrid shaking with grief and remorse, great tears leaking down into his beard'; and 'he rushed towards Harry and seized his hand, tears in his eyes'. Hagrid (along with Neville who sobs quite a lot), is the most lachrymose of the male characters, conforming to the stereotype of the gentle maudlin giant. Otherwise tears are associated with females: 'Aunt Petunia burst into tears' 'she was in tears'; 'Harry strongly suspected she had burst into tears'.

Turning to *shriek* and *scream* as Behavioural processes, Hermione seems the most frequent Behaver/Actor, closely followed by Dudley and Voldemort. She screams four times and shrieks once, Dudley screams twice, Voldemort screams and shrieks once, Quirell screams once and Aunt Petunia shrieks once. Notice that Harry doesn't scream, any more than he cries: 'Harry would have screamed, but he couldn't make a sound'.

Looking at this small selection of the data we can see crying is disproportionately ascribed to females who also display more frequent tendencies to scream and shriek.

3.2.2   Overt ideologies and ideological categories of the text

To some extent the author may have been aware of the cultural pitfalls of political incorrectness and attempt to overtly counter them in the text, for example the Gryffindor's Quidditch team is composed of males and females in roughly equal proportions. However, I don't suppose anti-speciesism had emerged sufficiently as an ideology to have affected J. K. Rowling's consciousness of political correctness.

We turn now to the more obvious ideological positions which can easily be detected in the text. Various representational preoccupations are apparent on reading the book, but concordancing techniques can make us much more aware of these obsessions and 'overwordings' (Goatly 2000: 340). I look at four areas: rules and conventions; competition; food; and architecture.

Rules and conventions

One of the main preoccupations of the book is the attitude to rules and conventions. Mr Dursley is damned for his obsession with the normal and conventional. He loves the ordinary and hates the weird and unpredictable. Many of the concordance lines for *normal, ordinary* and *weird(o)* represent his 'fictional point of view' (Leech and Short 1981): 'Mrs Dursley had had a nice, normal day'; 'Mr Dursley, however, had a perfectly normal, owl-free morning'; 'they were perfectly normal, thank you very much'; 'Mr Dursley tried to act normally'; 'he kept pointing at perfectly ordinary things like parking meters'; 'This was just an ordinary street full of ordinary people'; 'his eyes fell on a huddle of these weirdos standing quite close by'; 'your parents, well, they were weirdos, no denying it'.

But, paradoxically, Hogwarts, the school, is a place obsessed with rules as well, as though the existence of powerful magic forces necessitates regulation for their control and for protection against them. *Rules* often take the participant role of Goal with the verb *break* [8]. The concern about breaking or not breaking the school rules can be seen in the overwording of modals of obligation (prohibition) *must* and *should*: ' "you mustn't go wandering around the school at night" '; ' "we've got half an hour before lunch, we should be in the library" '; ' "I don't think you should be breaking any more rules!" '; 'Please note that all pupils' clothes should carry name tags'; ' "First-years should note that the forest in the grounds is forbidden" '; ' "no magic should be used between classes" '.

We also have many modal adjectives/past participles of permission, *allowed* [19], and obligation, *supposed* [6], often used with the negative to represent prohibition, like *forbid/forbidden* [11]. These prohibitions and controls apply to Harry when he lives with the Dursleys: 'By the time he was allowed out of his cupboard'; 'he'd never been allowed to eat as much as he liked'; 'of course he was forbidden to ask questions'. But they also apply to the pupils of Hogwarts: ' "first-years aren't allowed them." '; 'they were sure it wouldn't be allowed'; 'FIRST-YEARS ARE NOT ALLOWED THEIR OWN BROOMSTICKS'; ' "Students aren't supposed to know about the Philosopher's Stone" '; 'And now they knew why it was forbidden'; 'the forest in the grounds is forbidden to all pupils'. Ironically, therefore, the same kinds of prohibitions exist both in the Dursley's world and the school which is represented as an escape from it.

Prohibitions apply notably to Hagrid, even to his existence: 'He thought of Hagrid, expelled but allowed to stay on as gamekeeper'; ' "I'm – er – not supposed ter do magic, strictly speakin" '; 'Hagrid looked too big to be allowed'.

Much of the thrill of the exploits of Ron and Harry arises from the well-intentioned breaking of the rules. In this respect the two boys show themselves more socially deviant than Hermione, in keeping with stereotypes about male and female behaviour. It is to Hermione's credit, we suppose, that she becomes more willing to break the rules as her friendship with Harry and Ron develops: 'Hermione had become a bit more relaxed about breaking rules'.

We can conclude that Hogwarts, like the Dursleys' house, is a world of tight and tyrannical control, though more benevolent than the latter. It is the kind of school A.S. Neill believed contributed to the Second World War, the antithesis of his Summerhill (Neill 1968).

Competition

It is, of course, constitutive rules (Searle 1969 etc.) which make possible the main sport at Hogwarts – Quidditch. This leads us to consider a second main aspect of life at Hogwarts. A look at the predominant lexis associated with competition shows how important it is (Tables 3.1 and 3.2), namely team competition between the four houses (competition in exams is relatively unimportant). The competition is epitomised by *Quidditch* [60 tokens] *matches* [24] in which different *sides* [40] *play* [35] *win* [32] or *lose* [49]. By doing so the different *houses* [84], *Gryffindor* [107], *Slytherin* [62], *Hufflepuff* [22] and *Ravenclaw* [12] win *points* [58].

Table 3.1. Frequency of tokens for houses

LEXICAL ITEM	Frequency
GRYFFINDOR	107
HOUSE	84
SLYTHERIN	62
HUFFLEPUFF	22
RAVENCLAW	12

Table 3.2. Lexis of competition for points

LEXICAL ITEM	Frequency
QUIDDITCH	60
POINTS	58
LOST	49
SIDE	40
PLAY	35
WIN	32
TEAM	31
MATCH	24
GAME	20
EXAMS	15
CHESS	12
PLAYERS	11
MARK	9
TROPHY	6

But not only are points awarded for sport and other achievements, they are also deducted as a form of collective punishment. The concordance lines for *points* give us a fair idea of this main preoccupation of the book. They are Goals or Values of the Material or Relational (Possessive) processes most commonly of the verbs *lose* [11], for example: 'any rule-breaking will lose house points'; ' "Fred and George have lost loads of points" '; ' "think of the points you'll lose Gryffindor if you're caught" '; *win* [3], e.g. 'Hopes of winning fifty points for

Gryffindor faded quickly'; '"You each win Gryffindor five points"'; *take* [5], e.g. 'Harry left, before Snape could take any more points from Gryffindor'; '"Snape's always taking points off Fred and George"'; *award* [4], e.g. '"I award Gryffindor house fifty points."'; '"I therefore award ten points to Mr Neville Longbottom."' Notice that Dumbledore does the awarding to and Snape tends to take points away from Gryffindor.

The climax and resolution of the tale comes at the end of the year when the headmaster Dumbledore awards the cup to the house with most points (Rowling 1997: 222ff), underlining the importance of the intense rivalry and hatred between houses, especially Gryffindor and Slytherin. This produces a mind-set not far removed from that of the participants in the Palestine-Israeli conflict, with tendencies to collective punishment and fascism on both sides.

Food

Hogwarts has many of the characteristics of the typical boarding school boys' novel, not least in its obsession with food (Billy Bunter might be a precursor in this respect). The wordlist for items of food is extensive and varied (Table 3.3).

Table 3.3. Food lexis frequencies

EAT	24	LUNCH	5	WALNUT	2
CHOCOLATE	16	TOAST	4	TRIFLE	2
EGG	15	SANDWICHES	4	TASTED	2
CAKE	14	PUMPKIN	4	TART	2
FLAVOUR	11	POTATOES	4	SUGAR	2
BREAKFAST	11	PEAS	4	RATIONS	2
FOOD	10	HAMBURGER	4	PORRIDGE	2
SWEETS	9	FUDGE	4	NIBBLE	2
SAUSAGES	9	FEED	4	MILK	2
FEAST	9	CREAM	4	MARMALADE	2
SWALLOWED	8	WINE	3	LIVER	2
LEMON	7	TURKEY	3	KETCHUP	2
BACON	7	TREACLE	3	JELLY	2
PASTY	6	PIE	3	HUNGER	2
HUNGRY	6	JAM	3	HAM	2
SHERBET	5	HUMBUGS	3	GRAVY	2
ROAST	5	CHICKEN	3	CRUMPETS	2
PUDDING	5	YORKSHIRE (Pudding?)	2	CHOPS	2
MARS	5			CABBAGE	2

However, the food here is quintessentially English. Though in ethnicity there are some token gestures towards multi-culturalism in the student population – Parvati Patil, and Neville with his dreadlocks – this certainly doesn't apply to food. Is this because Hogwarts represents a deliberately archaic world with its steam train and Gothic architecture? For whatever reason, this is a world which either predates or ignores the culinary delights of chow mien, kebabs, moussaka, spaghetti, tom yam gung, madras curry, and other staples of the English high street.

Architecture

The obsession with architectural terms and the Gothic building of Hogwarts castle is another aspect of deliberate archaism. We might be aware of this obsession, but, again it becomes even more obvious when we consult a word list (Table 3.4). Freudian analysis would have a field day with all these openings and closings, lockings and unlockings of doors, the running along corridors, the climbing of towers, the hiding around corners, the vaults, the trapdoors, the forbidden corridors and the boys penetrating the girls' toilets.

Table 3.4. Architectural features lexis frequencies

DOOR	119	PLATFORM	25	TOWER	15
ROOM	96	CORNER	25	CHAMBER	15
FLOOR	57	CASTLE	23	STAIRCASE	14
WALL	52	KEY	22	UPSTAIRS	13
HALL	50	CUPBOARD	22	TOILET	12
WINDOW	44	CEILING	20	VAULT	10
CORRIDOR	38	HUT	19	TRAPDOOR	10
				STAIRS	10

3.2.3   Inductive discovery of representation and ideology

An inductive method involves the use of concordance data to reveal important categories of ontological and ideological representation which might escape an ordinary reading of the book.

Self-control

For example, while the prevalence of rules and the house/points system is extremely obvious from even a superficial reading of the novel, the related notion of self-control, or self-prohibition is less obvious and would probably only emerge from a consideration of concordance lines for *not/n't*. Here we have a bunch of examples in which Harry and our other heroes attempt to exercise self-control. Harry promises himself and swears to himself and makes a resolution 'not to meddle'. He thinks is best 'not to argue' is careful 'not to blink', fights/tries 'not to laugh', tries (hard) 'not to look at Malfoy', 'not to panic' and 'not to listen to her'. However, he and the other heroes are often unsuccessful in these attempts at self-control. Harry *couldn't help* [5] 'thinking', 'cheering', 'trusting him', 'noticing', 'overhearing' and 'couldn't keep his eyes off them', while Ron 'couldn't resist it'.

Thus we observe that the external system of rules, imposed by the school hierarchy and creatively broken by our heroes, is mirrored by internal attempts at self-control, which, are also transgressed when the pressure becomes too great.

Process patterns

Another way to reveal latent ideology is to look at patterns of verbs, using Systemic Functional Grammar transitivity analysis process categories, though doing this from a wordlist is a rather inexact method (see Table 3.5). Roughly speaking, it would seem to be the case that Material processes of action – in which the Actor has a real and important (if not irreversible) impact on the Goal – do not constitute the majority of the processes [2,430]. Material processes of travel in which we have Ranges rather than Goals are also very important [1,670]. Even more so the Mental/Behavioural outnumber the Goal directed processes [2,680]. And Verbal processes are equally important [1760].

Table 3.5. Frequency of process types

MATERIAL, EXCLUDING MOVEMENT	2429
MATERIAL, MOVEMENT ONLY	1674
MENTAL/BEHAVIOURAL	2680
VERBAL	1759

These general patterns might seem surprising in what is an action adventure novel. However a great deal of the action actually involves our three heroes moving themselves along and through and up and down all those architectural features we identified in the last section of 3.2.2 (Table 3.4), which thus become Ranges or parts of Circumstantial Adjuncts of direction (Table 3.6).

Table 3.6. Verbs of Material processes of movement

GO	308	SIT	82	RUN	52	STEP	38
COME	204	WALK	72	FOLLOW	49	FLY	52
LEAVE	113	FALL	57	WAIT	45	STAY	34
STAND	97	MOVE	56	REACH	43	HURRIED	32

Table 3.7. Mental process verbs

LOOK	421	REMEMBER	54	LEARN	29
KNOW	323	SMILE	48	BELIEVE	29
SEE	300	NOTICE	46	WORRY	27
THINK	244	PLEASE	42	EXPECT	27
LIKE	210	FORGET	39	LAUGH	23
WANT	136	SOUND	38	WISH	19
HEAR	106	HOPE	37	SURPRISE	19
FEEL	95	WONDER	36	UNDERSTAND	18
STARE	63	LISTEN	30	LEARN	29
WATCH	58	SUPPOSE	29	BELIEVE	29

The novel is also a mystery novel. Many of the Mental processes (Table 3.7) are to do with looking, watching for evidence, trying to learn and understand what is going on, wondering what the outcome of the adventures will be, and hoping it is a successful one. There is the additional experience of surprise that Snape is not, after all, the villain, and is not bullying Quirrell, but vice-versa.

The discovery of information, often from books in which Hermione is an expert, but also from observation, leads to the sharing of it among the three friends, which partly accounts for the importance of Verbal processes (Table 3.8). They share their information in the quest to understand and discuss and try to explain what it might mean.

Table 3.8. Verbal process verbs

SAY	915	MEAN	51	LIE	29	CURSE	19
TELL	190	WHISPER	48	ANSWER	26	WRITE	17
ASK	99	SPEAK	45	YELL	22	ADD	16
CALL	65	SHOUT	36	WARN	20	MENTION	12
TALK	51	MUTTER	31	EXPLAIN	20	AGREE	12

Time

Time is the most frequently occurring lexical item in any general-purpose corpus of English, for example the Cobuild WordbanksOnline. Despite that, it does seem that lexis to do with time is especially important in this novel (Table 3.9). Birthdays and Christmases recur annually. The year is neatly divided into terms, and holidays. The terms, with exams at the end and Quidditch matches punctuating them, are divided into weeks, and the weeks and days into timetabled periods. This is part of a larger pattern in which each of the seven novels in the Harry Potter sequence represents one year in his school life.

Table 3.9. Time lexis frequencies

TIME	146	SECOND	58	NEW	38
NEXT	96	YEARS	51	YEAR	37
LAST	84	MOMENT	50	WEEK	33
LONG	71	NIGHT	49	MORNING	32
DAY	71	PAST	44	CHRISTMAS	24
OLD	67	MINUTES	44	HOUR	22
LATE	60				

What is most apparent from concordance lines is the sense that there is never enough time to do things. *Late* is especially frequent as a Value in Relational Clauses: ' "It's gettin' late and we've got lots ter do tomorrow" '; 'They were a bit late arriving at Hagrid's hut'; ' "when you were late for class" '; ' "Hagrid's late" '; "'That's why yer late, is it?" ', ' "He's late, maybe he's chickened out," '; ' "We've got to go, we're going to be late." '; ' "I feared I might be too late." '; ' "It was a bit late to repair the damage" '; ' "It's too late to change the plan now" '.

The reason the heroes are late is that usually they do not have enough time to do things: 'Harry and Ron barely had time to exchange mystified looks'; 'They didn't have time to come and fetch anyone'; ' "She hasn't got much time," he added quickly'; 'Harry had even less time than the other two'; ' "We haven't got time to send Charlie another owl" '. Where time is the Goal it is therefore a commodity or gift that is highly valued: 'They couldn't afford to waste any more time'; 'which gave Harry time to dry his eyes on the sheet'; 'giving Harry time to run around it'. Their frequent and anxious racing against time is demonstrated by its occurrence in the Circumstantial Adjunct *in time*: Ron only just noticed in time' ' "I arrived in time to prevent that" '; ' "I arrived just in time to pull Quirrell off you" '; 'he caught it, just in time to pull his broom straight'; 'Snape turned on his broomstick just in time to see something scarlet shoot past'; ' "Hagrid collected that package just in time?" '

3.2.4 Summary

The world of *Harry Potter and the Philosopher's Stone* which emerges from concordance data is not a very attractive one to me, though it appears to be to juvenile readers. Let's summarise the findings in terms of the three ideological perspectives we established at the outset.

(1) From the external deductive ideological perspectives of feminism and environmentalism:

- The world generally conforms to sexist stereotypes, especially in the propensities to cry, though there are some deliberate attempts to make token gestures towards a more feminist attitude.

- Animals and plants are portrayed as dangerous, exploitable, and if not magic, insignificant.

The stance here, apart from the tokenism, is fundamentally sexist, and certainly speciesist.

(2) From its own overt ideological perspective:

- It is reminiscent in its excessive emphasis on rules and prohibitions and self-control of the Blake poem: 'I went to the garden of love/and saw what I never had seen/A chapel was built in the midst/…And "thou shalt not" writ over the door'.

- The regime of fierce competition between mutually hating houses breeds an unhealthy rivalry.

- It is parochially and archaically English, especially in its food and Gothic architecture.

The reader is, perhaps, expected to accept this world of authoritarian control, fierce rivalry and collective punishment, as natural and even exciting within the school context. And to enjoy the quaintness of the archaic, part of the commodification of history on which much of British tourism depends.

(3) From an inductive latent ideological perspective:

- The heroes often attempt to exert self-control, though not always successfully, as a mirror image of the external controls imposed on them.

- The heroes spend much time ranging over Hogwarts castle in a desperate race against time.

- They spend most of their remaining time in a state of mental turbulence, wondering, worrying and talking about things they don't understand.

These observations suggest that children are being asked to accept the tyranny of time and regulations as a bureaucratic mechanism of control, and the accompanying anxieties which such a control engenders.

3.3   Part 2. Questioning the SFG-corpus approach

In the second part of this chapter I wish to question the validity of this kind of Critical Linguistic approach to literary analysis and to locate it within a recent debate on Critical Discourse Analysis in relation to the role of concordancing, corpora-based textual analysis and the role of pragmatics.

Widdowson (1998) launched an attack on the ad hoc kind of Critical Discourse Analysis he found in some passages of Fairclough (Fairclough 1992, 1995). Stubbs (2001) developed a counter argument in which he claimed that concordancing techniques of the kind exemplified in Part 1 can give quantitative evidence to validate or challenge the kinds of analyses to which Widdowson was objecting. However, as Widdowson had pointed out (2000), there is an important role for Pragmatics in textual interpretation, so that meanings cannot be simply decoded from the surface of the text, as is the tendency both in Hallidayan analysis and concordancing. This means that the approach I have exemplified, and which I call Critical Linguistics, reinforced by the powerful tools of concordancing, may lead us to unwarranted conclusions.

How, then, might the analysis in part A have been faulty? The main problem seems to be the ignoring of propositional attitude (Sperber and Wilson 1995). Concordancing is a powerful way of gaining access to patterns of propositions at the representational level of discourse. But what is the author's attitude to these patterns?

The necessity for factoring in propositional attitude in text interpretation is nowhere clearer than in cases of irony and parody. In both these cases the surface of the text resembles almost to the point of identity an equivalent non-ironic statement or the genre or text which is being parodied. But in neither case can the author be seen as making assertions to which he/she subscribes or as observing the purposes of the genre being parodied. There is a humorous or critical distance between what is said and what is believed or endorsed.

So what of J. K. Rowling's propositional attitude to Hogwarts as she represents it in the clauses of this book? I am thinking particularly here of the linguistic representations analysed in 3.2.2 – overt ideologies and ideological categories of the text. Is the obsession with food and the highly developed house system a kind of parody of earlier school novels like Jennings and Billy Bunter? And what of her attitude to the competitiveness? In a later novel, *Harry Potter and the Goblet of Fire*, she has Harry sacrifice valuable time by rescuing Gabrielle, a competitor from a rival school, from an underwater death. Does this indicate that at the time of writing *Harry Potter and the Philosopher's Stone* she did not entirely celebrate the ultra-competitive aspect of Hogwarts' life? Or was it only later, in retrospect, that she felt she needed to move way from celebrating rivalry towards endorsing more co-operative values? It might seem that Dumbledore's climactic speech, in which he announces that the House Cup has just been won by Gryffindor (p.221), indicates that the house system and Gryffindor's winning is being celebrated not just by the hero but also by the author. But could this last minute success, against expectations, have something of the parodic about it? Doesn't it remind you of those interminable hours of school speech days and prize-givings, and make you shudder? And is it intended to?

My position on the kind of approach exemplified in part 1 of this chapter (3.2) is as follows. The Critical Linguistic approach using concordancing is extremely valuable if one is dealing with large quantities of text, and does, indeed provide quantitative evidence or patterns of representation or of ideological bias. It establishes aspects of or probabilities within a social *langue* or sub-code (Stubbs 2001: 168), for example the BBC World Service on nature (Goatly 2002). However, it may be more useful for some genres than for others (Goatly 1997: chapter 10). Stubbs (2001: 153) has pointed out that in some genres convention contributes relatively more to meaning than inference. For example, cases of irony in the language of air-traffic control are minimal (one hopes), and the same is likely to be true of news reports. In the novel, however, a non-instrumental or ludic genre, with its multiple levels of discourse and interpenetrating voices – character, narrator (implied author) – there are manifold opportunities for taking a complex propositional attitude to the meanings encoded in the text.

Children's novels, may, however, be a slightly different case. Children's capacity for detecting irony and parody are less developed than adults' (Winner

1988). And a writer cannot therefore rely on children recognising ironic distance. The writer may have that distance herself, and expect adult readers to recognise it, but it would be naïve of her to expect the children reading *Harry Potter and the Philosopher's Stone* to see Gryffindor's success, for example, as anything other than a fact to be celebrated. Moreover, as for the representations analysed in 3.2.1 and 3.2.3 of Part 1, if these stereotypes and patterns are latent and unrecognised, then the author will not have an attitude towards them. Unless she knows how she has marginalised grass and trees by placing them as Circumstances in most of her clauses she will not have an attitude which distances her from this marginalisation. The analysis in Part 1 is therefore justified on two counts: ideological representations latent even to the author will escape 'attitude' altogether; and, second, children may take the deliberate patterns of representation at face value. We can conclude that the values detected in Part 1 may have a significant effect on the construction and reproduction of ideology in young minds.

4 Marked Theme and its interpretation in A. E. Housman's *A Shropshire Lad*

4.1 Introduction

4.1.1 Why study Theme in *A Shropshire Lad*?

There are a number of reasons why *A Shrophire Lad* (hereafter *ASL*) invites analysis of marked thematic patterns. Firstly, any cursory glance at the poems in the sequence will show up a number of interesting phenomena in Housman's use of Theme, notably distinctively frequent

- marked Themes
- multiply-marked Themes
- preposed and postposed Themes.

The first stanza of poem 31 illustrates these tendencies:

> On Wenlock Edge the wood's in trouble
> His forest fleece the Wrekin heaves.
> The gale, it plies the saplings double
> And thick on Severn snow the leaves.

Theme position is not straightforwardly occupied by the Subject in any of the four clauses/lines. In the first the Circumstantial Adjunct provides the marked Theme; in the second the Theme is even more marked, being the Object; in the third the co-referring 'the gale' has been preposed before the 'it', the Subject of the clause; and in the fourth line/clause we have three marked Themes – Adjunct, Adjunct, Verb – preceding the Subject.

Secondly, of course, being poetry, which allows it a certain amount of licence, there is likely to be considerably more freedom in word order than in prose, and this will enhance the opportunities for marked Theme. Statistically this might mean that the probabilities of different syntactic elements being found in marked thematic position will be little different from prose in relative terms, but that the most marked of these, e.g. Object and Verb, will be more frequently represented in poems.

Thirdly, Housman spent most of his intellectual energy, not on the production of poetry, which was a minor sideline, but on the editing of classical Latin texts. It may be interesting, related to the second point about poetic licence, to discover whether the rules of classical rhetoric and the looser word order of classical poetry influence the use of marked Theme and thematic progression in his own poetry.

More generally, patterns of marked Theme (upper case henceforth) may be stylistically significant in a number of ways: pinpointing the structural organisation of individual poems; defining *ASL's* overall 'theme' in the non-technical, literary sense (lower case henceforth); and correlating with the shifts in poetic sub-genres between lyric and dialogue throughout the poem sequence. More specifically we can suggest for individual poems the effects on interpretation of marked, especially multiply-marked, Theme; what kinds of reader response might be suggested to a particular sequence which postpones, sometimes to an extreme extent, the subject of a clause? In considering these issues and questions Marked-Theme linguistic analysis can achieve stylistic status and bridge the gap between linguistics and literary criticism.

Sections 4.1.2–4.1.5 of this chapter defines the thematic management phenomena under consideration and the technical terms used. Section 4.2 gives details of the method of analysis and discusses theoretical problems arising from it, such as the definition of mood and the ambiguity of metafunction. In section 4.3 I move on to the results and discussion: in 4.3.1 I consider the method of development, the semantic content of marked Themes, and the relationship between this and literary critical comments on the importance of time, place and exile to literary theme; 4.3.2 and 4.3.3 proceed to an analysis of the use of marked Theme and multiply-marked Theme in the ten individual poems where they are most frequent, showing how their use relates to the schemes of classical rhetoric, and how they might affect reader response. In 4.3.4 I consider the fluctuating frequency of marked Theme throughout the sequence, and find that its use correlates with degrees of dramatisation or dialogism. Subsection 4.3.5 places the analysis in the context of earlier studies which relate thematic management and method of development to different genres.

4.1.2   Technical terms: theme, marked theme and method of development

As Firbas (1992) has pointed out, when talking about Theme we need to distinguish two possible notions of 'point of departure'. One notion is in terms of linear order. The other is in terms of interpretation, in which point of departure is a psychological concept, relating to low degrees of communicative dynamism. Adopting the first notion, I shall use *Theme* as a label based on the ordering of clausal elements, both for simplicity's sake, and because a considerable amount of the Systemic Functional work on Theme adopts this linear/syntactic definition. We may use the conventional terms *given* and *new* to indicate respectively lower and higher degrees of communicative dynamism; *given* refers to the interpretative or psychological point of departure.

Topical Theme (Halliday 1985: 53ff), as far as English is concerned, refers to the first element from among Subject, Verb, Complement/Object, Adjunct to occur in a clause. As the focus of this study is not interpersonal or textual Theme, the default interpretation of the word *Theme* from now on will be topical or ideational Theme. *Marked Theme* occurs in declarative mood clauses if an element other than Subject takes initial position in the clause; or in imperative and interrogative moods when an element other than Finite/Verb takes initial position.

Method of development (Fries 1992) is concerned with the semantic patterns set up in the successive Theme positions, the way in which semantic choices for Theme function as an organising principle of the text.

4.1.3   Degrees of markedness

If the markedness depends on degrees of improbability, then we can presumably say that some marked Themes are more marked than others (Halliday 1985a: 45). Intuitively, in the stanza quoted above, the marked Theme in line 1 of 'On Wenlock Edge' a Circumstantial Adjunct, is less marked than the marked Theme in line 2, 'His forest fleece' which is an Object. In English in declarative clauses, the Verb element is even less easy to get into marked Theme position than the Complement/Object. One normally has to have recourse to the thematic equative, e.g. 'Kill the king was what he did', or use non-finite participial clauses (Fries 1992: 11), e.g.:

> Loitering with a vacant eye
> Along the Grecian gallery
> And brooding on my heavy ill …

However, we can see that Housman exploits certain other grammatical resources besides thematic equatives and participial clauses to thematise the verb, notably the dummy Subject. Normally one would expect the dummy Subject *there* to introduce an existential process verb, but sometimes Housman uses it with material/behavioural process[1] verbs:

> There sleeps in Shrewsbury jail tonight, or wakes as may betide
> A better lad, if things went right than most that sleep outside. (9)

In some sense one might wish to make the claim with Fries (1983: 119) that marked Themes are more truly thematic than non-marked Themes. If Theme is 'everything located at the beginning of the sentence as a result of choice', then markedness of Theme or use of special resources to put Complements/Objects and Verbs in initial position betrays a deliberate choice; by contrast the default use of Subject as Theme may be quite automatic.

4.1.4   Additional grammatical resources for thematic management

I have already commented on the use of the dummy Subject *there*, participial clauses and thematic equatives in relation to the thematisation of verbs, though the latter are not an important resource in *ASL*. Preposed Themes, too, have been exemplified 'The gale, it plies the saplings double' (cf. Fries 1991: 15). These latter are one kind of *Theme substitution* (Halliday 1967, Matthiessen 1992: 76); another common kind is *postposed Theme*, e.g.

It has not died the war that sleeps on Severn side

We also need to mention the class of *predicated Themes*, for example:

'tis fifty years tonight that God has saved the Queen (1)
'tis little enough they leave (5)

In terms of marked Themes, predication of this kind is only significant if what is predicated is a clause element other than the Subject. So the quote from poem 49 is less significant for my purposes in this chapter than those from (1) and (5) which predicate Circumstantial Time Adjunct and Object respectively.

'Tis jesting, dancing, drinking spins the heavy world around (49)

4.1.5   Marked thematic clauses

So far I have been discussing the individual clause as the unit of informational structuring, but, when we turn to the clause complex or sentence as an information unit, we can make a case for labelling the initial clause in the complex as thematic (Fries 1983: 121). It is claimed that subordinate or hypotactic clauses have a higher probability of occurrence in non-initial position; this allows us to label subordinate/hypotactic clauses occurring in initial position in the clause complex as *marked thematic clauses.*

4.2   Method of analysis

4.2.1   Procedure

The sixty-three poems in the *ASL* sequence were analysed to identify the marked topical Themes in finite clauses, according to the definition given above. But the identification produced two separate kinds of list: in the first (hereafter referred to as *S*) multiply-marked Themes were counted once, with only the initial marked Theme being identified; in the second kind of list (referred to as *M*) the multiply-marked Themes were all counted, i.e. all of the experiential constituents in declarative clauses which preceded the Subject. For example, in

And thick on Severn snow the leaves

the S-type list would identify only one marked topical Theme, *thick*; whereas the M-type would identify three, 'thick', 'on Severn', and 'snow'.

Next the marked Themes in the basic S- and M-type lists were classified into the following categories and subcategories to give Table 4.1:

- ADJECTIVAL ADJUNCT
- ADVERBIAL ADJUNCT: accompaniment, beneficiary, place (direction, position, position/direction), manner, reason, state, state/time, time
- COMPLEMENT/OBJECT
- VERB

In addition the following Theme-management structures were noted:

- PREPOSED THEME
- POSTPOSED THEME
- PREDICATED THEME
- 'DUMMY' *THERE* + MATERIAL PROCESS VERB
- INFINITIVE CLAUSES
- PARTICIPIAL CLAUSES
- MARKED THEMATIC CLAUSES: concession, condition, place, reason, time

The last of these furnishes us with Table 4.3.

Subsequently the two basic lists were sorted in various ways. One way was to sort by category and then alphabetically in order to show word frequencies in the entire sequence (Table 4.2). For example, we can investigate how frequently the lexical item *far* is used as a marked thematic adverbial Adjunct:

Far and near and low and louder on the roads of earth go by, dear to friends
    and food for powder soldiers marching ...
Far I hear the steady drummer ...
Far in a western brookland that bred me long ago the poplars stand and
    tremble ...
Far behind a fading crest low in the forsaken west sank the high-reared head
    of Clee.
Far I hear the bugle blow
Far must it remove.
Far the calling bugles hollo, ...
Far, far must it remove.
Far from his folk a dead lad lies ...

Another way of sorting was to group members of categories and sub-categories poem by poem, in order to show significant patternings of categories of marked Theme and other thematic management structures in particular poems (Table 4.4). For instance the following section of the M-list of marked Themes shows the re-occurrence of verbs as the second of a multiply-marked Theme in poem (61).

> lie friends of mine
> lie Hughley people
> lie parted with Hughley tower above the kind the single-hearted the lads I
>   used to love
> slumber the slayers of themselves

Frequency of occurrence of particular classes of marked Theme and thematic management structures was used as a basis for selecting individual poems to be analysed for thematic patterning, and for the influence of classical rhetoric. The same was done for multiply-marked Themes (selected from Table 4.4) in order to analyse their literary effects and possible reader responses in some detail.

Finally, by counting the number of clauses in each poem and using the M-type inventory of marked Themes, I could calculate the percentage of marked Themes per clause in each poem (Figure 4.1). When counting these I limited myself to finite clauses, and ignored paratactically co-ordinated clauses with Subject ellipsis in the second clause, since the ellipsis makes it impossible to apply my definition of marked Theme. The calculation of marked Themes included predicated and preposed Themes only when a constituent other than Subject was preposed or predicated.

These calculations of relative frequencies of marked Theme for each poem allowed me to look at the overall fluctuations in the sequence, and to establish any patterns or sudden shifts, internal foregroundings whose significance might be worth investigation. In order to explain the patterns, I classified each poem into one of four groups on the basis of its degree of dialogism or dramatisation, and tested the hypothesis that the percentage of marked Themes per poem correlated inversely with the degrees of dialogism (Table 4.7).

4.2.2   Methodological matters arising from analysis

Ambiguity of metafunction

Matthiessen has convincingly explained how the textual metafunction uses the resources of the other two metafunctions, in much the same way as a wave uses water as its medium of transmission: 'grammatical constituency [experiential] can serve as a carrier of a textual wave just as prosody [interpersonal] can)' (1992: 52) (my material in brackets). This is one reason why certain initial deictic adjuncts such as *now*, *then* and to a lesser extent *here* and *there* can raise difficult problems of classification as either textual or topical Themes. I am not just referring to the ambiguity between place/time deixis and text deixis, according to the metaphor of a text as a path. Actually, it seems to me there is a more fundamental ambiguity based on the fact that any time or place ordering in the world (ideational) which is iconically reflected in the text (textual) can be interpreted as either ideational, giving rise to topical Themes, or textual. On the principle that the hegemony of text over psychology and context has already gone too far (see Goatly 1994) I am inclined to interpret the very frequent uses of *here* and *now*, *then* and *there* as topical, but their very frequency in thematic position, the mildness of their markedness, suggests they are to some extent textual too.

Turning to the conflation of interpersonal and topical Theme, we note a recurring structure in *ASL* in which a vocative, normally defined as an interpersonal Theme, functions also as a preposed topical Theme:

> Empty vessel, garment cast, we that wore you long shall last   (43)
> Hand, you have held true fellow's hands   (37)
> Oh lads, at home I heard you plain (38)

These, though in some sense interpersonal, were counted in the calculation of preposed Themes.

Systematic processing ambiguity of relative clauses

On the basis of the experience of analysis I wish to make the rather unconventional suggestion that in *ASL* Housman actually exploits relative clauses with deleted Object relative pronouns, as a means of creating a structure equivalent to marked Object Theme.

> eyes the shady night has shut cannot see the record cut

In processing this clause complex as far as *shut*, the absence of relative pronoun allows us to parse 'eyes' as the Object marked Theme of a main clause; only when we read on do we realise that 'eyes' is in fact the Subject of a main clause: 'eyes … cannot see the record cut'.

Exclamative and other ambiguities of mood

Martin (1992: 44) has made the suggestion that we need to split the mood signalled by the ordering Subject ^ Finite into two, the declarative and the exclamative. Presumably the criterion for recognising the exclamative mood is the use of: either *what/how* as a modifer to form a group functioning as Complement, followed by a Subject, followed by Finite relational process Verb; or *how* as a modifier of an adverb to form a group functioning as Circumstantial Adjunct of manner, followed by a Subject, followed by a Finite Verb (optionally followed by Object/Complement).

Whether one recognises two moods expressed by Subject ^ Finite or not will affect the analysis of marked Theme in structures like the following:

> how green the grass is all about (5)
> how thick the goldcup flowers are lying in field and lane (5)
> How soft the poplars sigh (52)

Recognising exclamative mood will mean they are unmarked, but if these exclamations are subsumed under declarative mood they have to be treated as marked.

A further problem in identifying mood arises with the following ambiguous structures.

> Be you the men you've been (1)
> Get you the sons your fathers got and God will save the Queen. (1)
> Come you home a hero (3)
> Oh come you home on Sunday (3)
> Or come you home on Monday (3)

It is difficult to define the mood here, partly because of possible archaism, but partly because in the context and with the provision of 'you' as Subject we have a choice between treating them as imperatives, or as equivalent to conditional declaratives. Even in present-day English there is something of the conditional about the first clause of

> Open an Account with Standard Chartered and win a Volvo.

In my analysis I treated them as marked Themes, rather than imperatives, arbitrary though that decision may have been.

Verbs as non-initial marked Themes

One notable feature of the details of Table 4.1 is the large discrepancy between the S-list and the M-list as far as Verbs are concerned, 10 as against 54. This reflects the fact that once an Adjunct has been used as marked Theme it is easier to promote the Verb to second position of the multiply-marked Theme. The resulting adjacency of Adjunct and Verb is particularly idiomatic when the Adjunct is semantically oriented towards the Verb,

> Out went the cat (my example)
> long will wait the fold (8)

or when the Subject of the clause is modified or qualified:

> Here and there will flower the solitary stars (63)
> Like a skylit water stood the bluebells in the azured wood (41)

Marlow points out that these Subject-Verb inversions are associated with balladic style, as in

> Up then crew the red red cock, and up and crew the grey. (Marlow 1958: 7)

4.3   Results and discussion

4.3.1   The semantic fields of marked Themes and their relation to literary theme

Both Tables 4.1 and 4.2 (and to some extent also Table 4.3) give a clear indication of the semantic fields which have significance for the overall method of development of *ASL*. As Fries says 'When a text is perceived to have such a method of development then the Themes of the component T-units will derive from some limited set of semantic fields' (Fries 1992: 3). He also points out that *topic* (what I call *literary theme*) and *method of development* should be distinct concepts (1983: 135), so that the semantic fields represented by our marked Themes, notably time and place, are not necessarily significant from the literary theme perspective. However, if one can show that the semantic fields frequently represented by the Theme are also frequently represented in non-Theme, then literary theme and method of development may, in certain cases, converge. So we should keep open the possibility that the semantics of marked Theme, linked to method of development of a text, have potential significance in establishing theme in the literary sense, at least as far as *ASL* is concerned.

In the case of Themes which are marked, there is an additional argument for claiming that their semantic patterns can be linked to literary theme or topic. Hasan (1989: 95–8) recognises a correlation between foregrounding and thematic meaning in the literary sense, and, of course, the markedness of the Themes under discussion is one kind of foregrounding. This section of the chapter will explore these questions of the convergence of literary theme and method of development.

Table 4.1. Frequency of marked Theme by class and subclass

CLASS OF MARKED THEME	M-TYPE	S-TYPE
ADJECTIVAL ADJUNCT	45	34
ADVERBIAL ADJUNCT	276	181
accompaniment	2	2
beneficiary	4	1
place	167	98
direction	31	18
position	93	52
position/direction	43	28
manner	17	11
reason	4	3
state	5	0
time	77	66
OBJECT	11	10
VERB	54	10
TOTAL	**386**	**235**

The semantic fields represented in (Adjunct) marked Themes in Tables 4.1 and 4.2 can be related to frequent comments of literary critics on the themes of *ASL*. Many of these comments may be summed up under the categories of time, place and exile. Housman seems obsessed with the following: the passing of time, contrasts between life and death, often the ironic, but happy deaths of the young, contrasts between past and present, unfaithfulness in love predicated on the passing of time; the depiction of a relatively idyllic countryside and its rustic inhabitants, in contrast with the town; and – bringing the two strands of time and place together – with the notion of exile, whether of the older man from the countryside of his youth, or of the soldier destined to die in foreign fields.

Table 4. 2. Item frequency in initial position of marked Theme

CLASS	WORD	NUMBER
ADJUNCT PLACE	*HERE*	19
ADJUNCT PLACE	*THERE*	16
ADJUNCT PLACE	*LOW*	3
ADJUNCT PLACE	*DOWN*	3
ADJUNCT TIME	*NOW*	20
ADJUNCT TIME	*THEN*	14
ADJUNCT TIME	*LONG*	5
ADJUNCT TIME	*TODAY*	3
ADJUNCT/ADJECTIVE	*FAR*	9
ADJUNCT/ADJECTIVE	*STILL*	6
ADJUNCT/ADJECTIVE	*SICK*	3
ADJUNCT/ADJECTIVE	*HIGH*	3
ADJUNCT/PRONOUN	*HOW*	5
PREPOSITION	*IN*	26
PREPOSITION	*ON*	17
PREPOSITION	*TO*	13
PREPOSITION	*WITH*	11
PREPOSITION	*BY*	10
PREPOSITION	*FROM*	7
PREPOSITION	*THROUGH*	6

Time

Of the Adverbial Adjuncts in Table 4.1 more than a quarter of the M-list and more than a third of the S-list are temporal. In Table 4.2, of the most frequent non-prepositional items in marked Theme position there are 48 tokens of time adverbs, *now, then, long, today, still*, out of a total 109 tokens. Table 4.3 shows that nearly half the marked thematic clauses are time adverbial adjuncts.

Table 4.3. Marked thematic clauses

Time	29
Condition	18
Reason	9
Concession	2
Nominal Group	2

The critics often draw attention to the role of time in *ASL* and the human reaction to it. An early critic, William Archer, identifies a major concern of *ASL* as 'the mutability of human feeling, the ease with which the dead are forgot, the anguish of love unrequited, and the danger that long life may mean slow degradation' (Gardner 1992: 79). Edmund Gosse refers to 'the unconquerable longing for what is gone for ever' (Gardner 1992: 25), what Leggett identifies as 'a longing for the redemption of the fallen world by the innocent world of the past' (Leggett 1978: 81) in the face of 'the inescapable nature of change and death' (Leggett 1978: 56). Leggett sees time in *ASL* as representing 'an opportunity or condition for painful discovery, for the move from expectation to disillusion, from innocence to knowledge', citing as examples 'When I was one and twenty' (13) and 'Bredon Hill' (21). Since temporal circumstances are the condition for these discoveries, it is hardly surprising that they should be often expressed in thematic position as circumstantial time adjuncts.

Place

In Table 4.1 we can see that the most frequent category of adverbial marked Theme is that of place adjunct, more than half in both the M-list (167/276) and the S-list (98/181). Most of these place adjuncts are unambiguously to do with position (M-list 93/167, S-list 52/98), around one-fifth are unambiguously to do with direction, implying distance or movement, and around a quarter are ambiguous as between direction and position. Table 4.2 shows place adjuncts, *here, there, low, down, far, high*, representing 53 out of the 109 tokens of non-prepositional words in initial marked Theme position. (To include prepositions would not be significant since their literal meanings are all to do with position.)

There is a degree of disagreement among critics in their comments on Housman's treatment of place. While an early reviewer claimed that 'Shropshire may be proud that its fields and streams have been sung by this genuine and individual poet' and Rupert Brooke valued 'Housman's earthiness, localised in Shropshire' (Gardner 1992: 17), many critics point out that there is not much particularity about what is described as Shropshire. Gardner reports William Robertson Nicoll's comments:

> Though Housman's poems from time to time mentioned the names of Shropshire towns and hills, his volume, such passing references apart, might have borne the name of any other English county, since Housman described neither the landscape nor the rustic inhabitants of Shropshire with any pretensions of particularity. (Gardner 1992: 6)

Housman himself admits that 'I am not a descriptive writer and do not know Shropshire well' (Gardner 1992: 188).

The general consensus seems to be that Housman does not describe Shropshire accurately or in its uniqueness, but uses place as a background for the depiction of human emotion:

> He is manifestly indifferent to local accuracy, and he writes relatively little about the natural world except in so far as it prompts or confirms a human mood. His real landscapes are of the heart. (Page 1983: 188)

It seems likely, from the evidence in Tables 4.1 and 4.2, that reference to place in *ASL* is most frequently found in Circumstantial Adjuncts, rather than as Subject or Object of clauses. This would be consistent with the observation that his 'landscape lives only when animated by human figures' (Gardner 1992: 92). I suggest that many of the poems depict movement through the countryside, with place figuring in the Circumstantial Adjunct (see analysis of multiply-marked Themes in poem 42 below) rather than directly depicting or describing landscapes in relational process clauses. And it may not be too fanciful to link this with Housman's own description of his method of composition:

> Having drunk a pint of beer at luncheon – beer is a sedative to the brain, and my afternoons are the least intellectual portion of my life – I would go out for a walk of two or three hours. As I went along, thinking of nothing in particular, only looking at things around me and following the progress of the seasons, there would flow into my mind, with sudden and unaccountable emotion, sometimes a line or two of verse, sometimes a whole stanza at once. (Gardner 1992: 249–50)

If this was his method of composition then this may have had some influence on the subject matter of his poems for many actually refer to walking (2, 3, 4, 5, 7, 10, 12, 14, 22, 25, 26, 29, 35, 36, 41, 50, 58) and there is a tendency to pile up direction adverbial Adjuncts, most extravagantly in 42, *The Merry Guide*, rather than to stop and describe natural features.

Exile and separation

The third thematic strand identified by critics brings together the themes of time and place into that of separation and exile. Exile and separation, though basically to do with place, also imply a change of time, and can come to symbolise a loss of youthful innocence or a loss of life.

Page (1983: 197) points out that the second half of *ASL* emphasises memories of being young, a memory of a blighted Eden with the pain and pleasure of innocence, and the gulf between youth and the present. This memory is symbolised in Housman — for example in the group of poems 37–41 — by exile from the home shire, the state of innocence. Poem 41, if we look at it closely, gives plenty of evidence of circumstantial adjuncts as marked Theme, showing this kind of contrast:

> In my own shire, if I was sad, homely comforters I had …
> In the woodland brown I heard the beechnut rustle down …
> On every road I wandered by, trod beside me, close and dear the beautiful
>   and death-struck year …
> Yonder, lightening other loads the seasons range the country roads …
> Here in London streets I ken no such helpmates, only men …

This claim that displacement, the contrasting of the place of innocence and experience, surfaces most prominently in the second half of *ASL* is borne out by the statistics in Table 4.4. The poems in which the number of marked Theme place adjuncts per clause are most frequent tend to be in the second half, in fact 7 out of 10. Indeed, there is some evidence that before publication Housman re-sequenced the poems in order to 'strengthen thee sense of relocation of setting from Shropshire to London' (Page 1983: 196).

In the soldier figure, the betrayed lover and, to a lesser extent the condemned or hanged criminal, Housman found ideal vehicles for depicting displacement and separation linked with time and death (Page 1983: 188–90). The obsession with soldiers and their death may have psychological explanations, but it is undoubtedly the case that his boyfriend Moses Jackson's abandonment of Housman for a career in the Indian Civil Service and, equally painful, a wife, gives the impetus to the theme of separated lovers. A good example is *ASL* 11, which treats these literary themes of unsatisfied love, departure and death in a distant spot. Incidentally, the syntax of the opening Theme realises the interpenetration of time and space: 'on your midnight pallet lying'.

The linking of the themes of time with the themes of place is of course facilitated by cognitive metaphors such as TIME IS SPACE, LIFE IS A JOURNEY (Lakoff and Johnson 1980; Johnson 1987; Lakoff and Turner 1989), and CHANGE IS MOVEMENT, what I have elsewhere referred to as *root analogies* or *metaphor themes* (Goatly 1997, Goatly 2007, Metalude). When Gosse commented that the major mood of *ASL* can be summed up as longing for what is '*gone*' for ever, he was in fact using a lexical item which exploits these conceptual metaphors, this root analogy referring both to movement in space and movement in time.

In this regard Housman's conception of one's lifetime and its 'passing' is very often tied to the metaphor of the wind. The wind is also part of Housman's pervasive geographical sense: for him exile and separation are concepts indivisible from the idea of movement in this or that direction, usually, because Moses Jackson emigrated to India, on an east-west axis (cf. *ASL* 31, 32, 38, 40, 42, Page 1983: 195).

Conclusion

We have now surveyed the ways in which critics have commented on the significance of time and place in Housman's poems in order to explain the extraordinary frequency of those semantic fields in the marked Themes of *ASL*. And we should return to the question posed at the beginning of section 4.3.1. It seems that method of development (marked Theme) and literary theme are intimately linked in Housman. Nevertheless, bearing out Fries's general contention, we can see that they are by no means identical. As we have noted, most of the critics cited accept that place is not the literary theme of *ASL*, but is rather the circumstance in which humans feel and suffer or from which they are exiled. Although time is more directly related to the literary themes of change, death and unfaithfulness, even here it is usually a symbolic circumstance for the persona's realisation of change or for his disillusion.

4.3.2   Thematic patterning in individual poems

In Table 4.4 the poems in bold, 14, 17, 31, 35, appear in more than one category, and this is a criterion for selecting them for detailed analysis from the perspective of method of development. In analysing these poems I have tried to indicate to the right the sorts of rhetorical classical schemes that Housman is using. Those which can be labelled straightforwardly are in bold. However, I wish to extend the use of these labels to cases which represent an antonymous meaning relation. In these cases I will use normal type. Doubtful cases will be accompanied by a question mark. Labels for rhetorical repetitions and tricks which do not involve marked Theme will be placed in parenthesis.

I shall also allow for intervening syntactic units between repetitions, so that the strict adjacency required for anaphora in classical rhetoric will not always apply. The fact that I am loosening somewhat the tight application of these labels indicates that Housman seldom applies the rules of classical rhetoric in a strict mechanical way, and that, as already suggested, he is intensely interested in contrast and antithesis, especially between times and places.

Table 4.4. Poems with most frequent repetitions of identical class of Theme (and of thematic management structures)

CLASS	POEM	SUB-GENRE	% PER CLAUSE
PLACE ADJUNCT	**35**	NO ADDRESSEE	67
	14	NO ADDRESSEE	62
	61	NO ADDRESSEE	60
	52	NO ADDRESSEE	45
	17	NO ADDRESSEE	43
	10	NO ADDRESSEE	38
	32	PARTIAL ADDRESSEE	36
	42	NO/PARTIAL	35
	38	PARTIAL IMPLIED	33
	55	NO ADDRESSEE	33
TIME ADJUNCT (PLUS TIME ADVERBIAL MARKED THEMATIC CLAUSES)	**17**	NO ADDRESSEE	57
	25	NO ADDRESSEE	40
	18	PARTIAL ADDRESSEE	38
	31	NO ADDRESSEE	29
	8	ADDRESSEE+VOCATIVES	26
	7	PARTIAL ADDRESSEE	26
PREDICATOR/VERB	**17**	NO ADDRESSEE	29
	61	NO ADDRESSEE	27
	35	NO ADDRESSEE	22
	14	NO ADDRESSEE	17
	3	ADDRESSEE +VOCATIVES	17
	36	NO ADDRESSEE	17
PREDICATED THEME	49	ADDRESSEE+VOCATIVE	15
	5	DIALOGUE	12
PREPOSED THEME	**31**	NO ADDRESSEE	11
	43	ADDRESSEE+VOCATIVE	9
	62	DIALOGUE	8
POSTPOSED THEME	16	NO ADDRESSEE	22
	37	PARTIAL ADDRESSEE	14

Before embarking on the analysis I will explain the classical rhetorical terminology, using Vickers (1970) and Leech (1969).

EPIZEUXIS:	immediate repetition
PLOCE:	intermittent repetition
ANAPHORA:	repetition of initial parts of syntactic units – AB.AC
SYMPLOCE:	repetition of both initial and final parts of syntactic units – AXB.AYB
ANADIPLOSIS (GRADATIO):	repetition of the final part of the first unit as the initial part of the second – AB. BC. (CD. DE. …)
EPANALEPSIS:	repetition of the initial part of a unit as the final part of that unit – AXA
ANTISTROPHE:	the reversal of the two parts of a unit in a later unit, so that the initial part becomes final and the final becomes initial – A(X)B.B(Y)A
POLYPTOTON:	repetition of words or lemmas with varying grammatical inflexions – *A, A-s, A-ing, A-ed*
PARISON:	syntactic parallelism, with or without lexical repetition

Besides these figures of repetition, I shall make use of the terms

APHESIS:	the reduction of the initial part of a word
PARALEPSIS:	the pretending to pass over topics but actually hinting at them
APOSIOPESIS:	the sudden breaking off, or interruption of the syntax
ANTIMETABOLE:	repetition of words in successive clauses

Poem 14

<table>
<tr><td>There pass the careless people</td><td></td><td></td></tr>
<tr><td>That call their souls their own:</td><td></td><td></td></tr>
<tr><td>Here by the road I loiter,</td><td></td><td>ANAPHORA ANTISTROPHE?</td></tr>
<tr><td>How idle and alone.</td><td></td><td></td></tr>
<tr><td>Ah, past the plunge of plummet,</td><td>5</td><td>**POLYPTOTON**</td></tr>
<tr><td>In seas I cannot sound,</td><td></td><td></td></tr>
<tr><td>My heart and soul and senses,</td><td></td><td></td></tr>
<tr><td>World without end, are drowned.</td><td></td><td></td></tr>
<tr><td>His folly has not fellow</td><td></td><td></td></tr>
<tr><td>Beneath the blue of day</td><td>10</td><td></td></tr>
<tr><td>That gjves to man or woman</td><td></td><td></td></tr>
<tr><td>His heart and soul away.</td><td></td><td></td></tr>
<tr><td>There flowers no balm to sain him</td><td></td><td>**ANAPHORA (PARISON)**</td></tr>
<tr><td>From east of earth to west</td><td></td><td></td></tr>
<tr><td>That's lost for everlasting</td><td>15</td><td></td></tr>
<tr><td>The heart out of his breast.</td><td></td><td></td></tr>
<tr><td>Here by the labouring highway</td><td></td><td>**ANAPHORA**</td></tr>
<tr><td>With empty hands I stroll:</td><td></td><td>SYMPLOCE?</td></tr>
<tr><td>Sea-deep, till doomsday morning,</td><td></td><td>PLOCE</td></tr>
<tr><td>Lie lost my heart and soul.</td><td>20</td><td>PLOCE (PLOCE)</td></tr>
</table>

'There pass the careless people' participates in a quadruple contrast: 'there' with 'here' line 3 and 'here' line 17, both contrastive anaphora; and 'pass the careless people' with its inverted Subject and Verb contrasts with 'I loiter' in both sense and order – the inversion suggesting a contrastive antistrophe. 'Pass', present tense, contrasts with the past participial adjective 'past' (l. 5), a case of polyptoton. There is also something of a contrast between the parison 'there pass' and 'there flowers' (l. 13), the first concerned with the plural 'people', the second the individual 'him' later revealed as identical with the 'I' (in much the same way as the 'English yeoman' of 31, line 11, becomes the 'I' in line 17). 'Here by the road I loiter' line 3, is echoed (symploce?) with a little amplification in 'here by the labouring highway … I stroll' of lines 17–18. By contrast 'past the plunge of plummet in seas I cannot sound' (1ines 5–6) is repeated in reduced form as 'sea-deep' in the last set of marked Themes (l. 19).

A number of other pieces of information are tied together, either explicitly or implicitly, in the multiply-marked Themes of the last two stanzas: 'with empty hands' suggests that while he may have given his heart, a major idea in the third and fourth stanzas, his lover did not reciprocate. 'Till doomsday morning' relates to the meanings of 'world without end' (l. 8), 'for everlasting' (l. 15). And 'lie lost' echoes the 'I cannot sound' (l. 6) and/or 'drowned' (l. 8), literally or metaphorically respectively, as well as 'lost' (l. 15). What is noticeable is how the last stanza ties together almost all the strands of given information, either by strict or contrastive anaphora/ploce/symploce.

Poem 17

Twice a week the winter through		
Here stood I to keep the goal:		
Football then was fighting sorrow		
For the young man's soul.		
Now in Maytime to the wicket	5	ANAPHORA
Out I march with bat and pad:		
See the son of grief at cricket		
Trying to be glad.		
		ANAPHORA, POLYPTOTON
Try I will; no harm in trying:		**EPANALEPSIS**
Wonder 'tis how little mirth	10	
Keeps the bones of man from lying		**(PLOCE/POLYPTOTON)**
Underneath the earth.		

The marked Themes 'the winter through' and 'in May time' clearly represent an anaphoric antithesis, both in terms of the season, and in terms of temporal duration versus point of time. 'Stood', the final element of the first thematic sequence, with a stasis which makes it something of a relational process (Martin and Matthiessen 1990: 373), contrasts with 'march' which is material and involves movement and effort. 'Stood' also introduces the symbolism of height contrasting with the final 'underneath the earth' (doesn't the ploce/polyptoton 'keep' imply that attempts to prevent a goal being scored by standing erect are about as futile as trying to be happy and avoiding death and burial, the ultimate goal?). A certain energy and emphasis arises from the anaphora (with polyptoton) of the lexical verb 'try' as highly-marked Theme, taking up the earlier 'trying' and preparing the way for the next to produce epanalepsis.

One ought perhaps to note that all the mentions of 'grief', 'sorrow' and the antonymous 'mirth' are confined to non-thematic position, an indication that the method of development and the literary theme, or at least the point, are quite distinct.

Poem 31

On Wenlock Edge the wood's in trouble;		
His forest fleece the Wrekin heaves;		
The gale, it plies the saplings double,		
And thick on Severn snow the leaves.		
'Twould blow like this through holt and hanger	5	(APHESIS)
When Uricon the city stood:		
'Tis the old wind in the old anger,		(APHESIS/PLOCE)
But then it threshed another wood.		
Then, 'twas before my time, the Roman		PARALEPSIS (APHESIS)
At yonder heaving hill would stare:	10	
The blood that warms an English yeoman,		
The thoughts that hurt him, they were there.		**PARISON**
There, like the wind through woods in riot,		**ANADIPLOSIS**
Through him the gale of life blew high;		**ANAPHORA/PARISON**
The tree of man was never quiet:	15	
Then 'twas the Roman, now 'tis I.		**ANAPHORA, PARISON** (APHESIS)
The gale, it plies the saplings double,		PLOCE
It blows so hard, 'twill soon be gone:		(APHESIS)
Today the Roman and his trouble		(PLOCE)
Are ashes under Uricon.	20	EPANALEPSIS ?

We notice that rhetorical figures of repetition do not appear obviously in the first stanza, despite the profusion of marked Themes, and this foregrounds it by comparison with other stanzas. It also suggests that the principle of syntactic and lexical variation is an important counterweight to Housman's repetitive tendencies, and that varieties of thematic marking contribute to it.

As with poem 17, the symbolism of height is made prominent by an initial marked thematic insistence on vertical height 'On Wenlock Edge' and a final rhematic prepositional phrase of relative depth 'under Uricon', a vaguely contrastive epanalepsis. In allegorical terms the wind, a superior force if not a hostile deity, can be seen as bending the young 'saplings double' with age from above, perhaps tearing out their white hair 'the leaves', which, in another marked Theme, fall downwards like snow 'on Severn', and inflicting punishment on them from above by threshing until finally they lie underground. A glance at poems 25–6 will give a clear idea of the importance to the whole sequence of this kind of vertical symbolism or, what Greimas calls 'axiological sememes' (Greimas 1966: 138).

The second marked Theme, 'his forest fleece', provides the point of departure for the lexical set which includes 'saplings', 'leaves', 'holt', 'hanger', 'wood', 'tree', and 'saplings'. Incidentally 'the tree of man', foreshadowed by the pronoun 'his' in this Theme, achieves a foregrounded prominence by being one of only two non-pronominal unmarked Themes, the only one beginning a line, and also by introducing the metaphor which is crucial for providing an equation between the two important lexical sets FOREST and MAN (see Goatly 1995b).

The use of preposed Theme in 'the gale, it plies the saplings double' along with the general tendency to use the (reduced or aphetic) *'t* as a dummy subject for wind or gale, may be an attempt to suggest the primacy of process (*wind* and *gale* are prototypical process nouns in any case). In addition, presenting it as a minor clause, as it were, makes it non-negotiable (Martin 1992: 42) because its existence is presupposed rather than asserted.

The succession of marked Themes 'thick on Severn snow' is significant in terms of thematic progression in picking up the 'on' prepositional phrase of line 1, though transforming it semantically to a direction adjunct, and by creating a little lexical set 'snow' and 'gale' to do with weather. I shall comment later on line 4 in relation to the effects of using multiply-marked Themes (section 4.3.3).

'Then' line 8 begins an anaphoric pattern of marked Themes 'then – 'twas before my time' (l. 9), 'then' (l. 16) culminating in the contrastive 'now' (l. 16). Along with tense this sets up a major developmental and organisation principle, a three-way time contrast, ending with the qualified optimism of the final three clauses of the poem, the last of which is introduced by the marked Theme 'today'. (One might paraphrase: 'my present pain will not last long, since the Roman's past suffering is finished from the perspective of today'.) The marked thematic 'there' (l. 13), picking up by anadiplosis the rhematic 'there' of the previous clause, is ostensibly a place adjunct but has to be interpreted, according to the conceptual metaphor POINT IN TIME IS POSITION, as temporal; for the whole point of the poem is that the persona is imagining the Roman in the same spatial position as him, staring at the hill, sharing the same deictic centre of place, but not the same deictic centre of time.

Incidentally, the aposiopesis of ' 'twas before my time' achieves a paralepsis, by pretending to pass over and negate the existence of the *I*, the persona, but actually introducing it. 'The blood that warms an English yeoman, the thoughts that hurt him' do not contract many obvious ties as far as thematic progression is concerned, except perhaps that 'hurt' may make some connection with 'trouble' and 'anger', and 'warm' may foreshadow 'ashes'. More importantly they exploit syntactic parallelism or parison, and, through the use of hypotactic clauses smuggle in the presuppositions:

>> blood warms an English yeoman
>> thoughts hurt (past) the Roman *or* thoughts hurt (present) an English yeoman

The second of these smuggled presuppositions is more problematic than the first. To start with, the tense of 'hurt' and the pronominal adjective reference of 'his' are ambiguous, neatly encapsulating the eternity of suffering and the identification of the Roman and the persona. But *qua* presuppositions, the first is much easier to accept than the second. The point of the parallelism is precisely to get us to accept that the painful properties of thought are as natural as the warming qualities of blood. 'Through woods in riot, through him' produces another parison or anaphora which prefigures semantically the metaphorical equations man = tree and gale = life, and 'like the wind' explicitly marks this metaphorical comparison.

'Then 'twas the Roman, now 'tis I' is an antithetical parison, with identical syntax but contrastive semantics, again exploiting marked Theme for time contrasts.

Poem 35

On the idle hill of summer		
Sleepy with the flow of streams,		
Far I hear the steady drummer		
Drumming like a noise in dreams.		(POLYPTOTON)
Far and near and low and louder	5	**ANAPHORA**
On the roads of earth go by		**PARISON**
Dear to friends and food for powder		
Soldiers marching, all to die.		
East and west on fields forgotten		**PARISON**
Bleach the bones of comrades slain,	10	
Lovely lads and dead and rotten;		
None that go return again.		(ANTIMETABOLE)
Far the calling bugles hollo,		**ANAPHORA**
High the screaming fife replies,		
Gay the files of scarlet follow:	15	**PARISON**
Woman bore me, I will rise.		(ANADIPLOSIS)

The relations between marked Themes and thematic progression in 35 is somewhat more straightforward than in 31. 'On the idle hill of summer' contrasts by parison with 'on the roads of earth' and 'on fields forgotten'; and also contrasts with 'low' (l. 5) and 'rise' (l. 16), but, more subtly, reinforces 'high' (l. 14). 'Sleepy with the flow of streams', opposes 'rise' in the sense of 'get up after sleep', and suggests 'dreams' of line 4. 'Far' is reinforced by anaphoric repetition (l .5) and (l. 13) and contrasted with 'near'. The marked Theme of line 4 has its 'near' phonologically and semantically echoed by 'dear' (through the metaphor theme AFFECTION IS PROXIMITY). It also exploits the ambiguity of 'low' in immediate contrast with 'louder' and more distant contrast with 'high' (l. 14). 'Louder' itself looks forward to 'the calling bugles hollo' (l. 13) and 'the screaming fife' (l. 14). The 'go by' is taken up in the unmarked Theme of line 12 (with its contrastive antimetabole) 'none that go return again', and also by 'follow' (l. 15). 'Dear to friends' makes a pathetic contrast with 'forgotten' in the next marked Theme. 'Food for powder' has more tenuous links, after being partially de-metaphorised, with 'comrades slain' and 'dead and rotten'. The parison 'East and west on fields forgotten' (l. 9) provides syntactic and semantic parallels with 'far and near and low and louder on the roads of earth' (l. 5), suggesting perhaps a set of ultimate psychologically-structured oppositions as in Table 4.5:

Table 4.5. Psychological place oppositions

Moses Jackson	Housman
East	West
Far	Near
Dear (to Housman)	Forgotten (by Jackson)
Fields	Roads

'Bleach' (l. 10) provides a point of later contrast with 'scarlet' (l. 15). 'Gay', at least in the sense it had at the end of the nineteenth century, is not significant for thematic progression, belonging to no obvious lexical chains. Its use as marked Theme does of course help to preserve the parison, the tightly controlled syntactic parallelism of Adjectival Adjunct + Modified Subject NP + Intransitive Verb, which gives way to the foregrounded final line. This is not only foregrounded locally, in terms of the obvious patterns of the previous three lines, but also in being one of two lines in the whole poem (with l. 12) which have no marked Theme, and which consist of two finite clauses. But note that whereas one of the clauses of line 12 is subordinate, the two in line 16 are equal in status and grandeur.

Summary of the uses of marked Theme

How can we sum up the main literary uses of progression involving marked Theme? In the poems analysed above we have identified at least the following uses:

- alerting the reader to symbolic patterns, especially of vertical position
- drawing attention to lexical patterns of similarity to give emphatic reinforcement
- pointing contrasts between time and place which are significant for literary theme
- presuppositional smuggling through subordinate clauses and the use of preposed Themes
- negatively, foregrounding the few clauses in which marked Themes do not occur

It is worth relating the third point above to Fries' arguments against Chafe's view that marked Theme is used for contrastive purposes (Fries 1983: 133). I think the analyses of individual poems' use of marked Theme given above (and below) would bear out the contention that the major use of marked Theme is contrastive (see also Winter's (1977) discussion of 'comparative denial'). However, I have shown that, besides contrastiveness, there are a number of other and concomitant uses.

Table 4.6. Proportion of multiply-marked Themes by poem

% of clausal multiply-marked Themes in ascending order	Poem number	Multiply-marked Theme/no of clauses
21	41	5/24
22	44, 59	6/27, 2/9
23	30	3/13
27	32*	3/11
29	17**	2/7
31	42*	7/23
33	35**	3/9
36	52*	4/11
39	36*	7/18
40	61*	6/15
54	14**	6/11

Note: * I shall use the statistics above as a criterion to choose the texts in which to investigate the effects of multiply-marked Theme. The poems marked ** have already been analysed.

4.3.3   Multiply-marked themes

Poem 42

This poem is too long to quote in full, so I list all the examples of clauses with multiply marked Themes (1–7) plus some significant other marked Themes (8–9).

1   Once in the wind of morning I ranged the thymy wold
2   There through the dews beside me behold a youth that trod
3   With mien to match the morning and gay delightful guise and
       friendly brows and laughter he looked me in the eyes
4   With kind looks and laughter and naught to say beside we two went on together
       I and my happy guide
5   Across the glittering pastures and empty upland still and solitude and shepherds
       high in the folded hill, by hanging woods and hamlets that gaze through
       orchards down on many a windmill turning and far discovered town, with gay
       regards of promise and sure unslackened stride and smiles and nothing spoken
       led on my merry guide (!)
6   By blowing realms of woodland with sunstruck vanes afield and cloud-led
       shadows sailing about the windy weald, by valley-guarded granges and silver
       waters wide, content at heart I followed
7   Like the cloudy shadows across the country blown we two fare on for ever
8   With the great gale we journey
9   Midst the fluttering legion of all that ever died I follow

These examples seem to create a number of literary effects. 5 and 6 use marked Themes to emphasise the extensiveness of space travelled, and therefore the length and the duration of the journey. 2, on the other hand, seems iconic of perception and reader response, as though the persona is directing the implied reader's gaze until it eventually lights upon his companion. 3, 4, 5 and 6 in their latter marked Themes, highlight feeling, while 3 also shares with 7 the identification of the travellers with nature. Notice, by the way, how the symbol of the wind is reinforced in 7 and 8, and to an extent in 5 and 6. 9 perhaps also hints at wind in 'fluttering' but certainly identifies the travellers and their journey with mortality. As we saw in our earlier analysis, mutiply-marked Themes like 5 are often used for cohesive purposes, in this case referring to the wind and the feeling of the travellers, in parallel with other marked Themes.

Multiply-marked Themes generate uncertainty as to which human participant will figure as Subject of the clause, but this uncertainty does not matter in this poem since both the persona and the guide are walking together in the same direction through the same countryside. (One can contrast this effect with that in poem 52, below.) Indirectly, then, the use of multiply-marked Theme underlines the solidarity of their relationship and harmony of mood, as well as their solidarity with all that is mortal (9). This underlining clearly exploits the conceptual metaphor PURPOSE IS DIRECTION, just as the poem as a whole plugs into the metaphors LIFE IS A JOURNEY or ACTIVITY IS MOVEMENT FORWARDS and EMOTION IS WEATHER. (For lexical details of these last two conceptual metaphors see *Metalude*.)

Poem 32

From far, from eve and morning		**ANAPHORA**
And yon twelve-winded sky,		**PARISON**
The stuff of life to knit me		
Blew hither: here am I.		EPANALEPSIS? ANADIPLOSIS?
Now – for a breath I tarry	5	**APOSIOPESIS**
Nor yet disperse apart –		**PARALEPSIS**
Take my hand quick and tell me,		
What have you in your heart.		
Speak now and I will answer;		(EPANALEPSIS)
How shall I help you, say;	10	(EPANALEPSIS)
Ere to the wind's twelve quarters		**PLOCE**
I take my endless way.		(PLOCE? ANTISTROPHE ANAPHORA)

This poem, like so many others, exploits the TIME IS SPACE conceptual metaphor through its opening anaphoric sequence. The piling up of these marked Themes is both iconic of the length of time (cf. 'endless' = eternal 1.12), and of the fact that in the beginning, at the point of departure, there is no *I*. The movement 'from far' to 'hither' is vaguely contrastively epanaleptic, and from 'hither' to 'here' anadiplotic. The succession of marked Themes in lines 4–5 creates a feeling of impatience as we scamper forward to find the Subject and Verb. As in poem 31, this aposiopesis (l. 5) produces a paralepsis, skating over, yet presupposing by provisional denial ('nor yet'), the persona's eventual dissolution. Lines 8 and 10 create some problems for analysis. There might be a case for counting these as marked Themes since the Verbs of the apparently projected clauses are placed before the Subjects. What seems to be happening here is a change from the more predictable structure in which a question is subordinated into declarative mood in one tone group, to the more unusual imperative + interrogative in two tone groups, i.e. two paratactic clauses:

/   /   /

Tell me what you have in your heart OR Tell me, what have you in your heart?

However, there is no question mark signalling the interrogative mood. The breaking out into the insistent speech of direct questions, amid the double directive underlines the impatience created by both the preceding aposiopesis, the other imperatives of lines 5–10, and the phonology (plosives) of line 7.

Lines 9 and 10 could be construed as a kind of epanalepsis, the 'speak' and 'answer' being contrastive, and 'speak' and 'say' repetitive. In lines 11 and 12 we have the use of ploce 'twelve-winded' + 'the wind's twelve quarters' both made prominent by their position in marked Themes (and an incidental use of ploce in 'take'). The double use of ploce creates a feeling of antistrophe, or even epanalepsis, if we regard the whole poem as the unit under consideration.

Poem 36

White in the moon the long road lies,		
The moon stands blank above;		PLOCE
White in the moon the long road lies		**PLOCE**
That leads me from my love.		
Still hangs the hedge without a gust,	5	**ANAPHORA**
Still, still the shadows stay:		**EPIZEUXIS**
My feet upon the moonlit dust		
Pursue the endless way.		
The world is round, so travellers tell,		
And straight though reach the track,	10	
Trudge on, trudge on, 'twill all be well,		**(EPIZEUXIS)** (APHESIS)
The way will guide one back.		
But ere the circle homeward hies		
Far, far must it remove:		**EPIZEUXIS**
White in the moon the long road lies	15	**PLOCE**, EPANALEPSIS
That leads me from my love.		

The tightly controlled anaphora, epizeuxis and ploce in this poem are emphasised by their position in marked Theme. One effect of the multiply-marked Themes is an iconicity of perception of reader response: we see the whiteness, we see the moon causing it, and only then do we identify the road on which it is shining. Placing 'moon' before the 'road' probably emphasises the enormity of space and the circularity of movement in line 13, the circularity here contrasting paradoxically with the straightness of the path (l. 10). The multiplication of marked Themes in lines 13–14 underlines both the extent and the conflicting directions of movement. The extent, duration and monotony of movement are further highlighted by the use of epizeuxis in 'trudge on, trudge on' and 'far, far'. These movements also contrast against the background of the stillness of the hedge and shadows, and their circularity is conveyed in the poem's ternary form, with epanalepsis created by the ploce of the final clause complex.

Poem 52

Far in a western brookland
That bred me long ago
The poplars stand and tremble
By pools I used to know.

There in the windless night-time,   5   **PARISON PARALEPSIS**
The wanderer, marvelling why,
Halts on the bridge to hearken
How soft the poplars sigh.

He hears: no more remembered
In fields where I was known   10   **PARISON** PLOCE
Here I lie down in London   ANAPHORA
And turn to rest alone.

There, by the starlit fences,   **ANAPHORA** PARISON
The wanderer halts and hears   (PLOCE)
My soul that lingers sighing   15
About the glimmering weirs.

This poem through its anaphoric marked Themes exemplifies the contrasts between the distance/the past (stanzas 1, 2 and 4) and the proximate/present (stanza 3). The anaphora is also coupled with parison in places, repeating syntactic formulae with some variation:

STANZAS 2 + 4:   ADJUNCT + PREP. PHRASE ADJUNCT

STANZA 1:   ADJUNCT + PREP. PHRASE ADJUNCT: [QUALIFYING RELATIVE CLAUSE [PREP. PHRASE ADJUNCT]]

STANZA 3:   ADJECTIVE/PARTICIPIAL CLAUSE [PREP. PHRASE. ADJUNCT [QUALIFYING RELATIVE CLAUSE]] + ADJUNCT

The sequence of marked Themes here creates subtle effects by disguising reasoning and withholding syntactic information, so making unsettling readjustment necessary when reading. For example, it turns out that line 5 involves a crucial paralepsis; tucked in unobtrusively as the modifier of a prepositional phrase 'windless' provides the reason why the trembling and the sighing of the poplars is to be marvelled at. There is something paraleptic about the next sequence in lines 9–10, too, as the 'I' is introduced surreptitiously, almost apologetically as part of a relative clause made less prominent by multiple downranking.

The sequence of marked Themes in stanza three creates a hiatus of uncertainty about the Subject; and given that the stanza begins with a clause of which 'the wanderer' is Subject, followed by a colon, it may be something of a surprise to find 'I' as Subject. Besides which, the syntax of the marked Themes is ambiguous; we are unsure whether the Adjunct 'in fields where I was known' is oriented towards the Verb 'remembered' or towards a later syntactic constituent.

Though it has nothing to do with marked Theme as such, it is worth noting how the triple ploce of line 14 allows the reader to assume that 'hears' will once again be used intransitively. The greatest surprise in the poem derives from the line-initial provision of the Object 'my soul'.

Poem 61

<table>
<tr><td>The vane on Hughley steeple
Veers bright, a far-known sign,
And there lie Hughley people,
And there lie friends of mine.</td><td></td><td>**ANAPHORA/PARISON**</td></tr>
<tr><td>Tall in their midst the tower
Divides the shade and sun,
And the clock strikes the hour
And tells the time to none.</td><td>5</td><td>PLOCE?</td></tr>
<tr><td>To south the headstones cluster,
The sunny mounds lie thick;
The dead are more in muster
At Hughley than the quick.</td><td>10</td><td></td></tr>
<tr><td>North, for a soon-told number,
Chill graves the sexton delves,
And steeple-shadowed slumber
The slayers of themselves.</td><td>15</td><td>ANAPHORA

PLOCE?</td></tr>
<tr><td>To north, to south lie parted,
With Hughley tower above,
The kind, the single-hearted,
The lads I used to love.</td><td>20</td><td>**ANAPHORA**
PLOCE?</td></tr>
<tr><td>And south and north, 'tis only
A choice of friends one knows,
And I shall ne'er be lonely
Asleep with these or those.</td><td></td><td>**ANTISTROPHE**
(PLOCE)</td></tr>
</table>

The multiply-marked Themes in lines 3–4, 15–16 and 17–20 put emphasis on the persons involved by placing them in Rheme position. Other elements of the marked Themes are involved with a kind of ploce, so that 'lie' (ll.3–4) contrasts with 'tall' (l. 5), 'steeple' (l. 1) and 'tower' (l. 5). Both these latter, in non-thematic position, are repeated in marked-thematic position in lines 15 and 18. The most marked of the marked Themes in lines 13–14, the Object 'chill graves' is important in reinforcing the distinction between sun and shadow, south and north, which is underlined by the contrastive and repetitive anaphora. But the antistrophe (l. 21) reverses the south ^ north ordering, thereby suggesting that the way the suicides and other dead are 'parted' is irrelevant to the poet. (This is well symbolised by the last line: we do not know where he is standing, to north or south and hence have no inkling of the deictic centre which would clarify the reference of 'these or those'.) To the dead, and those contemplating death, the division between shade and sun is as inconsequential as the time the clock tells.

Summary of the uses of multiply-marked Theme

We might summarise the literary effects of multiply-marked Themes as follows:

- emphasis on the distance and extent of movement and time
- tying together of significant and diverse lexical strings
- paralepsis, or the unobtrusive introduction of critically important information (often the existence of the *I*, the speaker)
- the creation of a sense of impatience or urgency, linked to the impatience of the reader in trying to locate the Subject
- a concomitant emphasis on the Subject, the person in non-Theme or Rheme position
- iconic representation of aspects of perception, the gradual focusing on participants from among circumstances, the creation and cancelling out of perceptual misconceptions
- the reprocessing of syntax and meaning, adjusting of syntactic interpretation, or the creation of semantic surprises.

The last four of these effects, which to some extent overlap, put an emphasis on reader response, and may be exemplified in other places in *ASL*. A very interesting example is 1.4 of poem 31, the text of which appears as part of our discussion in section 4.3.2.

> thick on Severn snow the leaves.

The iconicity of perception here is partly achieved by the syntactic ambiguity of 'snow'; we may momentarily believe that it is a noun and that we have reached the Subject of the clause, until we realise it is a metaphorical verb and the real Subject is the noun 'leaves'. This could be an attempt to suggest that the persona initially sees the leaves falling and misidentifies them as snow, until they land on the river and are finally recognised as leaves. Another example of the same kind of effect on the reader, emphasis on the addressee's response, can be found in the last lines of 15:

> There, when the turf in springtime flowers,
> With downward eyes and gazes sad,
> Stands amid the glancing showers
> A jonquil, not a Grecian lad.

Here the double-take is caused by the physical metamorphosis of Narcissus into a daffodil.

Misconceptions or confusions of syntax, though probably not iconic of misperception, can also be seen in the following sequence from stanza 4 of 28:

> When Severn down to Buildwas ran
> Coloured with the death of man,
> Couched upon her brother's grave
> The Saxon got me on the slave.

There is a deliberate difficulty in processing 'her', which has to wait to be resolved until we reach the final word of the stanza 'slave'. Perhaps this is meant to mirror the confusion and paradoxical mixing of enforced death and enforced pregnancy, and the bitter irony in making the grave a place of conception. There is also something of the presuppositional overload we identified earlier in this long succession of marked Themes, and a paralepsis involved in implying her brother's death through a participial clause.

This chapter has not yet devoted much space to the analysis of postposed Themes, so it is worth showing that this device can be used for similar effects of momentary syntactic and referential uncertainty. This is especially so when a pronoun appears as the unmarked Theme, and is only made explicit in the postposed phrase:

(8)   We'll sweat no more on scythe and rake my bloody hands and I

(16)   he does not move, the lover of the grave, the lover that hanged himself for love

(16)   It nods and curtseys and recovers when the wind blows above, the nettle on the graves of lovers that hanged themselves for love

(23)   They carry back bright to the coiner the mintage of man the lads that will die in their glory and never be old

(26)   As we came by a year ago my love and I

(28)   It has not died the war that sleeps on Severn side

(37)   Still you'll help me hands that gave a grasp to friend me to the grave

(37)   when I forget you, hearts of gold

(42)   we two went on together I and my happy guide

(62)   and faith/'tis pleasant till 'tis past, the mischief is that will not last

(62)   it sleeps well, the horned head

The frequency of this structure in *ASL* is rather distinctive, but space prevents further discussion of its detailed particular effects in context.

Summary: the use of classical rhetoric in relation to marked Theme

We have examined Housman's use of classical schemes of repetition in eight poems, and seen that there is not the kind of persistent use that we would find in seventeenth century English poetry (Vickers 1970: chapter 5). No doubt this has something to do with the poetic fashion at the turn of the nineteenth and twentieth centuries, which culminated in the Georgian predilection for everyday colloquial language (Ross 1965). Nevertheless we see many kinds of scheme represented in marked Theme position; repetitive anaphora and ploce are the most common, parison is frequent, there is some contrastive anaphora and paralepsis, but the use of the other schemes is infrequent.

However, all these schemes seem to be an available resource which Housman applies to varying degrees in different individual poems, and it is difficult to generalise about their use on the basis of eight poems taken from the least dialogic groups. It may well be that if one were to analyse further one would find a great deal more tightly controlled parison (and perhaps epizeuxis) in the balladic dialogic group of poems, such as 8 with its final stanza:

> Long for me the rick will wait,
> And long will wait the fold,
> And long will stand the empty plate,
> And dinner will be cold.

As Marlow points out this is a distinctively balladic style with its echo of Sir Patrick Spens:

> And lang lang may the maidens sit ... (Marlow: 71–3)

But even in the eight poems analysed, we have discovered that, if he wishes, Housman can produce the tightly controlled structures and method of development of 36 with its epizeuxis and ploce, or 52, with its parison, anaphora and ploce, and 61 with its anaphora, ploce and antistrophe. And yet at other times he seems deliberately to refrain from repetition of word forms and grammatical structures, a kind of elegant variation (e.g. the opening two stanzas of 31, and most of 17), and his repetition and contrast become semantic rather than lexical or syntactic; indeed many readers of the sequence have complained of his monotony in saying the same things in a variety of ways. Perhaps the most important point to emerge is that the repetitive schemes he does use are usually associated with marked Theme, and this would suggest that his rhetoric and choice of marked Theme are intimately connected.

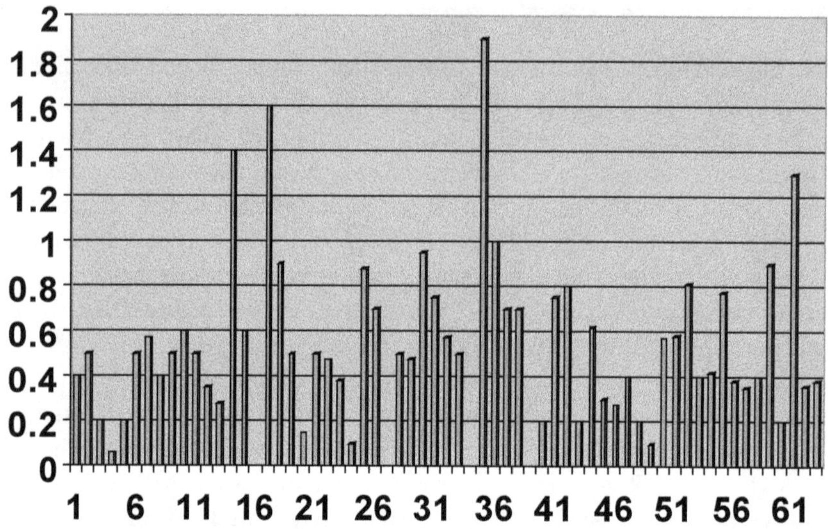

Figure 4.1. Frequency of marked Theme per clause in the 63 poems of the ASL sequence

4.3.4   Patterns of marked Theme in the sequence and degrees of dialogism

One way of interpreting Figure 4.1 stylistically is to notice where the major changes in marked Theme frequency occur in the sequence and to ask what might be the significance of these shifts. To do this effectively one needs to register the existence of a number of sub-genres within the *ASL* sequence. J.B. Priestley (Gardner 1992: 145) was the first to notice different sub-generic strands: the lyric, the ballad and the epigram, though it is not clear to me that epigrams, when used as part of poems as they are in *ASL*, define a subgenre in the same way as ballads and lyrics do. I would suggest that a more useful division may be made in terms of the degree of explicit dialogism in the poems, what Priestley refers to as the 'degrees of dramatization' (Gardner 1992: 144). We can use the label 'lyric' for poems at the minimally dialogic end of the scale, that is those in which a persona, the poet, seems only to be talking to an (implied) reader. At the other extreme are poems which Housman encloses in single inverted commas and which consist mainly of dialogues. To some extent these fall into Priestley's ballad category. Close to this dialogic extreme is a third category in which the personal poet is clearly addressing someone other than the implied reader, the addressee being identified in vocatives, typically *lad* or *soldier*. The remaining poems are difficult to categorise but exhibit one or more of the following characteristics: while not explicitly using vocatives,

they often imply the existence of an addressee through the use of *you* and/
or the imperative mood; sometimes they are addressed to unreal or absent
addressees or to the persona's soul; or they are poems which are mainly in the
lyric genre, but parts of them are representations of speech by speakers other
than the poet/persona.

One of the more interesting findings of my analysis is that frequency of
marked Theme correlates significantly with these four groupings; on average
the more dialogic the poems the less frequent the use of marked Themes. The
figures are found in Table 4.7. For confirmation of these tendencies we may
refer back to Table 4.4. Though this subcategorises marked Themes and takes
a different perspective on frequency by rank ordering poems, it nevertheless
confirms our findings with respect to sub-genre classification and frequency
of marking.

What is of equal significance, as far as Table 4.4 is concerned, is the apparent
tendency for preposed Themes and predicated Themes to be found in the more
dialogic poems, and less where there is no addressee, creating a complemen-
tary pattern with marked Themes. A count of the clear examples of preposed
and predicated Themes in *ASL* in fact confirms that 25/37 belong to those
poems which fall into the sub-genres DIALOGUE and ADDRESSEE WITH
VOCATIVES.

What little work there has been done on the relative frequencies of predicated Themes (Francis 1990) suggests that they occur more often in newspaper
editorials than in letters to the editor, and more frequently in letters to the editor
than in news reports. The general view seems to be that genres such as editorials,
which encode author intervention, are more likely to use predicated Themes
than those which set out to be objective (Fries 1992: 4). It is presumably their
use to express greater involvement and interpersonal emphasis which accounts
for their relative frequency in the group of poems which are dialogic or have
clear vocative reference to addressees.

Table 4.7. Frequency of marked Themes

SUB-GENRE	FREQUENCY OF MARKED THEME PER CLAUSE (*M-list*)
NO ADDRESSEE/LYRIC	73
PARTIAL OR IMPLIED ADDRESSEE	54
ADDRESSEE WITH VOCATIVES	28
DIALOGUE (? BALLAD)	23

4.3.5   Housman as a poet of the vernacular?

We can use our four-way division of the poems, and our findings about inverse correlation between marked Theme and dialogue, and positive correlation between predicated Themes and dialogue, as a context in which to discuss the question of Housman's 'colloquial' style.

Critics make some curiously impressionistic remarks about the colloquial tone of Housman's verse. Many praise him for being a poet of the vernacular, writing in the style of natural speech. These critics claim that there is 'not a touch of literary artifice in his work from end to end' (Gardner 1992: 88) or that he writes 'pure spoken English with hardly any admixture of poetic verbiage' (Elroy-Flecker, Gardner 1992: 101), that his poetry has the true ring and cadence of ordinary natural speech (Gardner 1992: 151) or that 'he is quite prepared to write a passage in a completely colloquial, almost slangy style' (Iolo Williams, Gardner 1992: 211). It is difficult to accept these comments as applying across the board to all poems in *ASL*, though they may be more applicable to those in the dialogic and addressee-with-vocative groups. I certainly cannot accept, after my exhaustive analysis, that 'few poets are so sparing of their inversions; stanza after stanza will run on almost as if it were written in prose' (Gardner 1992: 232). Possibly most of these comments are based upon lexis rather than grammar, patterns of lexis being more easily perceived than grammar by the linguistically naïve language user or critic.

Other critics take an opposing view saying 'the general effect of his language is far removed from the conversational' (Marlow 1958: 20–1), and these tend to be rather more perceptive about the extreme repetition, which is unnaturally 'carried even beyond Roman bounds' (Lucas, Gardner 1992: 182). Perhaps the most sensible comments are those that point to a 'mingling of the traditional poetic and the colloquial poetic' (Gardner: 231), or these balanced remarks of Harold Munro's:

> Where it includes poetical devices or the use of inversion, these are so
> discriminately managed as to render them either unobtrusive or else
> noticeably and characteristically proper to their context. (Gardner 1993: 110)

This final comment is endorsed by my analysis of individual poems, where I have shown the effects Housman achieves by the use of noticeably multiply-marked Themes. If we interpret Munro's 'context' in terms of degrees of dramatisation, we find that most uses of 'inversion' (if we interpret this as marked Theme) are found in the lyric poems not the dialogic ones; all the above poems I analysed are in the least dialogic categories.

4.3.6   Relation of findings to earlier work on genre and Theme

It is appropriate, finally, to relate my findings to earlier work on the correlation between genre and thematic properties. The major writings here are Fries (1983, 1991, 1992) and Ghadessy (1993). Fries (1983) makes two interesting points relevant to our previous analysis of place adjuncts. He shows that descriptions of locations typically contain sentences which begin with references to locations (Fries 1983: 125). More significant still is his Text D in which relative location is the method of development (Fries 1983: 128) and in which 'the description takes the form of a verbal tour and uses verbs of motion' (Fries 1989: 126). This description of Text D is uncannily similar to the general pattern in many of the *ASL* poems, in respect of Fries's 'relative location' (Shropshire/place of exile) as method of development, and in respect of the use of 'verbs of motion'.

Fries (1992) and Ghadessy (1993) provide summaries of other studies by Berry (1987), Francis (1990), Wang Ling (1993), Bäcklund (1990), Xiao (1991) and Nie Long (1991). Berry identified the first 25 place-names occurring in the genres of coffee party conversation, committee meeting discussion, travel brochure and a guidebook, and found that it was only in the coffee party and the travel brochure that place-names figured as marked Theme. While in the brochure place-names were split almost evenly between occurrence in an Adverbial and in the Subject, in the guidebook there was a tendency for them to occur in the Subject position as unmarked Theme. Nie Long confirmed the notion that guidebooks have Themes which provide a locational orientation for the reader, indicating that around 43 per cent of the phrases showing spatial location (presumably by place Adjuncts) occurred in thematic position. Nie Long also identified 57 per cent of the Themes in the guidebook text as marked ideational. Bäcklund, in a study of comparative frequencies of line text and scene text in a playscript, found 21 per cent of the Themes in scene text were marked ideational. The Nie Long guidebook text and the scene text appear to display patterns of marked Theme relatively similar to those in *ASL*. The same conclusion could be drawn from a comparison between *ASL* and the sample guidebook text in Matthiessen (1992: 60–1).

Ghadessy has a number of findings and reports which give significant comparisons with our data. Twelve per cent of the Themes he found in written sports commentary were marked circumstantial Themes, and of these 70 per cent were time Adjuncts and only 4 per cent were place Adjuncts. He comments that 'In the use of marked ideational Themes, sports commentary (13 per cent) is more like obituaries and expository prose and unlike programme and narrative' (Ghadessy 1993: 14).

Turning to Fries's own 1992 study which compared three obituaries, a concert program, four narratives and an expository text, the highest frequencies of marked Theme were found as follows in column I of Table 4.8. There is no semantic breakdown of marked Themes in Fries's report, but, taking all Themes together, spatial location and temporal location Themes give the figures in columns 2 and 3. One would guess that most of the thematised exponents of temporal and spatial location would be marked thematic Adjuncts.

The tentative conclusion seems to be that *ASL* resembles the Program Note and the historical narrative in respect of the use of temporal location as a method of development, but resembles the *A Farewell to Arms* passage (a descriptive or orientational extract of the narrative) in terms of its penchant for marked thematic place Adjuncts. Of course *ASL* shows a higher percentage of both kinds of Adjunct than any of the narratives analysed by Fries, but it is interesting that it seems to resemble narrative genres in making place or time important aspects of its method of development.

Table 4.9. Comparative studies of marked Theme and Themes of space + time

	Marked Theme %	Spatial Location %		Temporal Location %	
Napoleon (historical narrative)	36	5		18	
Program note	30	0		30	
A Farewell to Arms (descriptive/narrative)	12	12		8	
The Bathtub (narrative)	26	11		16	
Average for all narratives	24				
A Shropshire Lad	51				
		S-list	M-list	S-list	M-list
		42	43	28	20

Overall comparisons with other studies would suggest that the texts of *ASL*, particularly the lyrical ones, with their emphasis on movement through and away from the countryside of Shropshire, the passing of time and the journey to separation, exile and death, have a method of marked Theme development similar to scene text, certain guidebooks and the descriptive sections of narratives.

Note

1   For the terminology of Process types please refer to section 2.1.1.

5 A stylistic analysis of Elizabeth Jennings' 'One Flesh': poem as product and process

5.1 Introduction

This chapter attempts to exemplify a double-faceted approach to stylistic analysis of a short poem by Elizabeth Jennings. It begins traditionally by posing the question 'what impression does the poem make and what are the linguistic means by which this impression is created?' This question, it is suggested, can have two kinds of answer, depending on whether the poem is treated as a product/object to be viewed from a distance, or as a process of reading. The first approach is more in keeping with a formalist stylistics which emphasises the poetic function or message/code, while the second is more in line with a reader-response/pragmatic stylistics which emphasises the addressee or addresser-addressee interaction (the conative function).

Section 5.2 of this chapter considers the linguistic features which are salient when we treat the poem as an object, and which are responsible for the overall impression, at a distance. The chapter continues, in 5.3, by considering the traditional notion of foregrounding, demonstrating how the last sentence of the poem is multiply foregrounded. In 5.4 I show that in the case of this particular poem the effect of foregrounding is best explained in terms of text as process, rather than product, that is through the impressions and reader responses made in the course of a reading. To do this it analyses the ways in which syntax processing, arrest and release function; how transitions from one discourse unit to another are signalled and recognised by the reader; how the reader's expectations are constantly being defeated and undermined, through conflicting presuppositions, and through the use of non-factive and negative linguistic devices. The chapter concludes with a pragmatic exploration of the nature of the final foregrounded question, showing how it represents the culmination of the doubts expressed earlier, while, paradoxically, seeming to express certainty.

But before we proceed to this analysis I would like to place the distinction between process and product in the context both of stylistic and epistemological theory. Taking stylistic theory first we can remind ourselves of the position of Jakobson for whom poetics and the poetic function put the emphasis on the message or text. Jakobsonian stylistic analysis more or less defines the poem as

97

object, whose textual patterns are produced by projection from the paradigmatic to the syntagmatic axis (Jakobson 1960: 370–2) (Figure 1.1). These patterns are independent of the reading process in that the patterns found, though syntagmatic, produce the kind of timelessness of a Grecian urn, of non-linear art. The poem becomes a ritual object so that the processing order will be reversed by the re-reading or re-hearing.

The second context in which the object-process distinction can be located is Popper's epistemological theory, and Leech's (1983) development of it. Leech develops Popper's notion of three worlds of knowledge into four, by adding a world of societal knowledge to the worlds of physical, mental and objectively scientific knowledge of Popper (Table 5.1). The crucial question at stake is what kind of existence a poem might have, or which of these worlds it might inhabit. Those who view the poem and its meaning as an object might well regard it as having a kind of autonomy, in Leech's words: 'the knowledge contained in books and logarithm tables may exist outside the subjective knowledge of any living individual' (1983: 55). And Leech goes on to make the following point about language:

> A language may exist even though no one person exists who can speak read or understand it. Although at face value this seems absurd, there is nothing odd about saying that the Etruscan language exists, even though the Etruscan language is at present not known by anyone in the world. In fact it would be rather perverse to take the contrary view, and to claim that when the community of Etruscan-speakers died out, the language thereby ceased to exist; for if scholars decipher Etruscan writings in ten years' time, their achievement will not be in inventing the language but rather in rediscovering it (1983: 55).

I take it that what Leech claims here for languages is also true of texts and their meanings, according to the view which sees objective rationality as a possibility.

Whether one accepts the possibility of a world of objective fact and scientific rationality is not my main concern here. Heisenberg's uncertainty principle (Prigogine and Stengers 1985) and the persuasive arguments of Lakoff (1987) among others suggest that the psychological and physical world interfere to such an extent with our theorising and our cognition, that this objective world is inaccessible, if not unreal. And many would believe (Whorf 1956, Lucy 1992, Fairclough 1989) that the social world and the value systems inherent in language and thought make the quest for objective truth a non-starter.

Table 5.1. Leech (Popper)'s 4 (3) worlds of knowledge

	World 1	**World 2**	**World 3**	**World 4**
Inmates of these worlds are:	Physical and biological objects/states	Mental (subjective) objects/states	Societal (intersubjective) objects/states	Objective facts, existing independently of particular objects, minds, societies
Communication functions:	Expressive	'Signalling' or conative	Descriptive	Argumentative or metalingual
Historical transmission and accumulation of information	Genetic	Learning	Cultural transmission	Linguistic transmission by TEXT
Unit of transmission	Species	Individual	Society, tribe, culture	Linguistic (scientific?) community
Adaptation to environment by:	Natural selection	Conditioning	Social and technological advance	Error elimination through argument (scientific method)

The alternative, then, is to view a text as having no existence except as it is processed by the reader with the writer's possible intentions in mind. This makes the text the inmate of worlds two and three, the social, in that the dialogic partner is essential, and mental, in that processing effort and the accessing of background assumptions by the reader are the factors for judging relevance.

With these stylistic and epistemological contexts in mind we can proceed with analysis.

One Flesh
Lying apart now, each in a separate bed,
He with a book, keeping the light on late,
She like a girl dreaming of childhood,
All men elsewhere – it is as if they wait
Some new event: the book he holds unread,   5
Her eyes fixed on the shadows overhead.

Tossed up like flotsam from a former passion,
How cool they lie. They hardly ever touch,
Or if they do it is like a confession
Of having little feeling – or too much.   10

Chastity faces them, a destination
For which their whole lives were a preparation.

Strangely apart, yet strangely close together,
Silence between them like a thread to hold
And not wind in. And time itself's a feather   15
Touching them gently. Do they know they're old,
These two who are my father and my mother
Whose fire from which I came, has now grown cold?

5.2   Stylistic analysis – text as object/product

Leech and Short (1981) recommend the following procedure for the analysis of short texts:

> to begin with some general first impression of the passage and then to make selective use of the checklist [of linguistic features] in order to bring to the attention what appear to be the most significant style markers of each. (82)

This procedure is the mechanism for beginning the journey around Spitzer's 'philological circle' (Figure 1.2) in which general literary impressions are validated by linguistic analysis, and where this linguistic description in turn will yield further aesthetic/literary appreciation (Leech and Short 1981: 13–14). The emphasis on 'general impression' and the notion of a 'circle', indicate that such an approach tends to treat the poem as a product or object rather than a temporal process. To be more explicit, 'general' impression suggests an impression which is left with the reader after the reading has been finished. And 'circle' implies re-reading, an escape from the linear temporal process in which a reader experiences the text for the first time.

For myself, the general impression created by the poem is of inactivity and separation. What does linguistic analysis yield which might account for this impression?

5.2.1   Inactivity and verbs

One contribution to the sense of stasis and inactivity can be detected in the nature and frequency of the clause types. Table 5.2 divides the clauses in the poem into finite and non-finite, the non-finite including participial (infinitive) and 'verbless clauses'. What is noticeable is the high frequency of non-finite clauses, particularly in stanzas 1 (lines 1–8) and 3 (lines 13–16). This frequency creates an impression of inactivity since verbs are typically used to refer to changes of some kind, whether dynamic actions or not. So verbless clauses are more likely to describe a state or a circumstance than an event which brings change. The same is true for participial clauses, since participles are half way to becoming adjectives, and describe a relatively permanent quality rather than a change.

When we turn to consider the verbs within these clauses, we notice that very few describe a Material process in which an Actor effects some change upon a Goal within the physical environment, and those that do do not have the parent as Actor. 'Touch' (line 8) might be an exception to this were it used transitively, but the intransitive reciprocal use suggests lack of a volitional agent (cf. *the two snooker balls touched*). In any case the touching is all but negated by 'hardly ever'. When 'touch' is used transitively 'time' is the subject and 'parents' are the object. Even there the process is so gentle as to be almost imperceptible. 'Tossed up' (line 7), being a past participle, necessarily has the parents as Goal or deep object rather than Actor or deep subject. '(Not)wind in' (line 15) is a transitive verb describing a material process, but with negative polarity.

Table 5.2. Finite and non-finite clauses

Non-finite 'verbless'	Non-finite participial (infinitive)	Finite
STANZA 1		
each in a separate bed (1)	lying apart now (1)	it is as if… (4)
he with a book (2)	keeping the light on late (2)	they wait some new event (4–5)
she like a girl (3)	dreaming of childhood (3)	
all men elsewhere (4)	her eyes fixed on the shadows overhead (6)	the book he holds unread (5)
STANZA 2		
	tossed up like flotsam from a former passion (7)	how cool they lie (8)
	having little feeling or too much (10)	they hardly ever touch (8)
		if they do (9)
		it is like a confession (9)
		chastity faces them (11)
		for which their whole lives were a preparation (12)
STANZA 3		
strangely apart (13)	a thread to hold and not wind in (14–15)	time itself's a feather (15)
strangely close together (13)	touching them gently (16)	do they know…(16)
silence between them like a thread…(14)		they are old (16)
		who are my father and my mother (17)
		whose fire…has now grown cold (18)
		from which I came (18)

'Holds', 'hold' (lines 5 and 14) are transitive and have the parents as subject, and therefore are the best candidates for an exception to the rule, but a little consideration suggests that the meaning has more to do with the maintaining a position than bringing about dynamic change (contrast *grasp*). Other verbs resemble 'hold': 'keeping' and 'wait' are to do with suspension of action, while 'lie', 'faces', 'fixed' are to do with position.

Most of the remaining verbs describe mental/behavioural processes ('know', 'dreaming') or relational/existential ones ('is', 'is', 'were', ''s', ''re', 'are', 'have', 'grow' – meaning 'become')[1]. 'Came' is significantly different as it does indicate change and movement (though more to do with 'movement' in time rather than space). It shares this quality with 'grow', and significantly both of these occur in the final line of the poem. However, the subject of the verb 'came' refers to the speaker not the speaker's parents.

To sum up, lack of finite verbs, and paucity of material process verbs indicating perceptible change are perhaps the major factors in inducing an overall impression of the couple's inactivity.

5.2.2   Inactivity and sound effects

The sense of immobility can also be enhanced by the use of sound effects of various kinds. One important immobilising device may be a high frequency of long vowels/diphthongs. Any slowing effects of phonologically long vowels/diphthongs will be enhanced if the long vowels are stressed, and if they are open/followed by nasals or lenis fricatives, rather than stops or fortis fricatives.

The slowing effect of long vowels/diphthongs is particularly apparent at two points in the poem. The last sentence of two and a half lines throws up nine of these, an average of 7.6 per line, whereas the average number of diphthongs/long vowels in the first fifteen lines of the poem is 3.7. The concentration of such vowel quantities is thrown into sharp relief by the pattern of vowel length in the previous sentence, 'And time itself's a feather touching them gently', where we have only one long vowel/diphthong (underlined). This gives the question, the last sentence, a certain deliberateness (and the uncertainty of deliberation), a time and space in which to wonder. A similar effect is produced in lines 7–8 where the first four syllables of line 8 are constituted by long vowels/diphthongs, whereas the previous line has only two. 'Tossed up like flotsam from a former passion/How cool they lie'. The contrast in vowel quantity might mirror the contrast between their former turbulent passion and their present proneness for inertia. In both of these sentences the rallentando effect is further enhanced by the rhythm. When the poem was read aloud both readers put a full stress on the last three syllables of the poem, and one of the readers put intermediate degrees[\ ] or full degrees [/] of stress as follows on

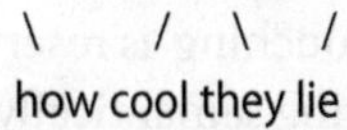

It is also important to note that in both line 8 and line 18 the words are all monosyllables, and are either left open or closed by nasals and voiced lenis fricatives, rather than by stops.

The final feature which produces rallentando efects in the poem might be the caesura, or the phonological punctuation (see Halliday 1989: 37). We shall discuss this in 5.2.4, as part of our attempt to identify the linguistic features responsible for a sense of separation and fragmentation.

5.2.3   Separation and lexis

If one of the general impressions created is of inactivity, another is surely that of separation. Most obviously, of course, the lexis is responsible for this. In Table 5.3, an attempt to sketch out some of the major lexical sets, we see two which are particularly prominent: touch and position.

Table 5.3. Lexical sets

Humans	Time	Position	Touch	Warmth	Light
girl	now	lying	holds	cool	light
child (hood)	late	apart	tossed	fire	shadows
men	new	separate,	touch	cold	
father	former	elsewhere	**feeling**	**feeling**	
mother	hardly ever	fixed	hold	passion	
	preparation	overhead	touching		
	time	lie			
	old	faces	one		
grown	**grown**	apart	(two)		
	keeping	close	whole		
	wait	together			
		between	(gently		
	destination	**destination**	thread		
	came	**came**	feather)		

As announced by the ironic title, and reinforced by the first line, the poem is an attempt to measure a relationship using spatial metaphors. At one extreme is the state of 'one flesh' where the parents embrace so intimately and completely in the sexual act that they are united. At the other extreme they are 'apart', 'separate', 'these two', for her 'all men elsewhere'. Between these two poles they 'touch', awkwardly if not accidentally, and are 'close together'. Somewhat pathetically he 'holds his book' instead of her. Purposeful 'touching' is reserved for time's effect on them. 'Tossed up' is particularly interesting semantically on the touch-separation dimension: to toss something one must first touch and hold it and then let it go, as their passion has done to them. Within this opposition between separate cool duality and passionate union even the conjunction 'and' in the environment of 'two' achieves significance: 'these **two** who are my father **and** my mother'.

The theme of separation and wholeness, along with the sense that these measure a relationship, can be observed in the premodifying quantifiers (ordinals) and their equivalent pronouns:

> **all** men elsewhere
> **some** new event
> **little** feeling or **too much**
> their **whole** lives
> **one** flesh
> these **two**
> **each**

The use of these quantifiers would hardly be noticeable, perhaps, were it not for the fact that they outnumber epithets ('separate', 'new' and 'former') in premodifying position.

5.2.4   Separation and phonology

Metre and sound repetition help to reinforce the sense of separation established by the semantics of the lexis. Crucial here seems to be the use of the caesura, which I shall associate with punctuation internal to the line. Jennings appears to be using punctuation phonologically, rather than syntactically (see Halliday 1989: 37). If she were using it syntactically then one would expect, for example, to find commas between 'mother' and 'whose', and between 'fire' and 'from' (lines 17–18), marking the fact that the postmodifying clauses are non-restrictive. Or for her to place a comma between 'like a girl' and 'dreaming of childhood' (line 3) in order to indicate that both postmodify 'she' directly, rather than allowing us to entertain the unlikely idea that 'dreaming of childhood' recursively postmodifies 'girl'. I feel entitled, therefore, to interpret punctuation as a graphological code for phonological effects, the most important of these being the caesura.

The most popular position for the caesura is after four or five syllables (lines 1, 2, 4, 5, 8, 11, 13, 15, 16), fracturing the lines into two separate halves. Underlining this symbolic break are a number of sound repetitions, more or less juxtaposed, cementing the integrity of each of the two halves:

1   separate bed
2   light on late
4   it is as if they wait
5   he holds unread
10 of having little feeling
13 yet strangely close together
15 and not wind in
15 time itself's a feather
16 touching them gently
18 fire from which I came

To sum up, we have seen that when we carefully re-read the poem looking for patterns which defy diachrony there are a number of repeated linguistic features which contribute to the overall impression of inactivity and separation, notably: clause types/verbs; phonology/sound effects; and lexical sets. We turn now to consider the kinds of emphatic patterning traditionally known as foregrounding.

5.3   Foregrounding the final sentence

Hasan has suggested that works of literature have two levels of subject matter of 'what the text is about' (1989: 87). The first, the level of verbalisation, simply involves the literal understanding of the language. So, at this level, the Jennings' poem would be about someone observing the cool but curiously intimate private behaviour of her parents and wondering whether they realise they are old. On the second level, the level of theme, we might, non-definitively, suggest that the poem is about the effect of time on passion. But how do we decide on the significance at the second level?

To do so we are expected to select certain parts of the text as capable of bearing a symbolic significance. Hasan claims that, in order to make that selection, we should be guided by the principle of foregrounding. The parts of the text which are multiply foregrounded are more likely to have symbolic significance.

If this is the case, then there is no doubt that the most symbolically significant section of the poem, the part which is most crucial for establishing what the poem is about at the second, thematic level, has to be the final sentence. It is foregrounded in the following ways:

1)   frequency of long vowels/diphthongs
2)   position of the caesura
3)   rhyme scheme
4)   frequency of monosyllabic words

5)   frequency of finite verbs
6)   multiple levels of subordination
7)   interrogative mood
8)   variety of tenses
9)   equative use of the copula
10) explicit, non pronominal person reference
11) use of first person pronouns/possessive adjectives
12) adjectives used predicatively

We have already touched on point 1). As for 2), the caesura in line 18 breaks the line 6/4, rather than the more ususal 4/6. As well as the frequency of long vowels/ diphthongs there is a preponderance of monosyllabic words, which probably have a slowing tendency too. (Both readers took longer to read the third stanza than the other two – Reader A: 18–18–22 secs., Reader B: 22–21–23 secs.)

The rhyme scheme in the first two stanzas establishes a pattern of a rhyming couplet, BB, ending the stanza. The final stanza ends AB.

Despite the relative scarcity of finite clauses in the poem (see Table 5.2) the last sentence accounts for five out of the fifteen, among them 'grow' and 'came', those verbs which we identified as most strongly suggesting change or movement. Packing five finite verbs into one sentence is achieved by four levels of subordination:

```
1) do they know
2)                 they are old    these two
3)                                      who are my father and my mother
                                 whose fire        ...        has now grown cold
4)                                              from which I came
```

The personal involvement which the speaker finally admits in the poem 'from which I came' is made less prominent by nesting it at the lowest rank of sub-ordination, which also iconically suggests the enclosure of the child within the process of the parents' cooling passion.

Crucially this sentence furnishes the only clause in interrogative mood in the whole poem. It is noticeable, however, that its subordinate clauses are in declarative mood. The mixture of moods within one sentence may be in itself slightly unusual grammatically. We discuss the pragmatics of this question later (5.4.6).

Time gets recognition in other parts of the poem through reference to age ('childhood', 'girl', 'men') by adjectives and adverbials ('now', 'late', 'new', 'former') and by metaphor ('destination', 'preparation') (see Table 5.3). But in these lines it is acknowledged by the variation in tense, the only previous non-present tense being in line 12. In the last sentence we have present, past-in-present, and past.

The degree of pastness goes hand in hand with the levels of subordination, so that the clauses at the highest ranks (1, 2 and 3) are present, the lowest rank (4) past, and intermediate rank (3) past-in-present.

The verb *to be*, the copula, is here used equatively in an identifying clause: 'these two who are my father and my mother'. Generally speaking copulation, syntactic or otherwise, does not thrive.

The disclosure of the couple's identity depends on two other linguistic features unique to this section of the poem: reference to the couple by full noun phrases rather than pronouns; and the shift of pronoun/possessive adjective from third to first person (cf. Edwin Thumboo's 'Krishna' (Sinclair 1989)).

Finally, the adjectives, 'old' and 'cold', are the only ones used predicatively in the poem. Along with their prominent position in the rhyme scheme, they underline the metaphorical equation

old : young :: cold : hot

Given that these quite startling departures from the norms of the poem multiply foreground the last sentence, what kind of symbolisation can we give these lines to confer on them a thematic value, abstract them away from their specificity, the level of verbalisation? The problem seems to be that there is no concrete description here which lends itself to symbolisation in the way of, for example, Robert Frost's 'The Road Not Taken' (Hasan's example), where the literal road becomes symbolic of a rejected alternative. In the Jennings poem the most concrete elements in this last line, the tactile images of fire and the cold, are not literal but are local metaphors, and hence cannot operate as symbols in the same way. For the moment, we could, perhaps, say that the foregrounding of these lines points to a theme such as wonder about the decline of the life force over time and doubts about old people's ability to recognise their age. But it seems to me that the prominence of the last sentence of the poem is better understood in terms of unfolding discourse process, rather than in terms of text as object.

5.4   Text as process – discourse pragmatics

Despite the developments in stylistic theory that we glanced at in chapter 1 and in 5.1. there is still an understandable tendency to treat the poetic text as a static object, a product. The reason for this is that poems are, if nothing else, memorable language, and are designed to be read or recited more than once, in a kind of ritual. As memorable rituals they seem to escape the linearity of time which we associate with most forms of speech, and invite us to treat them as objects, well-wrought urns, static and frozen. The kinds of analysis made in the first two sections of this chapter take a basically static view, presenting in table form, paradigmatically and simultaneously, what occurs syntagmatically and therefore (paradoxically) diachronically in a reading of the text. However, I now wish to consider a stylistic approach which emphasises the poem as a process of temporal discourse, an effect in the mind of the reader or listener.

Already, of course, by talking about the final sentence of the poem as being foregrounded, we may have been assuming that the poem should be understood as process. The foregrounding will not be noticed unless the background expectations have been established *prior* to the foregrounded section. Yet, it is doubtful whether we would consciously notice most of these foregrounded elements on a first reading. And in the remainder of the analysis it is the discourse processes of a first reading that I wish to concentrate on – largely because texts where disclosure of vital information is so obviously reserved for the final section have qualitatively different first and second readings. Take for example Jonson's *The Silent Woman*. And who re-reads a whodunnit?

5.4.1   Syntax as process: arrest and release

In 5.2. we noted that a general impression created by the poem was one of separation. This subsection suggests that in the process of reading the poem we experience fragmentation effects through the directionless, interrupted and 'bitty' syntax, which involves, what Sinclair (1966, 1989) has termed *arrest* and *release*. The confusion between arrest and release, is also part of the uncertainty effect induced as we process the text.

There are several aspects to this experience. Firstly there is the curious semi-grammatical effect of postmodifying third person pronominals (lines 1–3). Since we don't expect third person pronouns to be postmodified, the attempt to do so creates a sense of strain, as though syntactic relationships are attempted across a bridge that will not bear their weight. Further cracks in the syntax are created by a kind of delayed apposition,

a.   **each** in a separate bed, **he** with a book, keeping the light on late, **she** like
      a girl dreaming of childhood, all men elsewhere – it is as if **they**

We can process this as 'he' and 'she' jointly apposed to 'each' so that the verbless and participial clauses drive a wedge between the apposed pronouns. Or, alternatively, forced by the lack of a main verb, we might interpret 'he' and 'she' as jointly apposed to 'they', in which case not only do the non-finite clauses intervene but also the finite clause 'it is as if'.

b.   **chastity** faces them, **a destination** …

The dislocation is less pronounced in b., but even here the apposition would be more firmly and snugly established if the Subject and Object exchanged places:

> they face **chastity, a destination** …

c.   do **they** know **they**'re old, **these two** …

Again, with c., we have a verb (or two) sitting solidly as an obstacle between the apposed items.

We have already seen how, in the first three lines of the poem, the lack of a finite verb gives the text a directionless quality, and how we make what compensatory appositionary links we can. This lack of direction is manifest by various techniques which give the poem an unplanned, spontaneous feel, like unscripted commentary, as though many of the release structures represent afterthoughts. The paucity of premodifying structures within the noun phrase, particularly epithets (only 'new', 'separate', 'former'), places the burden of modification on postmodifying structures, as diagrammed. (Heads are underlined, postmodifiers in bold.)

> Lying apart now, <u>each</u> **in a separate bed**,
> <u>He</u> **with a book, keeping the light on late**,
> <u>She</u> **like a girl dreaming of childhood**,
> All <u>men</u> **elsewhere** – it is as if they wait
> Some new event: the <u>book</u> he holds **unread**,   5
> Her <u>eyes</u> **fixed on** <u>the shadows</u> **overhead**.
>
> Tossed up like flotsam from a former passion,
> How cool they lie. They hardly ever touch,
> Or if they do it is like a <u>confession</u>
> **Of having little feeling** – or too much.   10
> Chastity faces them, <u>a destination</u>
> **For which their whole lives were a preparation**.
>
> Strangely apart, yet strangely close together,
> <u>Silence</u> **between them like** <u>a thread</u> **to hold**
> **And not wind in**. And time itself's <u>a feather</u>   15
> **Touching them gently**. Do they know they're old,
> <u>These two</u> **who are** <u>my father and my mother</u>
> **Whose** <u>fire</u> **from which I came, has now grown cold?**

As we process these postmodifications and the delayed appositions of a. we are initially inclined to treat them as examples of arrest, since we expect a finite verb to arrive and complete the syntactic structure. However, ultimately, in the absence of arrival, the structures turn out to be examples of release.

This experience of unplanned afterthoughts is also conveyed by the co-ordinating of clauses and phrases: lines 9–10 'or', line 15 'and'. Subordinating conjunctions and clauses can often be used to achieve arrest, but they are rare here, so that few syntactic structures are tightly enclosed within others. Even those which do occur are within phrases which are already apposed to a previous phrase (lines 11–12, 17–18). However, in the final sentence there are multiple levels of subordination, tightly wrapping up, involving the *I* and its origins within the fire of the parents' passion.

The generally unarticulated, directionless and uncontaining syntax reflects the 'flotsam' image (line 7–8) which in turn is a metaphor for their present relationship. The wreck is broken up, nothing quite joined to where it ought to be by grammatical rule (postmodification of pronouns), nothing juxtaposed quite where it belongs (delayed apposition), nothing much contained within anything else (little subordination or restrictive postmodification, a preponderance of release), nothing much left of the original ship's plan or design.

5.4.2   Detecting moves between discourse divisions

What kinds of divisions might the first-time reader detect in the poem and by what means? S/he might be tempted to think that stanza division and discourse division coincide at lines 6–7. One argument in favour of this would be the shift from the present to the past at the beginning of the second stanza, 'now' (1) to 'former' (7). But just as we think we are moving into a past perspective we are brought full circle by 'lie' (line 8) back into the present and repeating the opening lexeme of the poem, in a kind of framing move. Syntactically, also, lines 7–8 resemble the first stanza with a thematised participial clause 'premodifying' the head of the later pronominal noun phrase.

So, syntactically, a better candidate for the beginning of a new section is line 8, where, the subject of the verb, 'they' is in Theme position. The 'hardly ever' which follows signals a shift from the specific present tense of simultaneous observation/commentary to the present tense of generalised habit. By lines 11–12 we have shifted even further from a consideration of their present general habits to consider the whole time span of their lives.

At the beginning of the third stanza the third discourse section of the poem begins. This is signalled by the same vocabulary that began the first section, 'apart', and the same kind of sentence structure in which we look in vain for a main finite verb.

Enough has already been said about the distinctive nature of the final section. The thematised interrogative operator 'do' signals unequivocally the change of mood. The occurrence of 'they' as subject contrasts with its absence in section three, and reminds us of the pattern in section 2.

Table 5.4. Markers of discourse sections

Section	Lines	Markers
1	1–8	non-finite clause as theme; delayed finite verb; time-span of the moment
2	8–12	'they' as theme; many finite verbs; time-span of habit/whole life
3	13–16	non-finite clause as theme; absent/delayed finite verbs; time-span of moment
4	16–18	interrogative 'do/they' as theme; many finite clauses; time span of youth to now

One might expect a first-time reader to notice at least some of the changes in Table 5.4, especially the changes in Theme, and to be aware that the poem seems to swing in style to and fro, with strong resemblances between sections 1 and 3, and between sections 2 and 4, and equally strong contrasts between sections 1 and 2, and 3 and 4. This oscillating in the style of discourse units is a counterpart to the hesitations about understanding, the vacillations and pattern of defeated expectations which I examine in more detail in sections 5.4.3 to 5.4.6.

5.4.3   Reference and deixis

This section deals with the crucial aspect of how reference and deixis operate as factors in the hermeneutics of progressive discourse. Two interlinked aspects of processing seem to be important here: the movement from anonymity to identification; and the movement from non-deictics to deixis. Unlike many of the other aspects of discourse process which I discuss in 5.4.4 – 5.4.6, reference and deixis create patterns of increasing certainty by the time the reader has processed to the end of the text.

What kinds of hypothesis can we make about the nature or identity of the people referred to as we read this poem? In the first clause we have no reference at all, simply predication 'lying apart now'. The only clues to the nature of the referents needed to complete this proposition will be found in the title of the poem: 'one flesh'. Since this is an allusive title, we will, in fact, have a rather rich fund of assumptions to draw on as clues:

> For this reason a man shall leave his **father** and be made **one** with his wife; and the **two** shall become **one flesh**. It follows that they are no longer **two** individuals: they are **one flesh**. What God has joined **together** no man must **separate**. (Matthew 19: 5–6. cf Genesis 2: 23–25)[my bolding of vocabulary found in the poem]

Drawing on the assmptions made available in the text alluded to, we will reach the hypothesis that two people are lying apart and that they are husband and wife. 'Now' with contrastive stress carries the presupposition that they were once sexually united, once one flesh. However, the 'now', if unstressed, might not be so interpreted on a first reading. Either way there is some confirmation of our hypothesis that a husband and wife are being referred to. The remainder of the first stanza tells us a good deal about their present physical circumstances and behaviour, but says nothing about their identity, and little about their attributes beyond suggesting that the wife is no longer a girl. The end of the first discourse section, lines 7–8, gives further confirmation that the state of sexual union mentioned in the title is in fact a previous state ('former passion') rather than, say, a future one. It is only at lines 11–12 that we gain any concrete evidence that the reason for their separateness, their chastity, is that they are towards the end of their lives. This evidence depends on the fact that the phrase 'their whole lives' suggests a relatively long life, and that 'destination' can be interpreted in terms of the root analogies LIFE IS A JOURNEY, DEATH IS A DESTINATION. The metaphorical treatment of time in section three underlines the notion that they are growing old.

By the end of the penultimate section the first time reader might well be in the following position as regards assumptions about the identity and nature of those referred to by the pronouns 'each', 'he', 'she', 'they', 'he', 'her', 'they', 'they', 'they', 'them', 'their', 'they', 'them', 'them': they are a married couple who were once physically united but now are towards the end of their lives and have little physical contact.

The final section confirms their age as a reason for their lack of physical contact: 'do they know they're old'. But it makes a radical change to the reader's interpretation of the poem by identifying them as the speaker's parents: 'these two who are my father and my mother'. Whereas certain hints and clues had prepared us for the fact that they are old, nothing had prepared us for the revelation that they are the mother and father of the speaker.

The focus on the speaker's involvement in the last foregrounded section is partly due to the identification of the couple, but also to the use of deixis. (*Deixis* is being used here in the strict sense of items whose meaning is incomplete unless one knows who is the speaker and what are the time and the place of utterance.) The first place deictic in the poem, only occurring near the end, is 'these' (line 17), indicating proximity to the addresser/scene of utterance. In the context of a poem where love is measured spatially, this proximity becomes symbolic of emotional attachment. It also stresses the mediating position of the speaker, who now seems closer to the people being described, both physically and emotionally, than the reader. Place deixis is followed by person deixis, 'my', as the people are finally identified as father and mother, and 'I'. Not only are place and person deixis prominent in the last section, but also time deixis, most obviously in the past and past-in-present tenses, and the adverb 'now'. The verb 'came', which apparently involves place deixis, in fact has more to do with time, as it can be glossed as 'originated'. Here the TIME IS SPACE metaphor is exploited. (I have drawn attention to this in the arrangement of items in Table 5.3, by the boldening of 'destination' and 'came' and their inclusion in both the position and time sets.) The effect of this sudden use of deixis rather than the earlier non-deictic pronoun reference is to give the final lines immediacy: more exactly, the speaker is unequivocally located in a scene of utterance which includes the people, now identified as her parents.

5.4.4   Non-factives and presuppositions

As a relatively distant observer or commentator in sections 1, 3, and even 2, the speaker shows some certainty about the physical universe she describes: the objects – the light, the book, the shadows, and the body language – posture, position, gesture, gaze. And in section 2, lines 11–12, she seems sure enough to issue general pronouncements about the course of human life, clinically certain that, after a certain age (or death), sexual activity stops. What the speaker cannot make up her mind about is the nature of their inner life. In order to represent her doubts to the reader she uses a number of contrafactive and non-factive markers, particularly similes, two of which are worth a more precise analysis to show how doubt is generated.

    a.   She **like** a girl **dreaming of** childhood

In a. we have one non-factive marker '**like**' (or counterfactive when we apply the standard implicature based on the maxim of Quantity: if the speaker knows the person is a girl she should say so), followed by, and apparently including, another counterfactive marker '**dreaming of**'. The counterfactive implications: 'she is not a girl', 'she is not a child' reinforce each other, providing we process the two phrases, 'like a girl' and 'dreaming of childhood' as separately postmodifying 'she'. However we are unlikely to process the phrases in this way, as the absence of a comma encourages us to take 'dreaming of childhood' as postmodifying 'girl'. If we succumb to such encouragement the anomalous 'a girl dreaming of childhood' cancels out the contrafactive implications of 'dreaming'. So we are unsettled and either have to do a retake of the syntax, or perhaps entertain the possibilities of: (i) dreaming of being what you already are; (ii) one's dreams turning into reality.

> b.   They hardly ever touch or **if** they do it is **like** a confession of having little feeling – or too much.

The first clause of b. involves the presupposition >> 'they do touch occasionally'. This makes the 'or' unexpected since it suggests two mutually exclusive propositions on either side of it: they touch or they don't touch. The 'if' reinforces the confusion since it standardly conveys the presupposition, >> 'they do or they do not (touch)'. As we already know that they do touch occasionally, a more consistent continuation would have been 'and/but when they do' rather than 'or if they do'.

Continuing with the clause complex we have 'it is **like** a confession', which, as with all similes or comparisons of this form, is ambiguous in terms of factivity, meaning either: 'all the evidence points to it being the case that' or 'though it appears to be it is not in fact the case that'. Given the first interpretation, we are to believe there is some evidence for the proposition that 'it is a confession of having little feeling or too much'. Now, while 'confession' is factive – confessing to something presupposes that what is being confessed to took place – in the religious sense it involves a change of mind or attitude to what was done, and an undertaking not to repeat it. Even this factive nominalisation involves, if not doubt, then reassessment.

Unlike the previous 'or' which was pragmatically infelicitous, this one is used perfectly standardly, but it creates a disjunction and therefore an opposition. In tandem with 'confession', and the implication of the reversal of behaviour from past to future which confession implies, we have a four way disjunction:

too much feeling in the past: less feeling in the future
too little feeling in the past: more feeling in the future

The remainder of the poem might suggest that we take the former of these.

5.4.5   Negative polarity, opposition and defeated expectations

These small-scale examples a. and b. of the cancelling out and multiplying of opposed contrafactive presuppositions, are part of a larger pervasive pattern of negativity and opposition. The following are absolutely negative in polarity: 'unread', 'not wind in'; other items indicate high degrees on the scale of negativity: 'hardly ever', 'little', while the meanings of some can scarcely be explained without recourse to negativity: 'elsewhere' (not here), 'silence' (no sound), 'chastity' (no sex).

The significance of much of the lexis of the poem also depends upon its position in a system of oppositions which runs throughout:

separate, apart	v	close together
light	v	shadows
passion	v	cool
fire	v	cold
he	v	she
one	v	two
father	v	mother
new	v	old
child(hood), girl	v	men
little	v	much
some	v	all

As it stands this list of oppositions demonstrates an object/product approach to the poem. To see how these lexical items of negativity and opposition work we have to examine their role in the discourse process; how they participate in the engendering and aborting of reader expectations.

We can begin with the title '*One Flesh*'. For the reader who picks up the allusion this will instantiate the verbal context of the above quotation from the Bible. The allusion might also be transferred to the Church of England marriage service which the poem echoes verbally:

to **have** and to **hold** from this **time** forth till death us do **part**.

Whatever the extent of the allusion's operation, we can be certain that we are intended to evoke a schema of sexual union. The expectations associated with the schema are immediately cancelled out by the first two words: 'Lying apart'. However, the contrastively stressed 'now' which follows (it was stressed by both my readers) gives the presupposition:

>> 'they did not previously lie apart'

which makes the 'one flesh' schema relevant to their past, though not the present. We might wish to speculate on the scope of the presupposition attached to contrastive 'now'

?>> 'he used not to have a book, keep the light on late; she used not to dream of childhood; she used to dream of other things; all men used not to be elsewhere'; etc.

The early positioning of 'now' seems to make it possible to draw these implications, though presumably only if further contrastive stresses are used to reinforce them. If, for example, we were to put contrastive stress on 'new' this would involve the presupposition

>> 'there were old events'

Sexual union is, for them, after all, an old event.

The next defeated or modified expectation concerns the 'reading in bed' schema, instantiated by 'each in a separate bed' and 'he with a book, keeping the light on late' and cancelled by 'the book he holds unread'. We may experience a parallel sense of unfulfilled expectations by having the 'sleeping in bed' schema instantiated by 'dreaming', and cancelled by 'her eyes fixed on the shadows overhead'. Furthermore the use of the colon seems to create a presupposition in itself: >> 'this behaviour resembles that of people waiting for an event'. The possibility of a future event, not entirely ruled out by the 'as if' but only made less than certain, is probably destroyed by line 11 which states dogmatically: 'chastity faces them, a destination'. Chastity is more of a non-event than an event.

We have already analysed the intricacies of defeated expectations and presuppositions in lines 8–10. But the contradiction between 'too little' and 'too much' bears further scrutiny. From the 'one flesh' perspective just touching hardly symbolises an adequate degree of feeling. From the 'chastity' perspective they might just as well admit that the last of life puts an end to sexual desire and activity, and forget about making any overtures of that kind.

In section 3 'strangely apart' is contradicted by 'strangely close together', unsettling the balance that had tipped down strongly on the side of chastity and lack of emotional involvement. It seems that this contrast can be viewed in two possible ways:

1   Literal.

    It is strange that they are now physically apart, since they were once so passionate, and strange that they are now so physically close (in the same bedroom) as they no longer desire sex.

2   Literal-metaphorical.

    It is strange that they are now apart since they were once so passionate, but in a strange kind of way they are close, metaphorically speaking, despite this physical separation.

The deliberately unsettling effect of the 'or' (line 10) is repeated by a similarly dislocating effect of 'and' in line 15. We expect people to wind in a thread, so that 'but' could have been anticipated. Even the defeat of our expectations in 'not wind in' is somewhat undermined by this choice of conjunction.

In section 4 the 'two' finally puts the nail in the coffin of the 'one flesh' schema. Just as finally, the 'fire' of the passionate young gives way to the 'cold' of the 'old'.

5.4.6   Pragmatic possibilities for the final question

We started this enquiry into the discourse pragmatics of 'One Flesh' with the question in our heads: what is the significance of the multiple foregrounding of the final sentence/section of the poem? We tentatively suggested that there might be some general symbolic value attached to the doubt presupposed by the interrogative mood. While this is a not unreasonable suggestion, a more valid perspective on this foregrounding would be to view the last section as a culmination of a discourse process. It is a suitable climax to the vacillation, defeated expectations, presuppositional readjustments and negative polarities which pervade the first three sections, particularly the uncertainties engendered about the inner life and state of mind of the parents. The doubts become urgent enough to force a change of mood, an interrogative, which seems more important precisely because, we now realise, the speaker is emotionally involved as the couple's child, an interested party. Increasing certainties about the identity of the couple, and increasing specificity conveyed by deixis, are all cast in doubt by the interrogative.

But pragmatically this question is far from simple. The first problem we need to resolve, if possible, is what kind of question this might be. Adapting some insights of Sperber and Wilson (1986: 251–3), and modifying them with Searle's notions of preparatory and sincerity conditions for questions (1969: 66) one might arrive at the following possibilities as in Table 5.5.

Table 5.5. A partial taxonomy of questions

QUESTION TYPE	PREPARATORY	CONDITIONS	SINCERITY CONDITION
	Speaker does not know p	Speaker believes hearer knows p	Speaker wants to know p
Self-addressed	Yes	No (S = H)	Yes
Deliberative	Yes	No	Yes
Indirect Q or Statement S	? [No]	No [No ?]	? [No]

The difference between self-addressed questions and deliberative questions is simply that there is no speakmate/interlocutor in the first case. But the speaker in deliberative questions e.g. 'Why do more shipping accidents happen on Saturdays than on other days of the week?' has no evidence to believe that the hearer is any more likely than s/he is to know the answer (columns 2 and 3). Nevertheless, the speaker would be interested to know the answer to the question (column 4).

There are certainly more kinds of indirect statements which interrogatives can be used for making, but I offer one in Table 5.5, bottom row. In this type of indirect statement the emphasis is upon the presuppositions behind the question rather then the question itself:

Why's she here again?	>>	'she's here again'
How come that window's open?	>>	'that window's open'
Do you realise it's raining?	>>	'it's raining'
Does he know he's driving on the wrong side of the road?	>>	'he's driving on the wrong side of the road'

This latter question/indirect statement, uttered, for example, to a fellow pedestrian as they see a car going the wrong way down a one-way street, is simply a way of drawing the attention of the interlocutor to the fact that the driver is driving in the wrong direction, and the speaker has noticed the fact. In these cases the question is more or less irrelevant as a question: the speaker and hearer may or may not know the answer and the speaker may or may not want to (see Q row in Table 5.5). As an indirect statement (see S row), however, it has the speech act conditions of an assertion: the speaker believes the presuppositions (columns 2 and 4), the hearer does not know or at least needs reminding (column 3).

Where does the final question fit, if anywhere, in this scheme of things? There remain three possibilities which, if we take into account the ambivalent nature of the literary discourse situation (Figure 5.1) can be expanded to four:

self-addressed question
self-addressed indirect statement
reader-addressed deliberative question
reader-addressed indirect statement

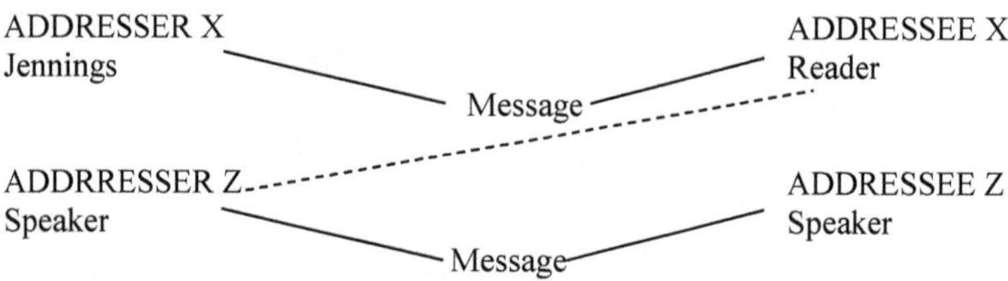

Figure 5.1. Discourse situation and levels in 'One Flesh'

Is it a self-addressed question, ADDRESSER Z to ADDRESSEE Z in Figure 5.1? This, initially, seems a likely solution: the speaker is genuinely asking herself whether they realise that age has finally crept up on them. However, the question seems just as likely to be an indirect statement; after all, the majority of clauses in the complex are declarative, and the *know* in the interrogative clause is a factive marker engendering the presupposition:

>> they are old

If this is a self-addressed indirect statement, it might have the following purposes: the speaker could be registering for herself the fact that she now realises they are old – she may have just realised it. But what would be the point of telling herself that these are her own parents and that she came from their passion? This could be a reminder: their cool behaviour to each other makes it difficult for her to believe that they are indeed her parents who once had a passionate enough relationship to produce her.

At the poet-reader level, it is as though we are eavesdropping on this self-address of the speaker for most of the poem (as diagrammed in Figure 5.1). From the addresser/ee X perspective the question is clearly intended as an indirect statement that the parents are old, that the people whose behaviour has been described in earlier sections are her parents (and that she is their child), and that she realises this. Could it also be a deliberative question addressed to the reader (or implied reader), Addresser Z to Addressee X (the broken line in Figure 5.1)? After all, despite the possibility of self-addressed questions, on the whole we associate questions with an addressee distinct from the speaker. The effect of taking it as a deliberative question addressed to the reader (implied or not) transforms the final section. We noted earlier how the deixis makes the last sentence more immediate: the poet identifies and identifies herself with her parents, becomes part of the situation she has been commenting on dispassionately. In posing a deliberative question she recognises the existence of the eavesdropping reader and so distances herself from him at the same time as she brings herself closer to her parents.

There is no fail-safe mechanism for categorising the final sentence of the poem, and all four possibilities seem to remain real ones. However, we have reached a tentative conclusion that, despite its pragmatic ambiguity, the final sentence seems to be making some kind of indirect as well as direct statements, both via the presupposition >> 'they are old', and through the declarative clauses which follow the interrogative clause. We could say, therefore that the sentence is an indirect statement masquerading as a question.

However, it seems equally possible to claim that the declarative clauses of the sentence are questions masquerading as statements. It is perfectly feasible to process the final clauses as though the illocutionary force of the question extends from the interrogative clause into the declarative and relative clauses.

these two who are my father and my mother whose fire from which I came has now grown cold?

This possibility takes two forms. On the one hand one can process them as declarative questions (Quirk and Greenbaum 1973: 195) licensed by the fact that the question mark occurs at the end of the clause complex, not after the interrogative clause. These questions could then be translated into the following interrogative form:

> Are these two my father and my mother?
> Has their fire grown cold?
> Did I really come from them?

There then arises the possibility that some of these clauses are interpreted as questions but not all. I have not space to spell out all the possibilities but such a combination would be likely to yield a paraphrase of the following kind:

> Either these are my father and mother and I came from them or their fire has grown cold. I am unsure of either but I cannot believe that both propositions are true.

The myriad pragmatic ambiguities of this final sentence are a fitting climax to the structures of doubt, hesitations in interpreting the parents' behaviour, and aborted schemata which characterise the first three sections of the poem. Despite its relatively purposeful and integrated syntax, its insistent monosyllables, and the apparently dogmatic and assured revelation of line 17, the final foregrounded section leaves us with a question mark hanging in the air.

5.5   Summary

Treating a poem as a permanent piece of ritual or cultural furniture as though it has an objective autonomous existence in Popper's 3rd and Leech's 4th worlds, and analysing it paradigmatically can give us valuable insights. But very often much is left unsaid if we deny ourselves the opportunity of investigating a poem in discourse process terms, as if it belongs in worlds 2 or 3, as we are naturally inclined to do with drama. It is the case in 'One Flesh' that patterns of foregrounding, established largely on the basis of treating the poem as a recycled object, will only achieve their significance when the poem is also considered in terms of reading and discourse processes. I hope the sketch of an interpretation above shows how the diachronic process approach and the synchronic formalist approach can complement each other as part of the stylistics enterprise. The first emphasises the addressee's pragmatic interpretative response on a first reading and the second discovers patterning in the message through re-reading and re-ordering the text. The first belongs more to reader response stylistics and the second to Jakobsonian formalist stylistics.

The remarks in this chapter about discourse processes remain something of a hypothesis, and it would be of interest to put them to empirical test. One means available for doing this would be protocol analysis of the kind exemplified in Short and Van Peer (1988) or Alderson and Short (1988), which would be particularly suited to the verification of the types of defeated expectation and the perception of discourse divisions that is hypothesised here, though other methods of reader response measurement might be needed for confirming the remarks about the nature of the final question.

6 The pragmatics of co-operation and politeness in two extracts from Harold Pinter's *The Birthday Party*

6.1 Introduction

In this chapter I hope to show how pragmatic theory, most obviously the Co-operative Principle, the Politeness Principle and negative face, but also aspects of conversational analysis such as pre-sequences and categories of silence, can be useful tools in the stylistics of drama. The theories and concepts can help us to describe what is going on in terms of the exchange of information, social positioning and characterisation of the participants, while also challenging the very notion of co-operation as an underlying norm. Pragmatic theories can also help to give us an explanation of the drama critic's impressionistic remarks about the style of Harold Pinter, namely his Pinteresque 'absurdity'. The stylistic approach in this chapter builds on that in the last part of the previous chapter, which emphasised the addresser-addressee relationship, by hypothesising the addresser's intended effect on the addressee of the dramatic utterances/silences, whether that addressee is a character or audience.

6.2 The style of Harold Pinter

How do non-stylistic critics or producers of Pinter characterise his style, in particular the style of the early plays, which Irving Wardle (1958) dubbed 'Comedy of Menace'? Communication, whether this is viewed in informational terms or interpersonal terms, often seems on the verge of breaking down, even if this is simply an exaggeration of much of our everyday talk, our 'slipshod contemporary idioms' (anonymous critic quoted in Peacock 2001: 75). Peacock puts it very well:

> Although initially critics considered Pinter's dialogue, with its
> circumlocutions, contradictions, repetitions, solecism, pauses and silences
> to be ultra-naturalistic, the type of speech that might be overheard on a
> London bus, as his work progressed they realised that its structure was in
> fact highly selective. Language now ceased to be a means of interpersonal
> communication or a carrier of factual information, but was merged with
> the dramatic action as a weapon in the characters' armoury of evasion,
> a 'stratagem for covering nakedness'. It revealed to the audience, not

the characters' motives or history, but only their current aims and fears. Pinter's characters do not wish to communicate: to do so would be to compromise their individuality, for, as Pinter himself explained, in his plays 'communication is a fearful matter'. (Peacock 1997: 46)

Or as Martin Esslin describes it, by denying its communicative purposes, Pinter, like other absurd dramatists, is bringing about a radical devaluation of language (Esslin 1980).

Informationally-inefficient communication is apparent in Pinter's dialogic silences, repetitions, contradictions and paradoxes, and in the importance of the hidden, the unstated, and the ambiguous (Hall 2001: 151, 146). Meaning seems to be more than usually underdetermined; in Pinter's own words 'If I'm being explicit, I'm failing' or more radically 'the speech we hear is an indication of that which we don't hear'. It follows that words can be a disguise and an evasion of communication, a resistance against 'being known' (quoted in Knowles 2001: 74, 77, 80). The importance to Pinter of this generation of uncertainty suggests to some that the radio play is a more suitable medium than the stage play, and partly explains Pinter's fondness for the use of blackouts on stage. (For example, in *A Slight Ache* the match seller is less mysterious and enigmatic on stage than in the original radio production (Guralnick 1996)).

Pinter's characters sense that the communication of information is a threat to individuality or autonomy, which partly accounts for pauses due to the refusal to communicate. 'The existential dilemma of Pinter's characters is the threat to their autonomy' (Peacock 1997: 56). In the early plays particularly, this inter-personal threat takes the form of invasions of territory: 'For the characters in Pinter's plays prior to 1969, territory is a personal sphere of influence and control and any intrusion into that territory therefore becomes a threat to per-sonality itself' (Peacock 1997: 53). Territorial disputes are simply one example of characters' opposed purposes. In general 'speech is at cross-purposes and combative' (Hall 2001: 145). And in the battle to dominate and reduce another's autonomy language can also become a weapon: 'by lowering language's informa-tional potential Pinter makes the audience aware of the strategic employment of language as a mode of defence, but at the same time he reveals its potential as a weapon' (Peacock 2001: 48).

To sum up, it is a combination of the generation of uncertainty, and interper-sonal threats to autonomy, realised both by linguistic structures of domination or by invasion of territory, and defended against by refusal to communicate, which lie behind the sense of menace and conflict in Pinter's early plays.

I now proceed to introduce various technical theories in pragmatics, which can be used as tools for elucidating and explaining further Pinter's early style, before applying them to two extracts from *The Birthday Party*. These theories will also be useful background to chapter 7.

6.3   The Co-operative Principle

Grice states the Co-operative Principle in general terms as follows: 'Make your conversational contribution such as is required, at the stage at which it occurs, by the accepted purpose or direction of the talk exchange in which you are engaged'. More specifically he claims that such co-operative communication (or other social activity) is realised by the application of four maxims:

The Maxim of **QUANTITY**
   i. *Make your contribution as informative as is required (for the current purposes of the exchange).*
   ii. *Do not make your contribution more informative than is required.*

The Maxim of **QUALITY**
   Try to make your contribution one that is true:
   i. *Do not say what you believe is false.*
   ii. *Do not say that for which you lack adequate evidence.*

The Maxim of **RELATION**
   Be relevant.

The Maxim of **MANNER**
   Be perspicuous:
   i. *Avoid obscurity of expression.*
   ii. *Avoid ambiguity.*
   iii. *Be brief (avoid unnecessary prolixity).*
   iv. *Be orderly.*

(Grice 1975: 45ff)

One particular problem in being co-operative arises with the maxim of Quantity. While with all the other maxims the speaker is likely to be aware of whether he/she is observing the maxims or not, in the case of Quantity one may not know whether the hearer already has the information one is about to give. For this reason, it is quite common in dialogue to employ a 'pre-announcement' to check whether the information is new (Levinson 1983: 349–56). Examples would be 'Do you know what happened to me today?' 'Have you heard the latest news about Jane?' 'Have you heard the joke about the nun and the kite?' While they have a checking function, such pre-announcements might also be employed as a call to attention, especially when the speaker is reasonably certain that the information will be new to the hearer, as in the first example.

   Grice's theory of communication is an inferential one, in other words he did not subscribe to a model of communication which emphasises the code as essential (see Jakobson's model in Figure 1.1., chapter 1). He is, in fact, rather more interested in phenomena like metaphor and irony, where the coded message is quite different from, if not the opposite of, the intended message. Because he emphasised the importance of inference, Grice showed how an inferential account of communication relates to his various maxims, whether they are observed or broken.

First of all he gave details of how inferences or implicatures may be arrived at if we assume that the speaker is observing the maxims. Levinson (1983) called these 'standard implicatures'. The two which concern us most are Quality and Quantity.

In his discussion of the standard implicatures of the maxim of Quality, Grice incorporates what Searle (1969), another famous pragmatician, called 'conditions' on speech acts. One of Searle's conditions – the sincerity condition – stipulates that for an assertion to be correctly performed, the speaker must believe the proposition in the assertion. A sincere assertion therefore upholds the Quality maxim 'try to make your contribution one that is true'. For example

'John was in jail three years ago'. – (sincerity condition) [standard implicature]
→
"S believes that John was in prison three years ago"

More interesting for our present purposes is how the standard implicatures or speech act conditions apply to questions. According to Searle a preparatory condition on *yes-no* questions is that the speaker does not know whether the proposition he is asking about is true or not. And a sincerity condition is that the speaker wants to know whether it is true or not.

'Do you have any sisters?' – (sincerity/preparatory conditions) [standard implicature]
→
"S wants to know if h has any sisters; S does not know whether the hearer has any sisters"

Also important for our analysis is the standard implicature on the maxim of Quantity. Logically 'I have two children' is consistent with 'I have four children', since, if I have four, I must have two. Why then do we normally interpret 'I have two children' to mean 'I have only two children'? Grice maintains that this interpretation is accounted for by the standard implicature on Quantity. For most assertions the implicature will be that the statement presented is the strongest or most informative that can be made. So that if I had more than two children I would be expected to say so (Levinson 1983: 106).

In explaining Grice's theories more emphasis is normally put upon the other ways of generating implicatures: that is by flouting a maxim (but see Levinson (2002) for extensive treatment of standard implicature). Flouting is a blatant breaking of a maxim, in the sense that the speaker believes that the hearer will realise a maxim is being broken, e.g. metaphor rather than lying. With flouting the speaker is still being co-operative, though in a less obvious way than if he/she observed the maxim. For example when William Golding writes 'the algebra was glue they were stuck in', he knows that algebra is not glue and expects us to realise that he knows algebra is not glue. Realising that this statement is not observing the maxim of Quality the hearer will access some meaning that is related to that of the proposition expressed in the utterance. We will therefore treat this as an intentional metaphor, and interpret it as 'the algebra was so difficult that they were "stuck" as though they were in glue', using the ambiguity of 'stuck' to find grounds of comparison.

While flouting breaks a maxim, but preserves the co-operation on which communication depends, there are other ways of breaking maxims which are more destructive of co-operation. Violation is a covert breaking of a maxim, where the speaker does not expect the hearer to know the maxim has been broken. Lying is a good example of the violation of the maxim of Quality, since successful lies have to remain undetected. Sometimes one or other interlocutor can give up co-operating in conversation altogether, and this is called 'opting out' (Thomas 1995: 72–6, 175).

6.4   The Politeness Principle

Grice and theorists like Sperber and Wilson (1995), who have streamlined his maxims into Relevance Theory, assume that the overriding purpose of communication is the efficient exchange of information, or expanding cognitive environments. However, it is quite clear that other social and interpersonal aspects of discourse are equally important. Consider the opening of George Bernard Shaw's *St Joan*.

ROBERT	No eggs! No eggs!! Thousand thunders man what do you mean by no eggs?
STEWARD	Sir, it is not my fault. It is the act of God.
ROBERT	Blasphemy. You tell me there are no eggs and you blame your Maker for it.
STEWARD	Sir, what can I do? <u>I cannot lay eggs</u>.
ROBERT	Ha! You jest about it.
STEWARD	No, sir, God knows. We all have to go without eggs just as you have, sir. The hens will not lay.
ROBERT	Indeed! Now listen to me, you.
STEWARD	Yes, sir.
ROBERT	<u>What am I</u>?
STEWARD	What are you, sir?
ROBERT	Yes: <u>what am I? Am I Robert, squire of Baudricourt and captain of this castle of Vaucouleurs or am I a cowboy?</u>
STEWARD	Oh sir, you know that you are a greater man here than the king himself.

ROBERT   Precisely. And now, do you know what you are?
STEWARD   I am nobody, sir, except that I have the honor to be your steward.
ROBERT   <u>You have not only the honor of being my steward but the privilege of being
                  the worst, most incompetent, drivelling, snivelling, jibbering, jabbering idiot
                  of a steward in France</u>.
STEWARD   Yes, to a great man like you I must seem like that.
ROBERT   My fault, I suppose. Eh?
STEWARD   Oh, sir, you are always giving my most innocent words such a turn.
ROBERT   I shall give your neck a turn if you dare tell me when I ask you how many
                  eggs there are that you cannot lay any.
STEWARD   Oh sir, oh sir-
ROBERT   No, not oh sir, oh sir, but no sir, no sir. My three barbary hens and the black
                  are the best layers in Champagne. And you come and tell me there are no
                  eggs! Who stole them? Tell me that before I kick you out through the castle
                  gate for a liar and a seller of my goods to thieves. <u>The milk was short
                  yesterday, too</u>: do not forget that.
STEWARD   I know, sir. I know only too well. There is no milk. <u>There are no eggs</u>:
                  tomorrow there will be nothing.

All the underlined utterances (and probably several others) break the maxims of the Co-operative Principle. We can really only understand these floutings in relation to questions of status, face, and (im)politeness, rather than in terms of co-operation. 'I cannot lay eggs' and 'there are no eggs' and 'the milk was short yesterday' break the maxim of Quantity; either we, the audience, know these first two facts already, or in the third case, the Steward knows it. In addition, Robert's two 'questions' do not observe the sincerity and preparatory conditions on questions, as he knows the answer and therefore does not wish to be informed of it. And finally Robert's insult 'you have not only the honour … in France' clearly breaks the Quality maxim, since Robert cannot have the evidence at hand about being the worst steward in France to make this a Quality statement.

Admittedly some of these breaches of the Co-operative Principle arise from the fact that this is the opening scene of the play, and what may be uninformative or infelicitous in terms of Robert–Steward communication, is not so for playwright–audience communication. For example, we as audience need to know that Robert is 'squire of Baudricourt and captain of this castle of Vaucouleurs' and that the cows are not producing milk and the hens are not laying eggs. However, it remains clear that the interpersonal dimension of the character-to-character communication is equally responsible for the unco-operative exchanges. We therefore need to take this interpersonal dimension into account in pragmatic theory.

Indeed, it soon became clear to discourse analysts that floutings or violations of the Co-operative Principle are not random, but depend on the systematic application of other principles to do with social relations. Leech (1983: 132–8), therefore, took up Grice's hint of the need for a 'Politeness Principle' to complement, or as part of, co-operation, with the six following maxims:

TACT (in directives and commissives)
    (a) Minimise cost to *other* [(b) Maximise benefit to *other*]

GENEROSITY (in directives and commissives)
    (a) Minimise benefit to *self* [(b) Maximise cost to *self*]

APPROBATION (in expressives and assertives)
    (a) Minimise dispraise of *other* [(b) Maximise praise of *other*]

MODESTY (in expressives and assertives)
    (a) Minimise praise of *self* [(b) Maximise dispraise of *self*]

AGREEMENT (in assertives)
    (a) Minimise disagreement between *self* and *other*
    [(b) Maximise agreement between *self* and *other*]

SYMPATHY (in assertives and expressives?)
    (a) Minimise antipathy between self and other
    [(b) Maximise sympathy between self and other]

We can see how these maxims might systematically account for breaking the Co-operative Principle maxims. For example, if someone asks us what we think of the presentation they just gave, and we thought it was poor, we are quite likely to sacrifice the maxim of Quality in favour of the maxim of Approbation. Or we might avoid expressing disapprobation by changing the subject, thereby breaking the maxim of Relation. And, even though we disagree with someone's statement, we might again sacrifice Quality to Agreement, and pretend to agree. We will quite often use roundabout and indirect forms when making requests, sacrificing the maxim of Manner to that of Tact.

Most of these maxims are self-explanatory. But for the purposes of this chapter it is worth saying a little more about Tact and Sympathy. All other things being equal, when directing someone to do something one ought to use grammatical forms which are relatively indirect or allow for optionality, in other words to avoid bare imperatives, e.g. 'Would you mind moving your chair?' instead of 'Move your chair'. However, one can still be polite and use the imperative where the action is of benefit to the hearer. So while 'wash my car' is impolite, because it involves cost to the hearer, 'have a sandwich' or 'take a seat' are perfectly polite, since they involve benefit to the hearer (Leech 1983: 107–8). In other words offers, suggestions and advice can take the imperative and still be polite and observe Tact.

Leech is not very clear about what constitutes Sympathy. I suppose we should include expressions which claim to share the feelings of the hearer: commiserations, condolences, congratulations and so on. Perhaps questions which show concern for someone's welfare or for a topic which is important to them may also be included under Sympathy.

6.5   Phatic communion

Leech's Politeness Principle is paralleled in many respects by Brown and Levinson's theories (1987). However, it is worthwhile highlighting their definition of negative face. Face is the public self-image that every member wants to claim for himself. One aspect of this is negative face: the basic claim to territories, personal preserves, rights to non-distraction – i.e. to freedom of action and freedom from imposition. I would like to stress the aspect of territoriality as part of negative face, since this will be important to our analysis and for our discussion of phatic communion.

The phenomenon of phatic communion is further evidence that rational and efficient communication of information is often sacrificed to equally important social and interpersonal factors. Remember from chapter 1 (Jakobson's functions, Figure 1.1), that phatic communion is communication whose purpose is opening, testing and maintaining the (physical or) psychological contacts between individuals. How often we say things such as 'Oh, it's you' or 'Here we are', which are non-informative or tautologous, simply to open communication channels.

In fact, phatic factors are particularly important at the opening and closing phases of an interaction, where psychological insecurity is at its greatest, and where negative face, and perhaps the rights to territories, are threatened.

> When one participant is static in space and the other is moving towards him … unless there are overriding special reasons, there seems to be a strong tendency, both in Britain and North America, for the incomer to initiate the exchange of phatic communion … the speaker realises that in some sense the static listener can be acknowledged as the owner of the territory … he acknowledges his own awareness of his invasion of the listener's territory… he declares, in effect, that his intentions are pacific, and offers a propitiatory token (Laver 1975: 226, quoted in Simpson 1989: 48).

Common propitiatory tokens including knocking on someone's door, shouting 'hallo' ('coo-ee' in south-east England in my mother's generation) if the door is open and you are entering a house, holding out one's right hand for it to be shaken and so on. Even if such tokens are lacking, it is incumbent upon the person approaching another's territory to be the first to speak and identify themselves.

Once this initial propitiation has been made, there are a number of topics which are common for initiating phatic communion. These include:

1   reference to factors specific to the context of situation with past, present or future reference, e.g. 'Foggy this morning, wasn't it?' 'Going to clear up this afternoon, they say'. 'Isn't it cold in this air-conditioning?'

2   direct reference to self-oriented or other oriented topics e.g. 'Gosh I'm hot!' 'You look good today!'

3   reference to on-going work, e.g. 'What are you doing?' 'This is too much like hard work for my liking' (Laver 1975, cf. Simpson 1989: 46).

I have now sketched in various pragmatic theories to do with co-operation, implicature, politeness and phatic communion. I hope to show how useful these can be for analysing two extracts of dialogue from *The Birthday Party*.

Extract 1

Act One

The living room of a house in a seaside town. A door leading to the hall down left. Back door and small window up left. Kitchen hatch down right. Kitchen door up right. Table and chairs, centre.

PETEY enters from the door on the left with a paper and sits at the table. He begins to read. MEG's voice comes through the kitchen hatch.

MEG	Is that you, Petey?	
Pause		
	Petey, is that you?	
Pause		
	Petey?	
PETEY	What?	
	Is that you?'	5
PETEY	Yes, it's me.	
	What? (*Her face appears at the hatch.*) Are you back?	
PETEY	Yes.	
MEG	I've got your cornflakes ready. (*She disappears and re-appears.*)	
	Here's your cornflakes.	10

He rises and takes the plate from her, sits at the table, props up the paper and begins to eat. MEG enters by the kitchen door.

	Are they nice?	
PETEY	Very nice.	

MEG	I thought they'd be nice. (*She sits at the table.*) You got your paper?	
PETEY	Yes.	
MEG	Is it good?	15
PETEY	Not bad.	
MEG	What does it say?	
PETEY	Nothing much.	
MEG	You read me out some nice bits yesterday.	
PETEY	Yes, well, I haven't finished this one yet.	20
MEG	Will you tell me when you get to something good?	
PETEY	Yes.	

Pause

MEG	Have you been working hard this morning?	
PETEY	No. Just stacked a few of the old chairs. Cleaned up a bit.	
MEG	Is it nice out?	25
PETEY	Very nice.	

Pause

MEG	Is Stanley up yet?	
PETEY	I don't know. Is he?	
MEG	I don't know. I haven't seen him down yet.	
PETEY	Well, then, he can't be up.	30
MEG	Haven't you seen him down?	
PETEY	I've only just come in.	
MEG	He must be still asleep.	

Extract 2

He looks at her, then speaks airily.

STANLEY	I've … er… I've been offered a job, as a matter of fact.	
MEG	What?	
STANLEY	Yes. I'm considering a job at the moment.	
MEG	You're not.	
STANLEY	A good one, too. A night club. In Berlin.	5
MEG	Berlin?	
STANLEY	Berlin. A night club. Playing the piano. A fabulous salary. And all found.	
MEG	How long for?	
STANLEY	We don't stay in Berlin. Then we go to Athens.	10
MEG	How long for?	
STANLEY	Yes. Then we pay a flying visit to … er … whatsisname …	
MEG	Where?	

STANLEY	Constantinople. Zagreb. Vladivostock. It's a round the world tour.	
MEG	(*sitting at the table*). Have you played the piano in those places before?	15
STANLEY	Played the piano? I've played the piano all over the world. All over the country. (*Pause.*) I once gave a concert.	
MEG	A concert?	
STANLEY	(*reflectively*). Yes. It was a good one, too. They were all there that night. Every single one of them. It was a great success. Yes. A concert. In Lower Edmonton.	20
MEG	What did you wear?	
STANLEY	(*to himself*). I had a unique touch. Absolutely unique. They came up to me. They came up to me and said they were grateful. Champagne we had that night, the lot. (*Pause.*) My father nearly came down to hear me. Well, I dropped him a card, anyway. But I don't think he could make it. No, I—I lost the address, that was it. (*Pause.*) Yes, Lower Edmonton. Then after that, you know what they did? They carved me up. Carved me up. It was all arranged. My next concert. Somewhere else it was. In winter. I went down there to play. Then, when I got there, the hall was closed, the place was shuttered up, not even a caretaker. They'd locked it up. (*Takes off his glasses and wipes them on his pyjama jacket.*) A fast one. They pulled a fast one. I'd like to know who was responsible for that. (*Bitterly.*) All right, Jack, I can take a tip. They want me to crawl down on my bended knees. Well I can take a tip … any day of the week. (*He replaces his glasses, then looks at* MEG.) Look at her. You're just an old piece of rock cake, aren't you? (*He rises and leans across the table to her.*) That's what you are, aren't you?	25 30 35 40
MEG	Don't you go away again, Stan. You stay here. You'll be better off. You stay with your old Meg. (*He groans and lies across the table.*) Aren't you feeling well this morning, Stan? Did you pay a visit this morning?	45

He stiffens, then lifts himself slowly, turns to face her and speaks lightly, casually.

STANLEY	Meg. Do you know what?	
MEG	What?	
STANLEY	Have you heard the latest?	
MEG	No.	
STANLEY	I'll bet you have.	50
MEG	I haven't.	

STANLEY	Shall I tell you?	
MEG	What latest?	
STANLEY	You haven't heard it?	
MEG	No.	55
STANLEY	(*advancing*). They're coming today.	
	They're coming in a van.	
MEG	Who?	
STANLEY	And do you know what they've got in that van?	
MEG	What?	60
STANLEY	They've got a wheelbarrow in that van.	
MEG	(*breathlessly*). They haven't.	
STANLEY	Oh yes they have.	
MEG	You're a liar.	
STANLEY	(*advancing upon her*). A big wheelbarrow. And when the van	65
	stops they wheel it out, and they wheel it up the garden path,	
	and then they knock at the front door.	
MEG	They don't.	
STANLEY	They're looking for someone.	
MEG	They're not.	70
STANLEY	They're looking for someone. A certain person.	
MEG	(*hoarsely*). No they're not!	
STANLEY	Shall I tell you who they're looking for?	
MEG	No!	
STANLEY	You don't want me to tell you?	75
MEG	You're a liar!	

6.6   Analysis of extract 1

The passage from the very beginning of the play creates a certain amount of apprehension on the part of Meg. Petey enters the territory that she is occupying, and by the normal rules he should give some propitiatory token and be the first to announce himself. However, Meg clearly hears him, but cannot identify him, which prompts her to ask him to identify himself. Only on the third attempt does she get a reply. (This is quite similar to Kidd's refusal to identify himself to Rose after knocking at the door in Pinter's previous play, *The Room*.) Petey's silences obviously cause unease, but how might we classify them according to pragmatic theory? According to Sachs, Schlegoff and Jefferson (1974) there are three possible kinds of silence. A gap, while either the speaker or one of the hearers who has not been nominated self-selects as next speaker. A lapse, where both interlocutors decide to suspend the conversation by not applying the rules for turn-taking. Or a significant silence, which violates the rule that if the current speaker selects the next speaker in the current turn, then the current speaker must stop speaking, and the next speaker must speak next. Although Meg self-selects when Petey fails to reply, as she would if there were a gap, these failures to communicate must be classified as significant silences, since Meg nominates Petey three times, and he therefore violates the rule. On the basis of what happens later in this opening scene, one might interpret his significant silences as optings out in Gricean terms – a certain unwillingness to engage in communication with Meg. With falling intonation the 'What' of line 4 might well indicate an irritated desire to opt out.

Silence in Pinter's plays has been the subject of much comment. Peter Hall makes a very interesting observation which suggests that all Pinter's pauses and silences are significant.

> He often uses nearly colloquial speech patterns. By the use of silence and of pauses, he gives a precise form to the seemingly ordinary, and an emotional power to the mundane …
>
> There are three very different kinds of pauses in Pinter. Three Dots is a sign of a pressure point, a search for a word, a momentary incoherence. A Pause is a longer interruption to the action, where the lack of speech becomes a form of speech in itself. The Pause is a threat, a moment of non-verbal tension. A Silence – the third category – is longer still. It is an extreme crisis point. Often the character emerges from the Silence with his attitude completely changed. As members of the audience we should *feel* what happens in a Pause; but we can and should be frequently surprised by the change in a character as he emerges from a Silence. … [T]he unsaid becomes sometimes more terrifying and more eloquent than the said. Pinter actually *writes* silence, and he appropriates it as part of his dialogue. The actor who has not decided what is going on in this gap will find that his emotional life is disrupted. The pause is as eloquent as speech, and must be truthfully filled with intention if the audience is to understand. (Hall 2001: 148)

These kinds of silence are so important to Pinter that, when he produced his own plays, he frequently overran by an hour or more (Peacock 2001: 74). The important point for us is that the type of analysis I perform here, in which inferences and pragmatic breaches and their inferences are teased out, needs the time and space to be appreciated by the audience at the playwright-audience level of discourse. Pinter insists on allowing such time in his productions.

So let's return to our analysis. It is not long before the dialogue apparently defies the Co-operative Principle and or the sincerity conditions on questions.

'Is that you?' (line 5), although a quite frequent expression at the beginning of dialogues, is an infelicitous question, since the only meaning of the deictic *you* refers to the addressee, and the speaker must know the answer before asking, though this anomaly is slightly reduced by the preface of 'Petey' in line 3. Similarly 'it's me' (line 6) conveys no information as the shifter or deictic *me* applies to whoever is speaking, and the utterance thereby breaks the Quantity maxim. One can hardly say 'it's not me'. There are two explanations of the frequency of these non-informative utterances. One explanation here may be that the identification of an unseen speaker is what is at stake. The situation is similar to that at the beginning of telephone conversations, at least fixed-line calls without caller ID, where besides issuing and answering a summons, and greeting each other, the speakers are displaying their voices for recognition (Levinson 1983). In these circumstances anything said in one's normal voice can take on informativeness about one's identity.

But perhaps we need another explanation. For the next exchange 'Are you back?'/'Yes' is another where the preparatory condition on questions – that the speaker should not know the answer – fails to apply, with the answer therefore uninformative. Indeed, Meg continues with these infelicitous questions and uninformative talk throughout this scene. 'Here's your cornflakes', assuming they are visible to him, and especially after 'I've got your cornflakes ready', must be somewhat redundant. The exchange 'Are they nice?' 'Very nice' 'I thought they'd be nice' suggests she is more or less certain of the answer before she asks it. Similarly infelicitous is the question 'You got your paper?' since she can see the paper propped up on the table where they are both sitting. These repetitions and recycling of known information might well achieve a comic effect.

Such is Meg's propensity to ask questions when she knows the answer already, that Petey tends to take this as quite normal. This accounts for the exchange 'Is Stanley up yet?' 'I don't know. Is he?' Petey, if we assume that the other preparatory condition on questions applies – that the speaker believes the hearer knows the information requested – must assume that Meg knows the answer to the question she herself has asked. She therefore has to insist on her own ignorance, 'I don't know', which makes her question more felicitous than Petey had assumed. However, without any further evidence provided by Petey she reaches the fairly firm conclusion that Stanley is not up and must be asleep. This suggests that, after all, the preparatory condition on the question, the speaker's ignorance of the answer, may not have applied. Any comic effect is intensified by this elaborate communicative circularity, where there is absolutely no progress in terms of the maxim of Quantity.

Another explanation for Meg's lack of informativeness or failure to observe the felicity conditions on questions is clearly that she is making all the phatic running. For phatic purposes we will often state the obvious or ask questions to which we know or can guess the answer. She clearly selects topics expected as phatic openers – other-oriented topics ('You got your paper?' 'What does it say?'), on-going work ('Have you been working hard this morning?'), and reference to factors specific to the context of situation ('Is it nice out?' and 'Is Stanley up yet?'). However, this phatic drive is very one-sided, as we saw at the very opening. Petey continues to give Meg a smaller quantity of information than she would like, as though he doesn't want to be disturbed while reading his newspaper. 'Is it good?' 'Not bad'. What does it say?' 'Nothing much'. We might conclude that he is trying to opt out. The longest answer he gives, 'No. Just stacked a few of the old chairs. Cleaned up a bit', is an unexpected answer, a dispreferred second, and perhaps not calculated to encourage Meg.

6.7   Analysis of extract 2

We turn now to the second extract, the dialogue with Stanley. Meg, Stanley's landlady, has a worse time of it here than she did with Petey. In the first section (ll. 1–23) he is not always informative, and threatening by implication, since the news of his job suggests she will lose a tenant. In the second section (ll. 24–45) he seems to be talking to himself, and ignoring her, and in the final section (ll. 46–76) he is positively menacing. We will see how this communication achieves its unfriendliness, not to say hostility by breaking the maxims of the Co-operative and Politeness Principles and in the final section, by the obsessive use of pre-announcements.

Like Petey, Stanley, even in the first section, seems rather reluctant to provide Meg with the information she wants, ignoring her rather than, like Petey, conveying minimal information. Stanley breaks the maxim of Quantity in line 10 (perhaps a flouting rather than a violation, since if they go to Berlin and Athens it must take a while) and more clearly violates it by not supplying an answer to 'What did you wear?' Stanley begins this extract hesitantly, perhaps breaking the maxim of Manner with his Three Dots and 'er' (line 1). Such hesitations are often markers of dispreferred seconds, one kind of preface (Levinson 1983), but can also be interpreted more generally as signs that the speaker is reluctant to convey information. If his job abroad means her loss of a tenant, then this is mock concern about breaking bad news to Meg. It may, however, be a hesitation due to the fact that he is fabricating the news as he goes along. This lying on the hoof could be our interpretation of 'Yes. Then we pay a flying visit to … er … whatsisname' which is a clearer breaking of the maxim of Manner.

Violations of the maxim of Quality, lies, are, almost by definition, hard to detect. Applying pragmatic theory to lines 15–18, we might detect a violation of Quality through the implicature of an inconsistency. 'Have you played the piano in those places before?' 'Played the piano? I've played the piano all over the world. All over the country. (*Pause.*) I once gave a concert'. Let's first of all assume that 'played the piano' means "played the piano in concerts". Now, there is no logical inconsistency between 'I once gave a concert' and 'I've played the piano in concerts all over the country' on the one hand, and 'I've played the piano in concerts all over the world' on the other. This is because if he played the piano all over the world he will have given a concert once (and many more times) and probably given concerts all over the country as well. However, we would normally detect an inconsistency here because we apply the standard implicature of the maxim of Quantity, which means one makes the strongest claim possible. By this standard implicature 'I once gave a concert' would be automatically interpreted "I gave a concert *only* once". This is inconsistent with 'I played the piano in concerts all over the world'. One of these statements must therefore be breaking, if not violating, the maxim of Quality.

A clearer case of breaching Quality can be found in 'I dropped him a card, anyway'. 'No, I – I lost the address, that was it'. The breaking derives from the inference that to drop someone a postcard one must have their address, and so the two statements are inconsistent, as marked by the 'no'. In this latter case of self-correction it would be hard to say the maxim had been violated since the correction is pretty obvious, and so it must probably count as a kind of flouting. In the first case, about the concert playing, whether it is flouting or violation seems less easy to decide.

Stanley's lack of observance of Quality often seems to overlap with his lack of observance of politeness. His claim to have played the piano all over the world clearly breaks the Modesty maxim, as does the possibly untrue recount of the adulation he received after the concert at Lower Edmonton (not very famous for its concert venues, though a place where Pinter himself broke the school record for the 220 yards sprint). His lack of Modesty might be, we feel, a compensation for the humiliation he received when 'they carved me up' (which is metaphorical, and therefore a flouting of Quality). He breaks the Approbation maxim with another metaphorical flouting of Quality – 'You're just an old piece of rock cake, aren't you?' – which suggests 'fruitcake', with the idiomatic meaning "crazy".

Meg responds rather more politely with apparent observances of the Tact maxim and Sympathy maxim. 'Don't you go away again, Stan. You stay here. You'll be better off. You stay with your old Meg'. She claims that staying with her will be for his benefit, which makes the imperative polite, though, since she is his landlady, it actually benefits her, so this may not observe Tact after all. She also expresses a certain amount of solidarity here, by nomination, 'Stan', and use of the pronominal adjective in 'your old Meg'. This is followed by an expression of Sympathy – 'Aren't you feeling well this morning, Stan? Did you pay a visit this morning' – showing concern about his state of health, more specifically the state of his bowels. But Stanley does not reciprocate this Sympathy.

The breaking of the Politeness maxims continues in the final section, although the breaches of these maxims are perhaps a by-product of violations of the maxim of Quality. The Agreement maxim is broken by Meg consistently throughout this extract: 'They haven't' (l. 62), 'They don't' (l. 68), 'They're not' (l. 70), 'No, they're not' (l. 72). Agreement (agreeing *with* rather than *to*) is probably the maxim closest to the Co-operative Principle, since it intrinsically involves matters of Quality. Moreover, twice calling Stanley a liar (l. 64, l. 76) involves three maxims. She shows not only disagreement, but also disapprobation of his habitual tendency to violate the maxim of Quality.

The maxim of Quantity is important in this extract, too. Stanley appears to be very studiously avoiding giving information that Meg already has by checking in advance through pre-announcements. In fact it is the use of these that contributes so much to the menace Stanley achieves in this section. Why should this be? Usually one pre-announcement is all that is required. But Stanley multiplies them: 'Do you know what?' (l. 46), 'Have you heard the latest?' (l. 48), 'Shall I tell you?' (l. 52), 'You haven't heard it?' (l. 54). Besides using these general formulae, Stanley continues to check in advance whether Meg knows the specific information that he is about to announce: 'And do you know what they've got in that van?' (l. 59) 'Shall I tell you who they are looking for?' (l. 73). The effect of this is to make Stanley seem reluctant to give information, and perhaps the intended implicature is that a full, bald and immediate statement of the facts would be too terrible for Meg to bear. Displacing a statement over several turns is one kind of delay associated with dispreferred seconds (Levinson 1983). However, this turns out to be a rather transitory concealment of hostility. For, in fact, of course, Stanley multiplies Meg's worry. By repeatedly checking that he is not breaking Quantity by giving information Meg already has, he is able to violate Quantity by rationing the amount of information he gives, and remain completely in control of what information emerges. Much of the information breaks Manner/Quantity by being too vague – 'someone' (l. 69), 'a certain person' (l. 71). Or it is unclear in reference '*They*'re coming today' (l. 56), which Stanley refuses to clarify despite Meg's demands for more information: 'Who?' 'And do you know what they've got in that van?' (ll. 58–9). Contrarily, information which Meg does not require he threatens to give (l. 74). He only gives the information she asks for when it suits his purposes: 'And do you know what they've got in that van?' 'What?'/'They've got a wheelbarrow in that van.' It is difficult to fit 'wheelbarrow' into any kind of script or schema involving men arriving in a van and knocking at the front door, which adds to the air of mysterious threat. In sum, Stanley exploits pre-announcements to withhold and provide just the amount and kind of information that prolongs fear of the unknown and enhances the power of vague puzzling threats.

I hope that I have demonstrated that a pragmatic approach to drama provides theoretical frameworks to help us describe how and to what extent information exchange and social interaction are taking place. As far as information exchange is concerned, we have seen that Quality is often in doubt: Stanley's contradictions, self-corrections, and possible fabrications make everything he says provisional. The maxim of Quantity is broken more than it is observed – Petey's failure to identify himself, his unwillingness to read out parts of the newspaper, Stanley's ignoring of several of Meg's questions, along with his use of pre-announcements to withhold information, and his failure to make explicit the identity of the men in the van and their purposes. Additionally, Meg asking questions to which she already knows the answer is hardly calculated to elicit any new information. Taken together the almost consistent breaking of these maxims generates much uncertainty and inexplicitness, which have been identified as a deliberate feature of Pinter's style. They comprise one of the strands leading to the atmosphere of menace, while also being a comic caricature of the non-compliance with the maxims which we encounter in everyday talk.

What also becomes clear is that the Co-operative Principle's assumptions about common purposes, 'the accepted purpose or direction of the talk exchange', refers to an ideal or idealised situation. Where interpersonal purposes of autonomy and domination are concerned there can be no common purposes between Meg on the one hand and Petey and Stanley on the other. In the first extract Petey violates Meg's autonomy by refusing to identify himself with a propitiatory token, thereby defying social norms and refusing to co-operate with Meg's attempts to identify the intruder. Later Meg threatens his autonomy/ negative face with infelicitous phatic questions about the cornflakes and the newspaper, which he wishes to read undisturbed. By resisting her phatic purposes and defending his autonomy he violates Quantity, or attempts to opt out. In the second extract Stanley similarly attempts to dominate by ignoring several of Meg's questions, and even ignoring her completely in the second section. These ignorings of Meg are themselves a form of passive domination. But more active attempts at domination and resistance to it are found in the breaches of the Politeness Principle of the second extract. Stanley's immodesty about his new job and his concert career, are an implied threat to leave Meg without a tenant. She counters this with what we finally decided was a breach of Tact, an attempt to get him to stay by claiming disingenuously it would be better for him. Meanwhile he has broken Approbation by insulting her with the 'rock-cake' metaphor. Stanley's pre-announcement strategies generate an intense menace, not to say desperation and humiliation in Meg, which she resists by breaking the maxims of Agreement and accusing him of being a liar. The second extract, especially the last section, demonstrates very clearly the way in which Pinter's characters use language as a weapon.

6.8   Summary and afterthought

To sum up, we have used theories of negative face, politeness, and phatic communion to describe more clearly and technically threats to autonomy, attempts at domination and resistance to it, and the significance of pauses/silence. We have used ideas from conversational analysis – the concepts of pre-announcements and dispreferred seconds to account for Stanley's hostile and menacing use of language. And we have used Grice's Co-operative Principle, especially the failure to observe the maxims of Quality and Quantity, to account for the miasma of uncertainty and asymmetry of purposes.

Of course, a play in which people were always perfectly co-operative and polite to each other would not be very exciting, and one might therefore expect drama to exaggerate asymmetry of purpose to enhance interest (Short 1996: 214). But even in everyday life purposes are less symmetrical than Grice might assume. For instance, let's take examinations as a communicative genre. Examinations have two different purposes for the participants in the exchange. The examiner wishes to grade the students, to produce a parabolic curve, which distinguishes the able from the less able. The student on the other hand wishes to achieve the best possible grade, which makes the purposes incompatible. The pragmatic effects of this can be seen in the nature of the communication. The examiner breaks the maxim of Manner by introducing a certain amount of obscurity of expression by, for example using technical terms to separate out those who have mastered them from those who have not. Exam questions often lack the essential preparatory condition of canonical questions, that the speaker does not know the answer to the question they are asking.

Religious leaders may deliberately break the maxims of Quality (Quantity/ Manner) by using metaphorical language in a misleading way. When Jesus' disciples return to Jesus by Jacob's well in Samaria, after having gone off to town to buy food, Jesus responds to their offer of food with 'I have food to eat that you know not of' – which is a metaphor one might not expect the disciples to detect. He seems to be attempting to single out those disciples who are on a spiritual wavelength and interpret this metaphorically, as with his parables. As Sarangi and Slembrouck (1992) have demonstrated, in dealing with bureaucracies the public want help, while bureaucrats want tidy classification, which may lead to lack of co-operation. More generally people in authority, including examiners, religious leaders, bureaucrats, wish to maintain their superiority and those under them may wish to challenge this superiority, and as a result purposes become asymmetrical.

One could even suggest that Gricean co-operative theory has its roots in a particular sub-culture which valued rationality (perhaps Oxford philosophers), and that is fails to obtain in other cultures, and certainly does not apply in situations of inequality. Edward Said, in *Orientalism* quotes, second hand, Sir Alfred Lyall's description of the 'Oriental' mind. Interestingly enough, Lyall depicts orientals as breaking many of the maxims of the Co-operative Principle, and the pre-figuring of Grice seems almost more than co-incidental (I have bolded certain significant phrases and commented on them in brackets):

> Thus, in the thirty-fourth chapter of his two-volume work *Modern Egypt* the magisterial record of his experience and achievement, Cromer puts down a sort of personal canon of Orientalist wisdom:

> Sir Alfred Lyall once said to me: "Accuracy is abhorrent to the Oriental mind. Every Anglo-Indian should always remember that **maxim [coincidence? probably].**" Want of accuracy, which easily degenerates into untruthfulness, is in fact the main characteristic of the Oriental mind.

> The European is a close reasoner; his statements of fact are devoid of any **ambiguity [maxim of manner: avoid ambiguity]**; he is a natural **logician** albeit he may not have studied logic [**Grice's article was entitled *Logic and Conversation***]; he is by nature sceptical and requires proof before he can accept the truth of any proposition [**maxim of quality: do not state that for which you have insufficient evidence**]; his trained intellect works like a piece of mechanism. The mind of the Oriental, on the other hand, like his picturesque streets, is eminently wanting in symmetry. His reasoning is of the most slipshod description. Although the ancient Arabs acquired in a somewhat higher degree the science of dialectics, their descendants are singularly deficient in the logical faculty. They are often incapable of drawing the most obvious conclusions from any simple premises of which they may admit the truth. Endeavour to elicit a plain statement of facts from an ordinary Egyptian. His explanation will generally be lengthy [**maxim of manner; be brief**] and wanting in lucidity [**maxim of manner: be perspicuous**]. He will probably contradict himself half a dozen times before he has finished his story [**maxim of quality**]. He will often break down under the mildest process of **cross-examination.**
> (Said 1978: 38, my bolding and insertions in brackets)

One might have various reactions to the above. It may be the case that, in this physical context of situation, that is under restraint in the office or court of a colonial administrator, in the institutional context of being cross-examined, and in the societal context of being subjected to colonial rule, co-operation would be unlikely. Or one could, following Pratt (1981), suggest that some societies, in any case, have different norms of conversational behaviour from others, and that value judgements should not be made on this basis. By the standards of other cultures are Cromer or Lyall, for example, ruthless, impolite, colourless in the way they talk? Gricean maxims could be based on the norms of a particular elitist Western sub-culture.

If breaking the maxims is natural, and yet also uncommunicative then this calls into question not only the notion of an underlying co-operativeness, but the very assumption that the only purpose of language(s) is communication. George Steiner (1975), himself multi-lingual, uses the multiplicity of the world's languages as evidence to the contrary:

> How are we to rationalize the fact that human beings of identical ethnic provenance, living on the same terrain, under equal climatic and ecological conditions, often organized in the same types of communal structure, sharing kinship systems and beliefs, speak entirely different languages? (p.54)

> Why does homo sapiens, whose digestive tract has evolved and functions in precisely the same complicated ways the world over, whose biochemical fabric and genetic potential are essentially common, the delicate runnels of whose cortex are wholly akin in all peoples and at every stage of social evolution – why does this unified, though individually unique mammalian species not use *one* common language? (p.50)

> It may be that the agonistic functions of speech inside an economically and socially divided community outweigh the functions of genuine communication … Languages conceal and internalize more, perhaps than they convey outwardly. Social classes, racial ghettoes speak at, rather than to each other (p.32).

> Obviously we speak to communicate. But also to conceal, to leave unspoken. The ability of humans to misinform modulates through every wavelength from outright lying to silence (p.46).

> My conviction is that we shall not get much further in understanding the evolution of language and the relations between speech and human performance so long as we see 'falsity' as primarily negative, so long as we see counterfactuality, contradiction, and the many nuances of conditionality as specialized, often logically bastard modes. *Language is the main instrument of man's refusal to accept the world as it is.* Without that refusal, without the unceasing generation by the mind of counter-worlds

… we would turn forever on the treadmill of the present. Reality would be 'all that is the case' and nothing more. Ours is the ability to gainsay to 'unsay' the world, to image and speak it otherwise. In that capacity, in its biological and social evolution, may lie some of the clues to the question of the origins of human speech and the multiplicity of tongues. It is not, perhaps, 'a theory of information' that will serve us best in trying to clarify the nature of language, but 'a theory of misinformation'. (p.218)

Nevertheless, I suppose we need a background assumption of co-operation if society is to be possible, and luckily normal life is not so fraught with social conflict as is drama. Perhaps it would be more entertaining if it were.

7 The limits of politeness: a butler's pragmatic dilemmas in Kazuo Ishiguro's *The Remains of the Day*

7.1 Introduction

Life in society is a delicate balancing act. We tread a tightrope swayed by the conflicting forces of truth, self-interest, concern for others and institutional demands. This is particularly clear in the area of pragmatics. Grice formulated his Co-operative Principle (6.3, Grice 1975) as if linguistic exchange was, at a deep level, simply a matter of the efficient communication of the truth. It was soon apparent that the floutings and violations of his maxims were not random, but could be accounted for systematically by postulating other sets of maxims such as those of Leech's Politeness Principle (6.4, Leech 1983), or by appeals to theories of positive and negative face (Brown and Levinson 1987). As we saw in chapter 6, when discussing Pinter's plays, linguistic and social behaviour cannot be explained by a single-minded desire for the truth, or reduced to maxims governing the untrammelled transfer of ideas about perceived states of affairs in the world.

The social dilemmas that we face are well illustrated pragmatically in situations where maxims of politeness and co-operation come into conflict with each other (Leech 1983, Lim 1992). Obvious examples are when our host asks us whether we enjoyed the rather bland meal he cooked, where there is a tug of war between Approbation and Quality; or when we wish to make a polite request and make it so indirect and Tactful that it breaches the maxim of Manner, either its sub-maxims of perspicuity or avoiding prolixity. The Politeness Principle and Co-operative Principle can also conflict with the Banter Principle, according to which we deliberately attack the positive and negative face of our speakmates, flouting (temporarily violating?) Quality by 'kidding' them and exaggerating our disapprobation of them as an expression of intimacy.

Some psychologists, like B. F. Skinner (1992), and scientists, such as Richard Dawkins (1989), would have us believe that concern for others and institutional demands are illusions. For them, the truth is that human behaviour is, at the root, largely determined by self-interest, the search for positive reinforcement, or the overwhelming imperative to ensure the survival of our genes or closely-related ones. Any self-sacrifice for the benefit of institutions or of others with whom we do not share genetic material is a wasted enterprise. It is tempting to interpret *The Remains of the Day* in these terms: Stevens' sacrifice of his whole life to the service of Lord Darlington can be seen as a terrible mistake. But to reduce the book to this kind of simplistic interpretation seems, to me, to be turning it into a melodrama. It is far more interesting than that. And so is life.

In this chapter I wish to explore how the butler, Stevens, in *The Remains of the Day* encounters situations in which the politeness we might expect from a butler is challenged and abandoned. His polite and dignified self-restraint in the service of Darlington and the institution of Darlington Hall come under pressure from self-interest, the 'truth' and the need for communication. And his subservience to this seat of power actually makes him less than polite to others whose demands conflict with his master's. The chapter attempts to show how politeness theory, as an explanation for the breaching of the maxims of the Co-operative Principle, can be a useful analytical tool for understanding character and theme. It therefore belongs to a stylistics that takes seriously the intentionality of pragmatics in the addresser-addressee relationship.

7.2   Observing and breaking the Politeness maxims

We introduced Leech's Politeness Principle in section 6.4. Let's start by looking at its maxims one by one and seeing how Stevens observes or breaches them.

7.2.1   Agreement

In certain scenes with his boss Stevens conforms to the kind of butler caricature associated with Jeeves in P. G. Wodehouse (O'Brien 1996: 789). In the following scene Darlington is broaching the question of the future duties of Stevens' father, after the latter's falling and spilling the contents of a tea tray. Despite his desire to vindicate his father, to show him approbation and give him positive face, Stevens nevertheless has to agree with Darlington's representation of the situation:

> 'As I say, sir, my father appears to have made a full recovery and I believe he is
> still a person of considerable dependability. It is true one or two errors have
> been noticeable recently in the discharging of his duties, but these are in
> every case very trivial in nature.'
> 'But none of us wish to see anything of that sort happen again.' (62)

Stevens, on the whole, seems to avoid disagreements whenever possible. For example, he reluctantly accepts the retrospective verdict on Herr Ribbentrop as a trickster, 'As I say, this is the commonly held view and I do not wish to differ from it here' (136), even though it implies his master's lack of judgment.

Caught in a pragmatic dilemma of having to listen to Mr Cardinal's criticism of Darlington's political alliance with Ribbentrop he does not openly disagree, though he ritualistically declines to agree:

> 'He's out of his depth you see, Stevens'
> 'Is that so, sir?'
> …
> 'His lordship is a dear, dear man. But the fact is he is out of his depth. He is being manoeuvred. The Nazis are manoeuvring him like a pawn. Have you noticed this?'
> 'I'm sorry, sir, I have failed to notice any such development.'
> 'Haven't you even had a suspicion? The smallest suspicion that Herr Hitler, through our dear friend Herr Ribbentrop, has been manoeuvring his lordship like a pawn, just as easily as he manoeuvres any of his other pawns back in Berlin?'
> 'I'm sorry, sir, I have failed to notice any such development.' (221–3)

Notice, incidentally, that this refusal to agree is prefaced with an apology, and framed as self-critical modesty, his own failure, mitigating the impoliteness.

There are two examples of disagreement that are especially significant. The person who provokes Stevens to disagreement is, in both cases, Miss Kenton. One important disagreement is over the wisdom of her hiring a new housemaid, Lisa.

> I recall that we became locked in disagreement for some time and perhaps it was only the fact that the matter of the dismissed maids was so recent in our minds that I did not hold out so strongly as I might against Miss Kenton. In any case, the result was that I finally gave way … (155).

Whether or not Miss Kenton hired Lisa deliberately for her looks, as a surrogate attempt to overcome Stevens' sexual repression, she certainly suggests that his objection to the hiring has a repressive motive, as the end of the following passage makes clear:

> 'No doubt, Mr Stevens,' she said to me, 'you will be extremely disappointed to hear Lisa has still not made any real mistake worth speaking of.'
> 'I'm not disappointed at all, Miss Kenton. I'm very pleased for you and for all of us. I will admit you have had some modest success regarding the girl so far.'
> 'Modest success! And look at that smile on your face, Mr Stevens. It always appears when I mention Lisa. That tells an interesting story in itself. A very interesting story indeed.'
> 'Oh really, Miss Kenton? And may I ask what exactly?'

'It's very interesting, Mr Stevens. Very interesting you should have been so
pessimistic about her. Because Lisa is a pretty girl, no doubt about it. And I've
noticed you have a curious aversion to pretty girls being on the staff.'
'You know perfectly well you are talking nonsense, Miss Kenton.'
'Ah, but I've noticed it, Mr Stevens. You do not like pretty girls to be on the
staff. Might it be that our Mr Stevens fears distraction? Can it be that our Mr
Stevens is flesh and blood after all, and cannot fully trust himself?' (155–6)

An earlier disagreement between Miss Kenton and Stevens arises in relation to
Stevens' father. Miss Kenton points out that Stevens' father has been remiss in his
duties and has muddled up the correct positioning of two statues of Chinamen.
Stevens is inclined to disagree with her, but through her insistence is forced to
admit that she had been correct:

'The Chinaman normally on the landing you will now find outside the door.'
'I fear Miss Kenton, that you are a little confused.'
'I do not believe I am confused at all, Mr Stevens.'
…
'You accept than, Mr Stevens, that I am not in error on this point.'
'I accept nothing of the sort, Miss Kenton.'
…
'Mr Stevens, that is the incorrect Chinaman, would you not agree?'
'Miss Kenton, I am very busy. I am surprised that you have nothing better to
do than to stand in corridors all day.'
'Mr Stevens, is that the correct Chinaman, or is it not?'
'Miss Kenton, I would ask you to keep your voice down.'
…
'Mr Stevens, will you kindly look at the Chinaman behind you?'
'If it is so important to you, Miss Kenton, I will allow that the Chinaman behind
me may well be incorrectly situated.' (58–9)

The Agreement maxim is, in a sense, the closest of the Politeness Principle
maxims to the Co-operative Principle, involving, as it does, questions of truth
or the maxim of Quality. To openly disagree, or to 'go into denial', is therefore
especially dangerous for a character who is otherwise using politeness as a
shield, because it may force one into argument and final discovery of the truth.
The case of the misplaced Chinaman illustrates Stevens' final facing up to the
truth even despite his initial disagreement or failure to accept it. His reluctance
presumably stems, not only from his filial respect, but also from the fact that
his father is a role model of a great butler, and it is painful to admit he is no
longer capable in his profession.

7.2.2   Sympathy

One controversial question in speech act theory concerns sincerity conditions for expressives, such as thanks, apologies and sympathising. According to Searle (1969) these speech acts are not felicitously performed unless the speaker has the corresponding feelings of gratitude, regret and sympathy when performing the locutionary act. If this is the case, then much of what we label as thanks, apologies and condolences are not the real thing. For example, why would we insist on children saying 'thank you', i.e. uttering the form of words, or why would the Chinese government, Korean 'comfort women' and allied ex-serviceman wish to wring out of Japan a verbal apology for atrocities committed during the Second World War? The alternative is to regard these acts as declarations, rather than expressives, that is to say as speech acts like christening and declaring a meeting closed, which achieve their effect simply by virtue of the correct form of words being uttered by the right person in the appropriate institutional setting.

Stevens certainly goes through the polite and superficial expressions of sympathy on occasions. On his motoring trip to the West Country he pulls up sharply in front of a hen in the middle of the road. When the hen's owner expresses gratitude that he did not run her over, and goes on to relate how their tortoise had been killed in exactly the same spot three years previously, Stevens says 'sombrely', 'How very tragic' (69). His ritual use of the word 'sad' to describe Darlington's friend, Herr Bremann's death may be equally 'insincere'. But when he uses the adverb 'sadly' to describe the death of Neighbours, a very popular rival butler of whom he disapproved (29), and the adjective 'sad' for news of Miss Kenton (now Mrs Benn's) separation from her husband, we detect some self-deception mixed with lack of sincerity. In this latter case he disingenuously goes on to say: 'It is of course tragic that her marriage is now ending in failure. At this very moment no doubt, she is pondering with regret decisions made in the far off past, which have now left her, deep in middle age, so alone and desolate' (48).

Leech does not explore the Sympathy maxim in much detail, though we might expand his notion to cover any verbal behaviour which appears to imaginatively identify with another's predicament or well-being. This would then cover the kind of phatic putting of others at their ease which Stevens can manage so 'admirably' on important social occasions, even, in the following instance, when he knows his father is dying elsewhere in the house:

> A moment later I spotted the young Mr Cardinal, not far away, still standing on
> his own, and it struck me the young gentleman might be feeling somewhat
> overawed in the present company. His glass was in any case empty, so I started
> towards him. He seemed greatly cheered at the prospect of my arrival. (107)

As with agreement, the grossest breaches of sympathy occur in communication with Miss Kenton. When she announces the death of her only living relative, her aunt, instead of sympathising with her he reprimands her (178–9). When she is upset about the sacking of the two Jewish housemaids at the insistence of Darlington, he fails to show her that he too finds it disturbing. To his later claim that the whole matter caused him great concern, she expostulates 'Then why, Mr Stevens, did you not tell me so at the time?'… 'Do you realize, Mr Stevens, how much it would have meant to me if you had thought to share your feelings last year?' (153–4). Most crucial of all, he fails the test of sympathy in comforting Ms Kenton when she is in tears, a failure which haunts him for the remainder of his life. One evening she announces her engagement, as, we suspect, a challenge to Stevens, which he, however, declines to take up. Later that night he suspects, with a kind of telepathy, that she is crying behind the door of her room, but he foregoes the opportunity to enter and comfort her. He remembers

> that moment as I paused in the dimness of the corridor, the tray in my hands, an ever growing conviction mounting within me that just a few yards away, on the other side of that door, Miss Kenton was at that moment crying. As I recall, there was no real evidence to account for this conviction – I had certainly not heard any sounds of crying – and yet I remember being quite certain that were I to knock and enter, I would discover her in tears. I do not know how long I remained standing there; at the time it seemed a significant period, but in reality I suspect it was only a matter of a few seconds. For, of course, I was required to hurry upstairs to serve some of the most distinguished gentlemen of the land, and I cannot imagine I would have delayed unduly. (226–7)

7.2.3   Approbation

Ishiguro's previous novel written in the first-person, *An Artist of the Floating World* (AFW), was set in Japan, where stereotypically the maxims of Approbation and Modesty have very high weightings. Indeed Leech (1983: 136–7) quotes at some length a conversation between Japanese housewives attempting to resolve the discomfort involved in the necessity for disagreement when one compliments the other's garden (Approbation) and the other attempts to politely refuse the compliment (Modesty). In this earlier novel we find expressions in keeping with this stereotype. One of Ono's pupils, for example, shows him extreme approbation, and part of that approbation stems from Ono's, the narrator's, apparent modesty, though this is not a modesty strong enough to prevent him narrating the adulatory speech:

> 'I have suspected for some time that Sensei was unaware of the high regard in which he is held by people in this city. Indeed, as the instance he has just

> related amply illustrates, his reputation has now spread beyond the world
> of art, to all walks of life. But how typical of Sensei's modest nature that he is
> unaware of this. How typical that he himself should be the most surprised by
> the esteem accorded to him. But to all of us here it comes as no surprise. In
> fact, it may be said that, respected as he is by the public at large, it is we here
> at this table who alone know the extent to which that respect still falls short.
> But I, personally, have no doubt. His reputation will become all the greater,
> and in years to come, our proudest honour will be to tell others that we were
> once pupils of Masuji Ono.' (AFW: 25)

It might be suggested that there is something of a pastiche of politeness in
Ishigiro's work and that the heightened sense of politeness in Japan is taken
over in the discourse style of Stevens. However, just as Housman did not know
Shrophire well (chapter 4), nor does Ishiguro know Japan well. He left Japan
for England at the age of six, and has only visited once. It may, in fact, be that
the quasi-archaic sense of English politeness which Ishiguro encountered in
England was a model for the excessive politeness he depicts in Japan in *Artist
of the Floating World*. This politeness behaviour was part of an aristocratic ideal
and class system that the Japanese aristocracy so admired, and perhaps imitated
(Asker 2003b: 302).

The operation of the maxim of Approbation in *The Remains of the Day* is
skewed by Stevens' respect and adulation for the powerful. The touchstone of
his professional life, more or less his whole life, is the pursuit of greatness, and
the answer to the question 'what constitutes a great butler?' The conclusion he
reaches is that you cannot be a great butler unless you belong to a 'distinguished
household', which he defines as a household which is a centre of power, a hub,
where 'mighty decisions' are debated and made, which only later emanate out
to the public (115–16). Stevens achieves this aim: 'Who would doubt at that
moment that I had indeed come as close to the great hub of things as any butler
could wish?' (227). He even goes so far as to call this desire to serve the centre
of political power 'moral' and 'idealistic': a tragic confusion between what is
good and great, since it turns out that through amateurism or naïvety the great
man he served had far from moral effects on government policy.

Stevens' instincts, then, are to accept power and to give the wielders of
power his uncritical approbation. This especially applies to Lord Darlington,
of course, whom he defends in the face of public criticism.

> I can say with conviction that his lordship was persuaded to overcome his
> more retiring side only through a deep sense of moral duty … I can declare
> that he was a truly good man at heart, a gentleman through and through, and
> one I am today proud to have given my best years of service to. (61)

> I for one will never doubt that a desire to see 'justice in the world' lay at the
> heart of all his actions. (73)

The extent to which power is the issue in these defences is evident when he discusses Darlington's association with Mosley and the blackshirts. It is not so much the immorality of their ideology which Stevens despises, but the fact that they never came near the centre of power:

> In any case such organisations were a complete irrelevance to the heart of
> political life in this country. Lord Darlington, you will understand, was the sort
> of gentleman who cared to occupy himself only with what was at the true
> centre of things. (137–8)

Stevens, of course, finds himself in a dilemma when David Cardinal expresses disapprobation of Darlington, since these are both powerful figures, but loyalty to his employer as well as the relative power differential win the day. Cardinal is appalled by Darlington's attempt to arrange a meeting between the Prime Minister and Hitler. Prompted for his reaction Stevens remains staunchly loyal:

> 'I cannot see what there is to object to in that, sir. His lordship has always
> striven to aid better understanding between nations.'
>
> …
>
> 'I am sorry sir, but I cannot see that his lordship is doing anything other than
> that which is highest and noblest.'
>
> …
>
> 'I am sorry sir, but I have to say that I have every trust in his lordship's good
> judgment.' (225)

Automatic approbation towards employers to some extent carries over to Stevens' new boss, Farraday, with his 'most kind suggestion' that Stevens should go on his motoring trip (3) (10), and his 'generous offer to "foot the bill for the gas"' (10). However, Farraday's new communicative style presents difficulties for Stevens. There are his Americanisms which fail to observe the correct technical housekeeping terminology – '"some sort of servants' rota"' instead of 'staff plan', 'putting sections of the house "under wraps"', '"give it a go with four"' – and which Stevens marks with slightly disdainful inverted commas. More disturbing is Farraday's lack of restraint, lack of respect for Stevens' negative face, in, for example, surmising correctly that Stevens' trip was in quest of a lady friend. Nevertheless, Stevens is disposed to make allowances and mute any disapproval. 'Embarrassing as those moments were for me, I would not wish to imply that I in any way blame Mr Farraday, who is in no sense an unkind person' (14).

Given the influence of power over his judgments, it is not surprising that Stevens is much less restrained in his criticism of his colleagues, peers, fellow-butlers and those serving beneath him. However, a few distinguished peers he unreservedly admires, for example Mr Marshall and Mr Lane (34) 'the two great butlers of recent times', or butlers like Mr Harry Graham, and Mr John Donalds, 'some of the finest professionals in England' (18). Among these he also includes his father, who was a model of self-restraint, loyalty, and dignity and whose conduct and standing as a butler he discusses at great length (34–42). His father's self-restraint was manifest when he declined his employer's offer to be relieved of the duty of serving the general whose military blunder had led to his son's, Stevens' brother's, death, and when, indeed, he went on to excel in his service to this general (39–40). His father's dignity and loyalty are manifest in his restrained disapproval of his employer's drunken guests' criticism of his employer, a disapproval which shows itself in his refusal to continue driving them for as long as they continue their unflattering remarks (38–9). In the pragmatics of politeness terms Stevens shows approbation of his father's loyal disapprobation of the guests' disapprobation of his employer. Because he holds up his father as a model of the dignified butler Stevens is loath to accept anyone else's disapprobation of his father, whether in the misplacing of the Chinaman or in his polishing of the cutlery (134).

Other recent trends in professional butlering life Stevens approves of less. The first is the fashion for employers to employ new-fangled butlers who can show off their general knowledge and grasp of current affairs: 'I have heard of various instances of a butler being displayed as a kind of performing monkey at a house party' (35). Stevens by contrast shows he holds no opinion on the delicate political issues of the day (92), repeatedly being unable to give an opinion when questioned by Mr Spencer (195–6). This is an extremely sensitive area for Stevens, since it is precisely his lack of political awareness and knowledge, his innocence and naïvety, which allows him to give unrelenting and unquestioning support to a Nazi sympathiser.

The second area where he displays sensitivity is in his criticism of house-maids and housekeepers who are on a constant lookout for romance. Explaining that Miss Kenton and his father had arrived at Darlington Hall at roughly the same time because the under-butler and housekeeper had left to get married, Stevens continues:

> I have always found such liaisons a serious threat to the order in a house. Since
> that time I have lost numerous more employees in such circumstances. Of
> course one has to expect such things to occur amongst maids and footmen,
> and a good butler should always take this into account in his planning;
> but such marrying among more senior employees can have an extremely

> disruptive effect on work. Of course, if two members of staff happen to fall
> in love and decide to marry, it would be churlish to be apportioning blame;
> but what I find a major irritation are those persons – and housekeepers
> are particularly guilty here – who have no genuine commitment to their
> profession and who are essentially going from post to post looking for
> romance. This sort of person is a blight on good professionalism.
> But let me say immediately I do not have Miss Kenton in mind at all when I
> say this. Of course, she too eventually left my staff to get married, but I can
> vouch that during the time she worked as housekeeper under me, she was
> nothing less than dedicated and never allowed her professional priorities to
> be distracted. (51)

This passage indicates that Stevens, in fact, disapproves of, or finds unsettling, those who, unlike him, refuse to sacrifice their emotional and sexual lives to their professional roles. It is only towards the end of the book that he briefly entertains the idea that his own sacrifice was in fact an unworthy one. Just as interesting is the way he hastens to deny this criticism is directed at Miss Kenton. At a subconscious level it probably is so directed, since it is apparent that he has a suppressed emotional and sexual interest in her, an unacknowledged 'unprofessional motive', the very reason for his trip to the West Country to meet her. Nor is it quite true to say that she 'never allowed her professional priorities to be distracted' during their time working together. Indeed, they were from time to time distracted by him, as we shall see.

In fact one of the most significant expressions of disapprobation of Miss Kenton are on the occasions when she invades the privacy of his room. In the first place she tries to brighten up his room by bringing him flowers. He obviously resents this, or resents his own defensive rejection of her attraction, for he responds:

> 'Miss Kenton I appreciate your kindness. But this is not a room of
> entertainment. I am happy to have distractions kept to a minimum.'
> 'But surely, Mr Stevens, there is no need to keep your room so stark and bereft
> of colour?'
> 'It has served me perfectly well thus far as it is, Miss Kenton, though I
> appreciate your thoughts. In fact, as you are here, there was a certain matter I
> wished to raise with you.' (52)

And he proceeds to reprimand her for calling his father by his first name, William, though this form of address conforms to the etiquette of housekeepers talking to under-butlers.

On another occasion she comes into his pantry and asks to see the book he is reading (which turns out to be a sentimental romance). She finally prises it from his grip, in the only instance of physical contact mentioned in the novel, but not before he has voiced his disapproval.

> 'Miss Kenton, I must ask you to leave me alone. It is quite impossible that you should persist in pursuing me like this during the very few moments of spare time I have to myself.'
>
> …
>
> 'But as a matter of principle, I object to you appearing like this and invading my private moments.' (166)

This incident conforms to a pattern in which Miss Kenton is the major irritant and threat to Stevens' negative and positive face.

7.2.4   Modesty

In both Stevens' narration and dialogue there is probably more evidence of a pattern of immodesty than of modesty. The immodesty includes pride by association. He is proud to be British: 'We call this land of ours *Great* Britain, and there may be those who believe this is a somewhat immodest practice. Yet I would venture that the landscape of our country alone would justify the use of this lofty adjective' (28). He is proud to have a father who is the epitome of the dignified and restrained loyalty necessary to great butlers (34). His name dropping shows his pride in being associated with those of high status: 'Perhaps I will convey a better idea of the tone of those evenings if I say that regular visitors included the likes of Mr Harry Graham, valet butler to Sir James Chambers' (18). When on his motoring trip he is mistaken for the owner, rather than the butler, of Darlington Hall, he refrains from disabusing his hosts and upholding Quality, partly, we suppose, because he is flattered. This perhaps represents his greatest immodesty (187–9).

Indeed what he feels distinguishes him is his service to the great:

> And one has a right, perhaps, to feel a satisfaction those content to serve mediocre employers will never know – the satisfaction of being able to say with some reason that one's efforts, in however modest a way, comprise a contribution to the course of history. (139)

Often this pride gives him an almost intolerable air of pretentiousness:

> As this date grew nearer, the pressures on myself, though of an altogether more humble nature than those mounting on his lordship, were nevertheless not inconsequential … I thus set about preparing for the days ahead as, I imagine, a general might prepare for a battle. (76–7)

Even simple achievements, such as polishing the silver to a standard of which Lady Astor calls 'probably unrivalled' (134) are important to him, but even more so if they have a beneficial effect on the political guests at Darlington Hall – 'Lord Darlington himself suggested that the silver might have been at least a small factor in the change of his guest's mood that evening, and it is perhaps not absurd to think back to such instances with a glow of satisfaction' (138).

Even when he is forced to accept that the political aims of Darlington were misdirected, he can still retreat into a pride in his carrying out his butlering duties to the highest standards, though in fact we might see this 'modesty' as a defence against shame.

> As far as I am concerned, I carried out my duties to the best of my abilities, indeed to a standard which many may consider 'first rate'. It is hardly my fault if his lordship's life and work have turned out today to look, at best, a sad waste … (201)

There is a sharp paradox involved in the operation of the Modesty maxim, especially when we have a first-person narrator. Since modesty is highly prized as polite, then, claiming it amounts to immodesty. Ono, for example, in *An Artist of the Floating World* claims, with a degree of inverted snobbery: 'For I was very lax in considering the matter of status, it simply not being my instinct to concern myself with such things. Indeed, I have never at any point in my life been very aware of my own social standing …' (AFW: 19). This paradox applies most obviously to 'false' modesty, when speakers deliberately understate their qualities, achievements or possessions, while believing they are greater than they say. Furthermore, as with sympathy, in cases of false modesty, the question arises of whether uttering a modest form of words counts as modesty or not, whether it is merely a ritual declaration or needs the sincerity condition of an expressive. False modesty can only count as modest if it is a declaration.

The typical pattern of intertwining or alternating of modesty and immodesty can be seen in this passage:

> I have myself devised many staff plans over the years, and I do not believe I am being unduly boastful if I say that very few ever needed amendment. And if in the present case the staff plan is at fault, blame can be laid at no one's door but my own. At the same time it is only fair to point out that my task in this instance had been of an unusually difficult order. (5)

The need for modesty is obviously on his mind, since he mentions boastfulness, even in the rather immodest first sentence. The second sentence, an admission of possible blame is modest enough, though the third diminishes the effect by giving an account or excuse for any failure on his part.

Quite typically Stevens, while making immodest statements, mitigates them or downtones them as much as possible, to give a veneer of modesty. Modesty is, after all, precisely what he values in the English landscape, 'It is as though the land knows of its own beauty, of its own greatness, and feels no need to shout it' (29). However, the pompous veneer of hedging, modalisation and diminution does little to endear him to the reader, except as rather pathetic in his self-obsession, and in his sense that he is the centre of attention for others who are monitoring and judging him.

> That is not to say I consider I became necessarily a 'great' butler; it is hardly for me, in any case, to make judgments of this sort. But should it be that anyone should ever wish to posit that I have attained at least a little of that crucial quality of 'dignity' in the course of my career, such a person may wish to be directed towards that conference of March 1923 as representing the moment when I first demonstrated I might have a capacity for such a quality. (70)

> Of course, it is not for me to suggest that I am worthy of ever being placed alongside the likes of the 'great' butlers of our generation, such as Mr Marshall or Mr Lane – though it should be said that there are those who, perhaps out of misplaced generosity, tend to do just this. Let me make clear that when I say the conference of 1923, and that night in particular, constituted a turning point in my professional development, I am speaking very much in terms of my own more humble standards. Even so, if you consider the pressures contingent on me that night, you might not think I delude myself unduly if I go so far as to suggest that I did perhaps display, in the face of everything, at least in some modest degree a 'dignity' worthy of someone like Mr Marshall – or, come to that, my father. Indeed, why should I deny it? For all its sad associations, whenever I recall that evening today, I find I do so with a large sense of triumph. (110)

The modest aspects of these two examples are, we feel, illustrations of false modesty, since he actually believes he has special qualities. But later in the chronology of the novel he increasingly allows himself to make straightforward and honest acknowledgment of faults and mistakes. For example he admits his blame for the dirty fork at Farraday's breakfast table (124), that in his staff plan for Farraday he was perhaps negligent in giving himself too much to do (9), and that during his motoring trip it was a foolish oversight not to keep enough water in the Ford's radiator and to run out of petrol (159–60).

But the really important instance of modesty comes when he is driven to accept that his life of service to Darlington really had no greatness or dignity in it after all.

> All those years I served him, I trusted I was doing something worthwhile. I
> can't even say I made my own mistakes. Really – one has to ask oneself–what
> dignity is there in that? (243)

If our reactions to the earlier immodesty and false modesty of Stevens are to
regard him as an obsessively self-important and pretentious bore, at this point
in the novel we come to a startling sympathy for him, and perhaps understand
that the earlier immodesty was a (subconscious) attempt to hang on to some
fragments of self-esteem in the face of a failed life.

7.2.5   Generosity

If the maximising of cost to self is the essence of the Generosity maxim, then
Stevens is supremely generous, having sacrificed most of his life in professional service for the benefit of Darlington. He portrays himself as the ultimate
professional completely 'inhabiting his role' as butler (169) to the extent that
everything which he undertakes is represented, however disingenuously, as
means to the end of better service to his employer. This includes the attempts
at banter (15, 245) which he hopes to perfect by discussion with Mr Graham
(19), the reading of romances as a way of improving his English (167–8), and
even the trip to visit Mrs Benn.

> What I mean to say is that Miss Kenton's letter set off a certain chain of ideas
> to do with professional matters here at Darlington Hall, and I would underline
> that it was a preoccupation with these very same professional matters that led
> me to consider anew my employer's kindly meant suggestion. (5)

But the extremes to which Stevens takes this service is seen in what he sacrifices
to his professional life: his morality and integrity; his relationship with his father;
and any possible emotional love life with Miss Kenton.

The conflict between morality and service is dramatised most clearly in
the incident of sacking two Jewish housemaids. When Miss Kenton is required
to send them to him for dismissal, she remonstrates forcibly, while he simply
accepts orders.

> 'I simply cannot believe it. You are saying Ruth and Sarah are to be dismissed
> on the grounds that they are Jewish?'
> 'Miss Kenton, I have just this moment explained the situation to you fully. His
> lordship has made his decision and there is nothing for you and I to debate
> over.'
> 'Does it not occur to you, Mr Stevens, that to dismiss Ruth and Sarah on these
> grounds would be simply – *wrong*? I will not stand for such things.' (148–49)

In the ensuing dialogue Stevens shows that he has, as he later regrets, delegated his political judgment and moral conscience to Lord Darlington.

> 'There are many things you and I are simply not in a position to understand concerning, say, the nature of Jewry. Whereas his lordship, I might venture, is somewhat better placed to judge what is for the best.' (149)

Service as butler to Lord Darlington with his father as under-butler seems inimical to their personal relationship. Converse between them becomes very embarrassing and infrequent (63–4). And when Stevens has to announce to his father that he will no longer perform the duties of an under butler, the communication is coldly and unpityingly efficient, impersonal in its use of passives [bolded].

> 'Principally,' I continued, '**it has been felt** that **Father should no longer be asked** to wait at table, whether or not guests are present.'
> 'I have waited at table every day for the last fifty-four years,' my father remarked, his voice perfectly unhurried.
> 'Furthermore, **it has been decided** that Father should not carry laden trays of any sort for even the shortest distances. In view of these limitations, and knowing Father's esteem for conciseness, I have listed here the revised round of duties **he will from now on be expected** to perform.'
> I felt disinclined actually to hand to him the piece of paper I was holding, and so put it down on the end of his bed. (65–6)

Of course, in one of the most memorable episodes in the novel his father dies of a stroke during the conference of March 1923, and Stevens is unable to be at his deathbed because he is attending to M. Dupont's painful feet, and putting David Cardinal at ease. It might appear that Stevens has no capacity for feeling or emotion towards his father, but in that case we could hardly talk of his making sacrifices in the service of Darlington. In fact he does find the death upsetting, and has to control and hide his tears (105). He regards the control he manages to exert as an achievement of restraint and dignity, and his professional conduct during the conference as the moment at which he comes of age as a butler.

Stevens appears to come closer to genuine human communication with Miss Kenton than with his father, but, as we have seen, foregoes the opportunity to comfort her. But this night when she returns from her evening off and announces her engagement, is the same night on which the most important guests visit Darlington Hall – the Foreign Minister, The Prime Minister, and Herr Ribbentrop. The excuse, if not the reason, for declining to enter the room of the crying Miss Kenton could then be that his professional duties would not allow it. He passes her door as he is on the way back from the cellars with wine, 'for of course I was required to hurry upstairs to serve some of the most distinguished gentleman of the land and I cannot imagine that I would have delayed unduly' (227). As with the March conference, Stevens regards this execution of his professional duties as a triumph in which 'I had managed to preserve a "dignity in keeping with my position"' (227) and as 'a summary of all that I had come to achieve thus far in my life' (228). In both these episodes Stevens uses professionalism as an alibi for lack of humanity.

7.3   Quality, Manner and self-deception

We might see the Politeness Principle as in conflict with the Co-operative Principle, rather than complementing it, especially if we highlight the latter's premium on efficient and logical exchange of information. Circumlocution is obviously one area which breaches the maxim of Manner, sometimes for purposes of politeness. It is a widespread phenomenon in Stevens' speech:

> 'he took the opportunity to inform me' (3) = he told me
> 'our shores' (6) = England
> 'a gentleman of generous dimensions' (85) = a big man

> 'Miss Kenton I wonder whether I may draw your attention to the fact that the
> bed linen for the upper floor will need to be ready by the day after tomorrow
> … I merely felt the need to satisfy myself that it had not escaped your
> attention' (79) =
> the bed linen for the upper floor will need to be ready the day after tomorrow
> … I just wanted to be sure you knew.

The most humorous passage where this indirectness misfires is when Stevens agrees to take on the task of telling the younger Mr Cardinal 'the facts of life':

> 'Excuse me, sir, but I have a message to convey to you.'… I coughed again and
> set my voice into as impersonal a tone as I could manage. 'Sir David wishes
> you to know that ladies and gentlemen differ in several key respects.'

This circumlocution leads to a misunderstanding by the younger Cardinal, since he interprets 'differ' to mean 'have different opinions' rather than 'have different qualities', and so replies: 'I really think I've thought of every possible permutation the human mind is capable of. I wish you'd reassure father of that' (83–4).

After five pages of very little progress, Steven continues in his evasive way:

> 'I have something to convey to you … If I may come straight to the point,
> sir. You will notice the geese not far from us … and likewise the flowers and
> shrubs. This is not in fact the best time to see them in their full glory, but you

> will appreciate, sir, that with the arrival of spring, we will see a change – a
> very special sort of change in these surroundings … Please excuse me, sir. As
> it happened, I had a word or two more to say on the topic of – as you put it
> yourself – the glories of nature. If you will indulge me by listening, I would be
> most grateful.' (89–90)

Stevens' style is not only characterised by a breaking of the maxim of Manner
by circumlocution, perhaps in the cause of politeness (dignified and formal
vocabulary, or avoidance of taboos), but it is also characterised by a high degree
of modalisation, which seems to pit the maxim of Manner against the maxim of
Quality. In short he seems reluctant to make bald plain unmodalised statements.
We have already noted this when he becomes involved in the struggles between
modesty and immodesty:

> Even so, if you consider the pressures contingent on me that night, you **might**
> not think I delude myself unduly if I go so far as to **suggest** that I did **perhaps**
> display, in the face of everything, at least in **some** modest degree a 'dignity'
> worthy of someone like Mr Marshall – or, come to that, my father. (110)

This is one instance of a general discourse pattern in which Stevens makes
a point of the accuracy of his narration and of the truth claims of his statements:

> … and I will try and quote accurately from memory. (33)

> I hope that you agree that in these two instances I have cited from his career –
> both of which I have corroborated and believe to be accurate – my father not
> only manifests, but comes close to being the personification itself, of what the
> Hayes Society terms 'dignity in keeping with his position'. (42)

> I cannot recall precisely the actual words … I could by no means hear
> complete exchanges; consequently it is hard for me now to recall precisely
> what I overheard… (94–5).

This apparent insistence on truth often leads him to self-correction or disclaimers about previous statements, perhaps calling into question the reliability of
his narration (Wall 1994, cf. Wong 2005: 55):

> But now that I think further about it I am not sure Miss Kenton spoke quite so
> boldly that day. (60)

> Incidentally, now that I come to think further about it, it is not quite true to say
> there was no dispute as to *who* were the great butlers. What I should have said
> was that there were no serious disputes among the professionals of quality
> who had any discernment in such matters. (29)

> In fact by calling it a problem I perhaps overstate the matter. (49)

Stevens claims an obsession with accuracy, regarding himself as 'one not prone to exaggerated statements' (77). One means of understatement, is the double negative: 'I was not unperturbed by the prospect of telling Miss Kenton I was about to dismiss two of her maids' (147), or 'a not inconsiderable sum' (6).

Such examples of self-correction are symptoms of Ishiguro's use in his first person narrators of unreliable and 'artificial memory … imaginative reconstruction based on psychic and historical observation' (Asker 2003a: 58). For example, it is found too in Ono's recollections and corrections and disclaimers in the previous novel: 'Did Miyake really say all this to me that afternoon?' (AFW: 56) 'Of course that is all a matter of many years ago now and I cannot vouch that those were my exact words that morning' (AFW: 69).

Narrative theorists (Fowler 1996, Toolan 2001, Simpson 1993) identify a cluster of linguistic features as constituting a certain narrative style: not only modals of probability and usuality, but also conditionals, descriptions of verbal and mental processes with first person pronouns, or subjective markers. This style is much used in *An Artist of the Floating World*: 'So I do not think I am claiming undue credit for my younger self if I suggest that my actions that day were a manifestation of a quality I came to be much respected for in later years …'(AFW: 69). The following passage from *Remains of the Day*, in which he sees an opportunity to lecture Cardinal on the facts of life, manifests many of these features, especially mental processes (in bold).

> It was around this point, in the midst of dealing with the many **demands being made upon my attention**, that **I happened to glance** out of a window and **spotted** the figure of the young Mr Cardinal taking some fresh air around the grounds. He was clutching his attaché case as usual and **I could see** he was strolling slowly along the path that runs the outer perimeter of the lawn, deeply absorbed in thought. **I was of course reminded of** my mission regarding the young gentleman and **it occurred to me** that an outdoor setting, with the general proximity of nature, and in particular the example of the geese at hand, would not be an unsuitable setting at all in which to convey the sort of message I was bearing. **I could see**, moreover, that if I were to go outside and conceal my person behind the rhodedendron bush beside the path, it would not be long before Mr Cardinal came by… (88–89)

A passage near the beginning of the novel exemplifies very clearly his use of verbal process verbs with first person pronouns (references to mental and verbal processes are bolded):

> The fact that **my attitude to this suggestion underwent a change** over the following days – indeed, that the notion of a trip to the West Country

> **took an ever increasing hold on my thoughts** – is no doubt substantially
> attributable to – and why should I hide it – the arrival of Miss Kenton's letter,
> her first in almost seven years if one **discounts** the Christmas cards. But
> **let me make it immediately clear** what I meant by this; what **I mean to
> say** is that Miss Kenton's letter **set off a certain chain of idea**s to do with
> professional matters here at Darlington Hall, and **I would underline** that it
> was **a preoccupation with** these very same professional matters that **led me
> to consider** anew my employer's kindly meant suggestion. But let **me explain**
> further. (4–5)

As the last quotation makes clear, Stevens' apparent obsession with the Maxim
of Quality and his indulgence in subjective markers are often a veneer for
self-deception (Wong 2005: 15), paradoxically making him a particular kind
of 'unreliable narrator' (Wall 1994). The most obvious of his self-deceptions
are perhaps his suppressed feelings for Miss Kenton, in the words of Ishiguro
'actually hiding from what is the scariest arena of life, which is the emotional
arena' (quoted in Wong 2005: 18). In the passage below we see him attempting
to persuade himself that these feelings do not exist:

> Our reasons for instituting such meetings [in the evenings for cocoa] was
> simple: we had found that our respective lives were often so busy, several
> days could go by without our having an opportunity to exchange even
> the most basic of information. Such a situation, we recognized, seriously
> jeopardized the smooth running of operations, and to spend fifteen minutes
> or so together at the end of the day in the privacy of Miss Kenton's parlour
> was the most straightforward remedy. (147)

When he suspects that Miss Kenton is meeting a suitor on her evening off,
he will not admit to being disturbed by jealousy at the thought of her possible marriage, but simply by the prospect of a disruption to his professional
duties: 'This was indeed a disturbing notion, for it was not hard to see that Miss
Kenton's departure would constitute a professional loss of some magnitude, a
loss Darlington Hall would have some difficulty recovering from' (171).

He deceives himself into thinking that his trip to see Miss Kenton/Mrs
Benn was for professional reasons,

> to determine whether or not Miss Kenton has any interest, now that her
> marriage, sadly, appears to have broken down and she is without a home, in
> returning to her old post at Darlington Hall. (180)

When recounting their meeting for tea, he protests that his enquiries into the
state of her marriage were purely of a professional nature: 'I would not have

dreamt of prying into these areas were it not that I did have, you might recall, important professional reasons for doing so' (234).

However, Miss Kenton realises some of his sexual repression and self-deception. Desperately she asks 'Why, Mr Stevens, why, why, why do you always have to pretend?'(154). She discovers that he is in the habit of reading romances (168), and suspects that his reluctance to employ pretty maids is because he does not wish his sexual appetites to be aroused (155–6).

Stevens' understatements, tentativeness, circumlocutionary tendencies, apparently in the cause of upholding Quality and Modesty maxims and avoiding taboos, and the general formality of his vocabulary make much of his narration seem pompous or insincere. Especially his excessive formality is thrown into sharp relief by contrast with his interlocutors, such as Dr Carlisle:

> 'So Harry was trying to tackle philosophical definitions. My word. I take it it
> was a lot of rot.'
> 'His conclusions were not necessarily those that compelled agreement, sir.'
> (210)

Even when disclosing his own thoughts and emotions he generally manages to preserve surface formality, masking the extent of the feeling beneath. At one point Stevens looks back at the opportunity he missed to comfort Miss Kenton when grieving at the death of her aunt, and indeed at his failure to make allowances for her emotional state affecting her work:

> But what is the sense in forever speculating what might have happened had
> such and such a moment turned out differently? One could presumably drive
> oneself to distraction in this way. In any case, while it is all very well to talk of
> 'turning points', one can surely only recognize such moments in retrospect.
> Naturally, when one looks back to such instances today, they may indeed
> take the appearance of being crucial, precious moments in one's life; but, of
> course, at the same time, this was not the impression one had. Rather, it was
> as though one had a never-ending number of days, months, years in which
> to sort out the vagaries of one's relationship with Miss Kenton; an infinite
> number of further opportunities in which to remedy the effect of this or that
> misunderstanding. There was surely nothing to indicate at the time that such
> evidently small incidents would render whole dreams forever irredeemable.
> (179)

The tension between the underlying emotion and the formal impersonality of the surface seems at its greatest in the last clause of this passage, where he is more or less admitting that he has destroyed his dreams of loving Miss Kenton forever.

The impersonality of the 'one' in this passage contrasts it with the personality of the 'I' in the following one (Wong 2005: 63), his account of Mrs Benn's avowal during their last conversation, and of its effect on him:

> 'But that doesn't mean to say, of course, that there aren't occasions – extremely desolate occasions – when you think to yourself: "what a terrible mistake I've made with my life." And you get to thinking about a different life, a *better* life you might have had. For instance, I get to thinking about a life I might have had with you, Mr Stevens. And I suppose that's when I get angry over some trivial little thing and leave. But each time I do so, I realize, before long – my rightful place is with my husband. After all, there's no turning back the clock now. One can't be forever dwelling on what might have been. One should realize one has as good as most, perhaps better, and be grateful.'
> I do not think I responded immediately, for it took me a while to fully digest these words of Miss Kenton. Moreover, as you might appreciate, their implications were such as to provoke a certain degree of sorrow within me. Indeed – why should I not admit it? – at that moment my heart was breaking.
> (p. 239)

What is intensely moving is the sudden transition from the formal understated tone of the penultimate sentence, to the frank, albeit clichéd, admission in the last sentence 'my heart was breaking'. Even if it is an admission, implying guilt, for a moment he reveals his emotional involvement honestly. One might see the effectiveness of these two passages as depending upon the move from an ' "extradiegetic" narrator who is "above" or superior to the story he narrates and a "homodiegetic" narrator who is part of or within the story he tells' (Wong 2005: 53). These are 'two contradictory voices that we hear simultaneously' (Wall 1994: 23).

7.4   Negative face, restraint and dignity

An alternative theory of politeness, covering much the same ground as Leech, but not formulated in terms of maxims, is Brown and Levinson's (1987) (see 6.5). Their theory is subsumed under the concept of face: positive face – the desire to be accepted and esteemed by others; and negative face – the right to territories, to remain undisturbed. We can relate much of Stevens' behaviour to concern with negative face, through the concept of restraint – one of the major planks in Stevens' belief system. Restraint operates along several dimensions: invisibility; decorum and normality; and inhibition of communication.

Stevens attempts to be as invisible and silent as possible. For example he dislikes disturbing Farraday when he is occupied: 'it nevertheless made sense not to broach the subject when he was preoccupied or distracted' (12). He believes that it is essential when waiting on table to maintain a 'balance between attentiveness and the illusion of absence' (72). When he interrupts David Cardinal in the library he, stereotypically uses a cough to discreetly announce his presence (83) – a propitiatory token in Laver's terms (see section 6.5). Given these concerns he becomes extremely embarrassed when his presence is suddenly manifest and he startles David Cardinal in the garden (89). In order to avoid intrusion he has a habit of listening at doors in order to avoid propitiatory knocking at an unsuitable moment: 'You may not yourself be in the habit of taking this small precaution to avoid knocking at some highly inappropriate moment, but I always have been and can vouch that it is common practice amongst many professionals' (94). Similarly, as we have noted, he foregoes the opportunity of disturbing Ms Kenton who is crying (202). He admires the shyness and modesty of Darlington who pretends not to want to intentionally communicate with him by standing reading an encyclopaedia at the foot of the stairs, so that their meeting can appear accidental (60–1).

Stevens' obsession with decorum and normality is noticeable in his attitudes to dress, his naming practices, and his suspicion of drinking, smoking and humour. He is very concerned about the correct clothes to take on his trip to Cornwall (11), and somewhat mortified, when, after running out of petrol he muddies his shoes and turn-ups by walking through a field: 'I deliberately refrained from shining my lamp onto my shoes and turn-ups for fear of further discouragement' (163). He obviously disapproves of M. Dupont's dress: 'He had arrived in the sort of clothes one often sees continental gentlemen wearing on their holidays, and indeed, throughout his stay, he was to maintain diligently the appearance of having come to Darlington Hall entirely for pleasure and friendship' (90). Stevens insists both in his dialogue and narration in giving correct formal titles – 'Mr Simpson, landlord of the Ploughman's Arms … Mr Rayne, who travelled to America as valet to Sir Reginald Mauvis' (15). He refers to 'Miss Kenton' 'Mrs Benn' passim ('Miss Kenton is, properly speaking, Mrs Benn' (47)). Only on his trip do we hear the given names of the characters Harry Smith and Richard Carlisle (both, incidentally characters with socialist leanings). Stevens seems to regard drinking and smoking, especially in the presence of ladies, as indecorous or risky to smooth human interaction: 'A few of the gentlemen, I noticed, were drinking spirits, and one or two, despite the presence of the two ladies, had started to smoke' (94).

The desire for normality, routine, and hiding any trace of disturbance to it, is best exemplified in his father's favourite story:

> The story was apparently a true one concerning a certain butler who had travelled with his employer to India and served there for many years maintaining amongst the native staff the same high standards he had commanded in England. One afternoon evidently, this butler had entered the dining room to make sure all was well for dinner, when he noticed a tiger languishing beneath the dining table. The butler had left the dining room quietly, taking care to close the doors behind him, and proceeded calmly to the drawing room where his employer was taking tea with a number of visitors. There he attracted his employer's attention with a polite cough, then whispered in the latter's ear: 'I'm very sorry, sir, but there appears to be a tiger in the dining room. Perhaps you will permit the twelve-bore to be used?' and according to legend, a few minutes later, the employer and his guests heard three gun shots. When the butler reappeared in the drawing room some time afterwards to refresh the teapots, the employer had enquired if all was well.
> 'Perfectly fine, thank you, sir,' had come the reply. 'Dinner will be served at the usual time and I am pleased to say there will be no discernible traces left of the recent occurrence by then.' (36)

On the more mundane level any traces of cleaning, such as dustpans left in view are regarded as 'unseemly' (56, 57–8).

The most extreme way of restraint, of avoiding a threat to others or one's own negative face, is to refrain from the face-threatening act at all, in which case you neither disturb nor are disturbed by others. Opting out of communication and failures or deficiencies in communication by Stevens abound. His communication with his father has more or less ceased or become embarrassing:

> My difficulty was further compounded by the fact that for some years my father and I had tended – for some reason I had never really fathomed – to converse less and less. So much so that after his arrival at Darlington Hall, even the brief exchanges necessary to communicate information relating to work took place in an atmosphere of mutual embarrassment. (63–4)

Stevens refuses to share with Miss Kenton his feelings about the dismissal of the Jewish housemaids (153). He also breaks off their evening meetings over cocoa (174–5). When Mr Spencer questions Stevens on economics and politics he replies with the mechanical formulaic repetition: 'I am very sorry sir, but I am unable to be of assistance on/assist in this matter' (195–6). During his trip Stevens displays a lack of communicative skills with the strangers he meets, for example he shows unwillingness to try to communicate with people at Mr Taylor's house: 'it would be far too complicated a task for me to explain myself more clearly to these people' (186). He realises he is deficient in his mastery of banter with Farraday. Too much communication is indecorous for Stevens in any case. Comparing the English countryside with Africa or America he talks of the 'unseemly demonstrativeness' of beauty spots in the latter continents (29).

One specific dimension of self-restraint and control can be summed up in the word *dignity*. 'If one looks at, say Mr Marshall or Mr Lane it does seem to me that the factor which distinguishes them from those butlers who are merely extremely competent is closely captured by the word "dignity"' (33). He recognises this quality in his father. When the latter's employer was being disparaged by his guests and his father stopped the car and opened the door until they promised to stop their unflattering remarks, one of the passengers, Mr Charles was impressed by how 'my father showed not one hint of discomfort or anger, but continued to drive with an expression balanced between personal dignity and readiness to oblige' (38). When his father is informed that he will no longer be able to wait on table after his accidental fall, 'my father's face, in the half-light, betrayed no emotion whatsoever' (65). Stevens defines dignity as a butler's ability not to abandon the professional being he inhabits and to show emotional restraint. Lesser butlers will abandon their professional being for the private one at the least provocation. And continentals are unable to be butlers because they are, as a breed, incapable of the emotional restraint of the English (42–3). The word 'inhabit' is somewhat revitalised as a metaphor when he defines dignity as 'not removing one's clothing in public' (210), symbolic of repression, and with overtones, indeed, of the Fall of Man and its resulting guilt or shame.

7.4.1   Challenges to self-restraint and dignity

There are four major challenges to Stevens' dignity, negative face and emotional restraint: his father's death; banter; Miss Kenton's behaviour; and the journey to the West Country to visit her.

Stevens struggles to maintain his dignity, continue with his duties and not to break down as his father lies dying during the conference. But at one point he is unsuccessful and weeps in the smoking room. When Darlington sees him slightly later his tears are noticeable:

> 'Stevens, are you alright?'
> 'Yes, sir, perfectly'
> 'You look as though you're crying.'
> I laughed and taking out a handkerchief, quickly wiped my face. 'I'm very

> sorry, sir. The strains of a hard day.' (105)

Characteristically he apologises, and refrains from indicating the real reason for his grief. After the actual death Miss Kenton is equally upset, and shows less control than Stevens.

> 'Mr Stevens, I'm very sorry. Your father passed away about four minutes ago.'
> 'I see.'
> She looked at her hands, then up at my face. 'Mr Stevens, I'm very sorry,' she said. Then she added: 'I wish there was something I could say.'
> 'There's no need, Miss Kenton.'
> 'Dr Meredith has not yet arrived.' Then for a moment she bowed her head and a sob escaped her. But almost immediately, she resumed her composure and asked in a steady voice: 'Will you come and see him?'
> 'I'm very busy just now, Miss Kenton. In a little while perhaps.'
> 'In that case, Mr Stevens, would you permit me to close his eyes?'
> 'I would be most grateful if you would, Miss Kenton.'
> She began to climb the staircase, but I stopped her, saying: 'Miss Kenton, please don't think me unduly improper in not ascending to see my father in his deceased condition just at this moment. You see, I know my father would have wished me to carry on just now.' (106)

Notice that he rationalises his restraint by claiming he maintains it in honour of his father. And in retrospect he looks back on the evening of his father's death as a triumph of his professionalism and dignity over personal emotion (110).

Banter might be seen as part of the repertoire necessary to 'speak the language of the world', but also represents a challenge to both positive and negative face, and its use in the mouth of Farraday is a tool in the exercise of power (O'Brien 1996: 793). In the more specific and technical sense, as used by Leech, banter is seen as an attack on the Approbation maxim, since it involves deliberate mock insults as an expression of intimacy. In a wider sense, as any attempt to use humour to lessen emotional distance, it represents an intrusion and a threat to negative face. This can be seen when the idea of banter first surfaces in the novel.

When Stevens first announces to Farraday his intention to go on a trip to the West Country, he is in something of a pragmatic dilemma. He cannot be immodestly presumptuous by pretending he is going to see Miss Kenton in order to persuade her to rejoin the staff, but this leads to Farraday, who has offered him the use of his car for the trip, teasing him: ' "My, my, Stevens. A lady-friend. At your age." ' This remark, which intrudes on his personal life and his negative face, makes him lose some control and feel awkward: 'how uncomfortable a situation this was for me'. And Farraday continues, this time more obviously threatening his positive face by mock disapprobation: ' "But then I really don't know it's right for me to be helping you with such dubious assignations" '. Although embarrassed, Stevens identifies these remarks as banter, a particularly American style of speech.

> I remember Mr Simpson, the landlord of the Ploughman's Arms, saying once that were he an American bartender, he would not be chatting to us in that friendly, but ever-courteous manner of his, but instead would be assaulting us with crude references to our vices and failings, calling us drunks and all manner of such names, in his attempt to fulfil the role expected of him by his customers. (14–15)

Here we have banter used in the strict sense of deliberate breaking of the Approbation maxim in order to induce intimacy. But later Stevens broadens the concept to include any witticism or humorous remarks which reduce personal distance. He tries out banter at the pub where he stays during his trip after running out of petrol, but not very successfully. He is warned by one of the regulars that he won't sleep well:

> ' … and then you'll get woken by his missus shouting at him right from the crack of dawn.'
>
> Despite the landlord's protests, this caused loud laughter all round.
> 'Is that indeed so?' I said. And as I spoke I was struck by the same thought
> – the same thought as had struck me on numerous occasions of late in Mr Farraday's presence – that some sort of witty remark was required of me. Indeed the local people were now observing a polite silence, awaiting my next remark. I thus searched my imagination and eventually declared:
> 'A local variation on the cock crow, no doubt.'

However, this 'witticism' falls flat.

> I was bitterly disappointed, I suppose, because I have been devoting some time and effort over recent months to improving my skill in this very area. That is to say, I have been endeavouring to add this skill to my professional armoury so as to fulfil with confidence all Mr Farraday's expectations with respect to bantering. (130)

Near the end of the novel Stevens is impressed by the crowd of strangers on the pier as the lights are turned on, and finds it curious and wonderful how people can so quickly warm towards each other. He suggests the warmth has as its basis mastery of the art of bantering.

> Perhaps it is indeed time I began to look at this whole matter of bantering more enthusiastically. After all, when one thinks about it, it is not such a

> foolish thing to indulge in – particularly if it is the case that in bantering lies
> the key to human warmth. (245)

Just after Miss Kenton has announced her marriage and resignation, and Stevens has responded with cool unfeeling professionalism, she deliberately insults and provokes him by saying how she spends her time laughing with her partner about Stevens' behaviour (219). This is not exactly bantering, but shares with it the breaching of the Approbation maxim to lessen interpersonal distance, in fact an attempt to break through his cool exterior to find a warm living emotional man beneath.

We have already noted ways in which Miss Kenton represents a threat to Stevens' self-contained politeness, negative face and emotional restraint. His dignity, self-restraint and professionalism in not allowing himself to be more than momentarily distracted by Miss Kenton crying behind her bedroom door, as he presides over the meeting with Herr Ribbentrop, are 'as a sort of summary of all that I had come to achieve thus far in my life' (228). We also saw how Miss Kenton provokes him to breaches of the Politeness Principle; their disagreement over the dismissal of the Jewish housemaids and the misplaced Chinaman; his failure to show her sympathy over her aunt's death; his disapprobation of her calling his father by his first name and of her invading his privacy when she brings him flowers or comes uninvited to his parlour and wrests the romance he is reading from his grasp, a threat to his negative face which he describes with a territorial metaphor as 'invading my private moments'. But there are other impolitenesses too: when he teases her about her threatened resignation over the case of the housemaids, a resignation which never materialises (150). Or when, after his humiliation over his father's fall with the tea tray, and just prior to the important 1923 conference, he goes around nagging her about preparations, implying criticism of her professionalism, which she regards as 'gratuitous comments' and which result, for a while, in the cessation of face to face communication (79–80).

It appears that the impoliteness between Stevens and Ms Kenton results from her attempts to break through his negative face, to invade his territory, both literally and symbolically. This would be in keeping with Wolfson's (1988) 'bulge theory', that we use the most polite forms of language and behaviour to those at a medium degree of horizontal social distance. As a converse of this theory her threats to politeness are bids to increase intimacy. It emerges towards the end of the novel that Kenton has been deliberately attempting to irritate him, and that her engagement and resignation, too, were in fact 'just another ruse to annoy you' (239). In turn he obviously irritates her by not responding to these attempts. For example when she apologises for mentioning the way Mr Benn and she laughed at him behind his back, he claims

> 'I have not taken anything you have said to heart, Miss Kenton. In fact, I
> cannot recall what it is you might be referring to. Events of great importance
> are unfolding upstairs and I can hardly stop to exchange pleasantries with

you.' (226)

There is an implication, if not an admission, by Stevens, that it is only when their relationship becomes personal that politeness is threatened. Anticipating the meeting in Cornwall he says:

> There is, of course, no reason at all to suppose that our meeting will be anything but cordial. In fact, I would expect our interview – aside from a few informal exchanges quite proper in the circumstances – to be largely professional in character. (180)

However, there is a reassessment of his relationship with Miss Kenton which leads to this journey to Cornwall, which gives it a symbolic significance – he is now about to invade her territory as she has done his in the past.

7.4.2   Stevens' journey of discovery

Stevens' physical confinement to Darlington Hall and its environs is perhaps symbolic of the professional, restrained and dignified persona he adopts in his butlering service. The journey he undertakes to Cornwall to visit Miss Kenton conversely symbolises freedom to allow his personal needs to overcome professional demands, manifest in his looking at the Cornwall section part of Symons's guidebook, *The Wonder of England*, shortly after Miss Kenton's departure (11), though he is reluctant to admit this (9, 13, 14).

Such a symbolism depends upon the powerful conceptual metaphor that FREEDOM IS SPACE or ABILITY TO MOVE or RELEASE, whereas NO FREEDOM IS LIMIT TO SPACE, ENCLOSURE or TYING/BINDING (see *Metalude* 2004 and sections 8.3.2 – 8.3.3). When he says 'I had gone beyond all previous boundaries' (24), we take this to mean an escape from his routine professional work, but also from self-restraint and emotional repression. At the very beginning of the journey where, for the first twenty minutes he is in familiar territory, he 'cannot say I was seized by any excitement or anticipation at all' (23), but before long he seems to become subject to emotions beyond his control, conveyed grammatically by becoming a Goal or Senser (for explanation of these participant roles see 2.1.1). The relevant clauses featuring Goals and Sensers are bolded below:

> **The feeling swept over me** that I had truly left Darlington Hall behind, and I must confess **I did feel a slight sense of alarm** – a sense aggravated by the feeling that I was perhaps not on the correct road at all, but speeding off in totally the wrong direction into a wilderness. It was only the feeling of a moment, but it caused me to slow down. And even when I had assured myself I was on the right road, **I felt compelled** to stop the car to take stock, as it

> were.

> I decided to step out and stretch my legs a little and when I did so, **I received a stronger impression** then ever of being perched on the side of a hill. (24)

He goes on to climb a hill for the view, and the man who advises him to do so pointedly, and perhaps with a sexual innuendo, says ' "I'm telling you, sir, you'll be sorry if you don't take a walk up there. And you never know. A couple more years and it might be too late" – he gave a rather vulgar laugh – "better go up while you still can" ' (25). He reaches the top of the hill:

> And I believe it was then that **I felt the first healthy flush of anticipation** for the many interesting experiences I know these days ahead hold in store for me. And indeed it was then that **I felt a new resolve not to be daunted** in respect to the one professional task I have entrusted myself with on this trip; that is to say, regarding Miss Kenton and our present staffing problems. (26)

This experience of the view, because it boosts his self-confidence and mission, is, perhaps, a variation on what Pratt calls 'the monarch of all I survey' mode of landscape description (Pratt 1989).

The journey takes on extra significance as a number of experiences challenge his dignity, self-restraint and positive face. The most important is the incident of running out of petrol. This in itself diminishes his self-esteem and positive face as 'it would not be unreasonable for an observer to believe such general disorganisation endemic to my nature' (160). But more important it leads him to spend the night in the village, and to encounter the socialist Harry Smith.

Harry Smith is important because his definition of dignity is diametrically opposed to Stevens'. While for Stevens dignity amounts to serving those in power unthinkingly and unquestioningly, for Smith dignity means being treated as worthy and equal, and being allowed to express opinions. Mrs Taylor, Stevens' landlady for the night, asks what makes a true gentleman, besides clothes and wealth, and Stevens replies that it is dignity. Smith retorts that ' "dignity isn't just something gentlemen have. Dignity's something every man and woman in this country can strive for and get." ' (186). He believes that the war against Hitler was a war for dignity and against slavery. ' "You can't have dignity if you're a slave. But every Englishman can grasp it if only he cares to. Because we fought for that right." ' (186). He continues:

> 'The way I see it, England's a democracy, and we in this village have suffered as much as anyone fighting to keep it that way. Now it's up to us to exercise our rights, every one of us. Some fine lads from this village gave their lives to give us this privilege, and the way I see it, each one of us here owes it to them to play our part. We've all got strong opinions here, and it's our responsibility to get them heard … that's why, sir, I give so much of my time now to making

sure our voice gets heard in high places. And if it changes me, or sends me to
an early grave, I don't mind'. (189)

Smith's disquisition on dignity provokes and upsets Stevens given the kind of
life of service (slavery) with which he associates dignity, and his failure to voice
his opinions, even if he had formed any, to those in high places to whom he
had access. Thus he has to reject Smith's ideas:

> Of course, one has to allow that Mr Harry Smith was employing the word
> 'dignity' in a quite different sense altogether from my own understanding of
> it. Even so, even taken on their own terms, his statements were, surely, far too
> idealistic, far too theoretical, to deserve respect. Up to a point, no doubt, there
> is some truth in what he says: in a country such as ours, people may indeed
> have a certain duty to think about great affairs and form their opinions. But
> life being what it is, how can ordinary people truly be expected to have 'strong
> opinions' on all manner of things – as Mr Harry Smith rather fancifully claims
> the villagers here do? And not only are these expectations unrealistic, I rather
> doubt they are even desirable. There is, after all, a real limit to how much
> ordinary people can learn and know, and to demand that each and every one
> of them contribute 'strong opinions' to the great debates of the nation cannot,
> surely, be wise. It is, in any case, absurd that anyone should presume to define
> a person's 'dignity' in these terms. (194)

Stevens proceeds to show how, in his own case, he had been quite content to
plead ignorance on important political matters. Darlington and Spencer had
contested Leonard's view that the best arbiter of policy was the will of the people.
In order to confute this, Stevens had been summoned and asked by Spencer to
give his opinions on the debt situation in America, the advisability of an arms'
deal between the French and the Bolsheviks, and whether a prominent French
politician's speech on North Africa was an attempt to defeat the nationalist
fringe of his own party. Stevens, as we have already seen, has no opinions on
these matters. Darlington apologises to Stevens for this interrogation the next
day, and continues

> 'Other great nations know full well that to meet the challenges of each new
> age means discarding old, sometimes well-loved methods. Not so here in
> Britain. There's still so many talking like Sir Leonard last night. That's why Mr
> Spencer felt the need to demonstrate the point.' (197)

Here the lack of education of the masses is being used as an excuse for fascism.

These passages illustrate the theme of the conflict between power and
morality. The ordinary people, who have no special access to the powerful,
need to have their voices heard in order to ensure policy is conducted according
to moral principles. Stevens, of course, regards his own greatness as a butler

as dependent on serving the great and the good, and that 'our best course will always be to put our trust in an employer who is wise and honourable'. However, unless one exercises one's duty to 'adopt such a critical attitude towards an employer' (200) how can one be sure one's employer is honourable? When David Cardinal suggests to Stevens that Darlington is being manipulated by Hitler through Herr Ribbentrop, Stevens shows no interest and claims ignorance 'I'm sorry, sir, I have not noticed any such development' (223) to which Cardinal replies: 'But I suppose you wouldn't, Stevens, because you're not curious. You just let all this go on before you and you never think to look at it for what it is'. This is a clear case of Stevens' approbation for his master overcoming the maxim of Quality or the facing up to the truth.

Almost to the end of the narrative Stevens still holds to the importance of loyalty to Darlington as the touchstone of his professionalism, and denies that he deserves to be criticised for this:

> How can one possibly be held to blame in any sense because, say, the passage of time has shown that Lord Darlington's efforts were misguided, even foolish? Through the years I served him, it was he and he alone who weighed up evidence and judged it best to proceed in the way he did, while I simply confined myself, quite properly, to affairs within my own professional realm. (201)

But at the end of his journey, after Miss Kenton's heart-breaking confidence that she wished she had married him instead of Mr Benn, and as he sits on the pier abandoning his emotional self-restraint by talking to a stranger, and crying in a way that he apologises for as 'unseemly' (244), Stevens radically reassesses his service to Darlington and admits his mistake:

> 'You see, I *trusted*. I trusted in his lordship's wisdom. All those years I served him I trusted I was doing something worthwhile. I can't even say I made my own mistakes. Really – one has to ask oneself –what dignity is there in that?' (243)

And yet he backtracks on this confession:

> The hard reality is, surely, for the likes of you and I, there is little choice other than to leave our fate, ultimately, in the hands of those great gentlemen at the hub of this world who employ our services. What is the point in worrying oneself too much about what one could or could not have done to control the course one's life took? Surely it is enough that the likes of you and I at least *try* to make our small contribution count for something true and worthy. And if some of us are prepared to sacrifice much in life in order to pursue such aspirations, surely, that is, in itself, whatever the outcome, cause for pride and

contentment. (244)

7.5   Summary and conclusion

Can we accept this final position of Stevens? I think not, even if we are almost persuaded. The point is that Stevens has sacrificed the maxim of Quality for the maxims of Approbation and Generosity towards his employer, tactfully maximising cost to himself by his repression of his emotional life, not to say of communication itself. Or in David Lodge's words 'his life has been based on the suppression or evasion of the truth, about himself and about others' (Lodge 1992: 155) And yet, the Politeness Principle is just as important for our social life as is the pursuit of truth, and so we cannot turn this into a simple melodrama where we condemn Stevens for being plain wrong. While we may ultimately and reluctantly judge him so, we sympathise with him, unlike the melodramatic villain with whom we have no sympathy (Frye 1967).

This struggle between, on the one hand, politeness, civilisation, formality, dignity, self-restraint and decorum, and 'not removing one's clothes in public' (210), which one might associate with the super-ego, and, on the other hand sexual desire, passing on one's genes, self-interest, expressiveness and taking one's clothes off, which one might associate with the id, is a long-standing one. But its ideological, economic and political dimensions are extremely important given the resurgence of a new sociobiology and its attempts to (re-) define human nature. The new sociobiology attempts to reduce humans to animals calculatingly working in their own self-interest to pass on their genes (cf. Goatly 2007: chapter 4). For example, Matt Ridley, in the influential book *The Origins of Virtue*, has what he would call a realistic view of human nature, that the truth is we are basically selfish, and that people who are not are exceptional.

> Just as we wish other people to turn the other cheek when hurt, but seek revenge on behalf of close relatives and friends, just as we urge morality far more than we act on it, so environmentalism is something we prefer to preach than to practise. Everybody, it seems, wants a new road for themselves, but less road-building. Everybody wants another car, but wishes there were fewer on the road. Everybody wants two kids, but lower population growth. (Ridley 1997: 216)

In this vein he discusses Wang Shou-yu the father of Jung Chang, the author of the popular biography *Wild Swans*, who, putting his belief in the revolution above his zoological instincts to favour only those with whom he shared genes, refused to show any partiality towards relatives. 'Communism would have worked if there were more such men … but most people are not like Wang

Shou-yu' (258–9). He regards people in general as 'calculating machines intricately designed to find co-operative strategies only when they assist enlightened self-interest' (Ridley 1997: 214).

B. F. Skinner, though not a sociobiologist, like Ridley dismisses religious morality, disinterestedness and the notions of self-sacrifice as irrational. In his famous book *Beyond Freedom and Dignity* (1971), he claims both the concepts in the title are unfortunate illusions, and that the reality of human behaviour is, and should be, determined by the striving for self-interested positive reinforcement and the avoidance of negative reinforcement. Skinner believed that we err when:

> We give maximal credit when there are quite visible reasons for behaving differently … If we commend a person who puts duty before love, it is because the control exercised by love is easily identified. (Skinner 1971: 50)

> We acknowledge this curious relation between credit and the inconspicuousness of controlling conditions when we conceal control to avoid losing credit or to claim credit not really due to us… (Dr Johnson questioned the value of this: spewing out a mouthful of hot potato, he exclaimed to his astonished companions, 'A fool would have swallowed it'.) In other words, we resist any condition in which we behave in undignified ways. (Skinner 1971: 52–3)

But the strength of *The Remains of the Day* is precisely that, though Stevens would be regarded by Harry Smith as an undignified slave, and Skinner would have us believe that the self-restraint of Stevens gives him only an illusory dignity, we cannot so easily dismiss his life of self-sacrifice in a cause which he regards as greater than himself and greater than his own emotional and sexual drives: 'a reader's verdict on his moral character necessarily remains elusive, primarily because Stevens' story is a human story about loss and fear of that loss. He has told it to elicit sympathy and understanding, and, despite the overwhelming evidence against his own misperceptions, Stevens emerges as a somewhat compassionate character' (Wong 2005: 65). In this respect Stevens resembles the artist Ono in *The Artist of the Floating World*, influenced by these opinions of Matsuda: 'in times like these, when people are getting poorer, and children are growing more hungry and sick all around you, it is simply not enough for an artist to hide away somewhere, perfecting pictures of courtesans' (AFW: 173). Ono subsequently devotes himself to socially-committed art, only to become a tool of the fascist and imperialist Japanese government. In both characters we admire the commitment and the instinct to serve, even though we recognise the delusion and its terrifying personal or social consequences.

8 Conceptual metaphor, its paradoxes, modifications and distortions in the poetry of John Donne

8.1 Introduction

This chapter concerns itself with the extent to which John Donne in his *Songs and Sonnets* and religious poems relies on and exploits metaphorical patterns variously known as conceptual metaphors, root analogies or metaphor themes. These are conceptually important metaphors whose importance is manifest in the frequent number of types of metaphorical lexical items realising them in the vocabulary of English, or in the frequency of tokens of them in text.

The chapter begins by explaining the theories of conceptual metaphor, of how metaphors inter-relate, and the lexical research which justifies the positing of particular conceptual metaphors or metaphor themes. It proceeds by showing how Donne was particularly interested in the mind-body relationship, and exploring how his poetry uses the RELATIONSHIP IS PROXIMITY/COHESION (RELIABILITY IS STABILITY) themes, and, through paradox, exploits the opposition between this theme and both FREEDOM IS SPACE TO MOVE, and the metaphorically-based symbolism of literal separation. The latter he attempts to overcome by the conceits of the annihilation of space, the phenomenon of reflection, the portability of pictures, and more particularly by the idea of RELATIONSHIP IS TRANSACTION, especially relevant, ideologically, in the economic climate of early capitalism.

In his poetry Donne regards distance as a threat to stable relationships, since if EXISTENCE IS PROXIMITY then conversely separation is death. But EMOTION IS MOVEMENT also threatens RELIABILITY IS STABILITY or RELATIONSHIP IS COHESION. So in the latter part of the chapter we are led to consider Donne's destructive metaphors for love (lovers) which imply its (their) transience, such as SEX IS VIOLENCE, FEELING/EMOTION IS BEING EATEN, and LOVE/PASSION IS HEAT or FIRE, the last of which, however, is rescued from its destructiveness by the image of purification through refining.

8.2   Metaphor

8.2.1   What are we talking about?

A simple definition of linguistic metaphor might run as follows:

> A metaphor occurs when a term is applied[1] unconventionally. And when that unconventional application is understood on the basis of a similarity or analogy. This similarity or analogy involves the conventional application of the term and the actual unconventional application.

J. P. Hartley opened his novel *The Go-Between* with the following famous sentence: 'The past is a foreign country; they do things differently there'. This sentence expresses three elements of metaphor. First there is the term that refers to what we are actually or literally talking about, 'the past'. This can be called the Topic or Target. Second there is the term which is applied to some entity with which the Topic is being compared, which does not belong to the literal level established by the Topic, 'a foreign country'. This can be called the Vehicle or Source. Third, there is a clause which helps us to see in what ways the Topic/Target and Vehicle/Source might be similar or analogous, 'they do things differently there'. This can be called the Ground.

8.2.2   The interplay of metaphors

I have written at length, elsewhere (Goatly 1997: chapter 9), on how topics and vehicles inter-relate, but I need to selectively introduce some of the terminology which I developed there, as it bears on the analysis in this chapter. Of most importance in this chapter will be the relations of Diversification and Multivalency.

We have cases of diversification when the same topic is referred to by different vehicles, vehicles that belong to quite different semantic fields or conceptual schemas. In Milton's 'Paradise Lost' Book 1, for example, Satan's legions are variously compared with locusts and autumnal leaves.

> PL1.301   His legions, angel forms, who lay entranced
> **Thick as autumnal leaves that strew the brooks**
> **In Vallambrosa, where the Etrurian shades**
> **High overarched embower;** (Book 1, lines 301–4)

> PL1.337   Yet to their general's voice they soon obeyed
> Innumerable. As when the potent rod
> Of Amram's son in Egypt's evil day
> Waved round the coast, up called **a pitchy cloud**
> **Of locusts** … (Book 1, lines 337–41)

Diversification is found in single texts, but can also be applied to more conventional metaphors in the dictionary. Using lexicographical evidence we can talk about the diverse ways in which a particular language, such as English or Chinese, structures a topic like FAILURE: DIVISION (*his plans to study in Oxford* **came unstuck**); FALLING (*further criticism of the* **tottering** *government is unnecessary*); SHIPWRECK (*their marriage is* **on the rocks**); SINKING (*bad weather could* **sink** *our plans for the garden party*); GOING BACKWARDS (*after months on a diet I've been* **backsliding** *lately*). Diverse metaphors may share grounds, or may vary their grounds along with the vehicle.

Multivalency is the opposite of diversification, because it occurs when the vehicle remains the same, but is variously applied to different topics. For example in stanza III, 'The Holy Ghost', of 'The Litany', John Donne uses fire as a vehicle for both pride/lust and the Holy Spirit:

> O Holy Ghost, whose temple I
> Am, but of mud walls, and condensed dust,
> And being sacrilegiously
> Half wasted with youth's fires, of pride and lust
> Must with new storms be weatherbeat;
> Double in my heart thy flame
> Which let devout sad tears intend; and let
> (Though this glass lantern, flesh, do suffer maim)
> Fire, sacrifice, priest, Altar, be the same.

From a lexicographical standpoint, we could notice how in the dictionary of English the vehicle LIQUID is multivalently applied to CROWDS (*the crowd* **flowed** *over London Bridge*), TRAFFIC (*there was* **a trickle** *of cars over the new flyover*), MONEY (*you'll have to* **dip into** *your savings*), EMOTION (*he* **poured out** *his feelings to his girlfriend*), and KNOWLEDGE/INFORMATION (*the main recommendations of the Butler report have been* **leaked** *in advance*).

Quite apart from the interaction of metaphors with each other, there is the widespread phenomenon of a deliberate confusion of metaphorical and literal levels. This is a frequently-used technique in advertising copy, and popular journalism, where we have puns which convey a literal and metaphorical meaning simultaneously, e.g. 'He'll be **worn out** long before his shoes are' in an ad for children's footwear. Or where the literal world of the text reminds us of the literal meaning of a conventional metaphor for example 'A beautiful new bathroom from Graham makes freshening up a positive pleasure. But with interest free credit as well it feels even better. Because that means you won't have to **splash out** too much'. In the ballad 'Tom Bowlin', the elegy on the dead sailor employs nautical images throughout, for example 'For though his body's **under hatches**/ His soul is **gone aloft**'. More specifically we have cases of a lexical item being used literally at one point in the text, and at another point as a vehicle term, a phenomenon I have elsewhere referred to as 'Literalisation of Vehicles' (Goatly 1997: 202–9). Though much used for comic effects, it can also impart a symbolic value to the literal referents, and we shall see how important this is in Donne's poems, especially his valedictory ones.

8.2.3   The theory of conceptual metaphor

Conceptual metaphor theory was first popularised by Lakoff and Johnson's *Metaphors We Live By* (1980). The first insight of the theory is that metaphor is everywhere (Paprotte and Dirven 1985), and though one might claim that it has its epitome in poetry, is not confined to it. We cannot escape from it even if we wanted to. Although many philosophers, such as Hobbes and John Locke, would have liked to do without metaphor, feeling that it confused thinking, ironically enough, the terms in which they inveigh against it are themselves loaded down with metaphors.

> But yet, if we would speak of things as they are, we must **allow** that … all the artificial and figurative application of words eloquence hath **invented**, are for nothing else but to **insinuate** wrong ideas, **move** the passions, and thereby **mislead** the judgment, and so indeed are perfect **cheat**. [*Essay concerning Human Understanding* Book 3, Chapter 10, p.105, my bolding]

Arguably 'move', 'mislead' and 'cheat' are being used metaphorically, 'eloquence hath invented' is a case of personifying metaphor, 'insinuate' depends upon a metaphor borrowed from Latin, where its literal meaning is "work its way in, penetrate", and literally we 'allow' actions rather than propositions.

We are especially reliant on metaphor when discoursing on abstract topics and the strong claim of conceptual metaphor theory would be that abstract thought is only possible through the use of metaphor. Though some have held up mathematical thought as an alternative to metaphorical thought, Lakoff has demonstrated that even mathematical concepts such as Boolean logic or set theory depend on the metaphor of containers or bounded spaces, with members inside the container and non-members outside it (Lakoff 1987: chapter 20).

One of the most important insights of conceptual metaphor theory is that these concrete vehicles for abstract topics do not occur randomly but fall into patterns, which we might call Conceptual Metaphor Themes or Conceptual Metaphors or Metaphor Themes, for short. These are conventionally referred to by the capitalised formula X IS Y.

The question arises, if metaphor is everywhere and vital to our conceptualisation of abstract ideas, where do the vehicles of these metaphors originate from? According to Lakoff's theory, they have their source in our bodily infant experiences. For example, even in the womb, and when we are released from it, we acquire a schema of space or lack of space, providing the vehicle of, for example, FREEDOM IS SPACE TO MOVE. We soon acquire the notion of proximity from being picked up and separated from our carers, so that RELATIONSHIP IS PROXIMITY. We experience gravity, so moving downwards is easier than moving upwards, giving us POWER IS HIGH, and sense vertical orientation as well whereby the higher a pile the more things are in it, so MORE IS HIGH. The first most obvious changes that we notice are movements, thus CHANGE IS MOVEMENT. As we develop through the first two or three years we acquire the ability to handle objects with more and more control, initially grasping with all fingers in a palm grasp, and progressing until we can pick up small objects between our thumb and index finger; this not only provides the source for UNDERSTAND IS HOLD/GRASP, but also the motivation for CONTROL IS HANDLE. We learn to crawl towards objects that we want, and eventually to walk unaided, giving us PURPOSE IS DIRECTION and DEVELOPMENT/ SUCCESS IS MOVEMENT FORWARDS.

How, then do we decide which topics to pair with which vehicles, when we begin to think abstractly? To understand this we have to introduce the idea of metonymy. Unlike metaphors, metonymies are relationships between meanings based on contiguity in experience, or, linguistically, on deletion rather than substitution. We might say for example 'I drank two bottles of wine' as shorthand for 'I drank the contents of two bottles of wine'. And this deletion depends upon the fact that bottles are a container for wine and therefore the three concepts are contiguous in our experience. By contrast, by calling Tony Blair 'the lapdog of Bush', I am metaphorically substituting 'Blair' with 'lapdog', two concepts which have no particular association or contiguity in experience. Many of the basic links in conceptual metaphors can be traced back to metonymies such as cause and effect, or activity and place. So, for example there is a well-established set of metaphorical vocabulary in English and other languages which conceptualises anger as heat. The origin of this is quite obviously one of cause and effect – when we become angry we do feel hot. And there are many lexical items which conceptualise activity as place, as when we talk of 'filling a position', or 'the office of the president' (cf. 'the President's office'). These metonymies, are, however, later developed metaphorically, so we can talk about anger 'flaring up', or about being on the 'verge' of doing something.

In his most important book on metaphor, *Women, Fire and Dangerous Things* (1987) George Lakoff uses the evidence of conceptual metaphors grounded in our bodily experiences to suggest an alternative to the philosophical traditions of Objectivism and Subjectivism. We cannot accept objectivism, because, although there is a reality out there we do not have unmediated access to it, as our thinking is inescapably mediated by the metaphors we use. Even scientific theories and models are basically metaphorical hypotheses, technically known as model-theoretic metaphors. These are, at best approximate versions of reality, and can only construct a hypothetical model of the reality they purport to describe, so that any new model-theoretic scientific metaphor will initiate a programme of research trying to establish exactly what the grounds of the metaphorical model are, and what features of the model do not apply.

On the other hand, we have no need to accept subjectivism and complete conceptual relativism, because, after all, our infant bodily experiences, which we use as tools for thinking, are universal, and to that extent we share a common metaphorical language. Experientialism, then, steers a middle course between philosophical traditions which assume that truth is something we can access independent of any description of it, and subjectivism which believes that truth is a matter of individual belief relative to circumstances (Lakoff 1987: 265–8).

8.2.4   Identifying conceptual metaphors and metaphor themes: METALUDE

The theory I have just summarised took as its starting point lexicographical evidence. And, as we have noted, conventional conceptual metaphors in the dictionary do not appear singly but in groups arranged around schemas, an insight taken from Goodman:

> Shifts in range that occur in metaphor, then, usually amount to no mere distribution of family goods but an expedition abroad. A whole set of alternative labels, a whole apparatus of organization takes over new territory. What occurs is a transfer of a schema. (Goodman 1968: 73)

However, some of the conceptual metaphor literature, such as *More than Cool Reason* (Lakoff and Turner 1989) with its list of conceptual metaphors at the back, and the database Master List of Metaphors at the University of Berkeley linked to the Conceptual Metaphor Home Page[2], do not specify any clear criteria by which to identify important conceptual metaphor themes. In my own research, I have tried to use some consistent criteria, somewhat arbitrary and inadequate though they may be. (1) To count as a significant conceptual metaphor the theme should be realised by at least 6 lexical items, taken from a dictionary of contemporary English. (2) There should be at least 200 tokens of this joint set of lexical items with the relevant metaphorical meaning in the Cobuild Bank of English/WordsOnline database[3].

Here is an example of one such conceptual metaphor theme, CHANGE IS MOVEMENT with the lexicographical evidence to back it up. If you change your opinion you **shift** (*attitudes to homosexuality shifted during the 1990s*), and if your refuse to change it you will not **budge** (*they won't budge on the issue of equal pay*), while **move** can mean both "change opinion or behaviour" (*old people are moving away from eating meat*). **Move on** means "start doing a new activity" (*we moved on from painting to wallpapering*), and if you "keep on changing" activities you **flit** from one to another (*she's always flitting from one hobby to another*). As far as matter is concerned **pass** means "change, be transformed" (*wax passes from liquid to solid when you cool it*).

Change in the direction of movement stands for change in general as in **turn** "change quality, character or colour" (*suddenly my mother turned nasty*), **turn into** "become, be changed into" (*the witch recited the spell and Peter turned into a frog*). Rotation through 180° or 360° expresses complete or continuous change: **turnabout** "complete change from one state or condition to its opposite" (*what accounts for the dramatic turnabout in the University's examination performance this year?*), **revolution** "complete change in society through force" (*the French Revolution destroyed the aristocracy*), **rotate** "regularly change the person who does a job" (*the headship of department rotates among senior members*), and if the rotation continues into a spin we have a **gyration** "frequent and sudden changes" (*the gyrations in government policy are amazing*).

Moving backwards and forwards indicates changes that cancel each other out. These metaphors are generally applied to opinions and attitudes: **swing** "change significantly" (*her mood can quickly swing from calm to hysterical*), **swing back** "change back to its original state" (*public opinion swung back behind President Bush*), as does a **pendulum** "change from one opinion to an opposite one" (*the pendulum will swing back away from the individualism of the 1980s and 1990s*), **oscillate** "change repeatedly from one attitude to another" (*his feelings were oscillating between desperation and hope*). But movement backwards and forwards applies to states as well as opinions, as in **seesaw** "continually change from one state to another and back again" (*the Dow-Jones index see-sawed up and down*), **ebb and flow** "frequently changing situation" (*the ebb and flow of fashion continues unchecked*), **get back to** "return to a previous state" (*I must try to get back to sleep*), and **reverse** "change to the opposite" (*the appeal court reversed the lower court's decision*).

Causing change is conceptualised as causing movement: **shake up** "make major changes in an organisation" (*the reform of institutions is one way of shaking up the country*), **world-shaking** "very surprising and important in changing perception or behaviour" (*911 was a world-shaking event*), **turn ... upside down/inside out** "change a system or way of life completely" (*my world was turned upside down by AIDS*), and **turn ... on its head** "cause to be the opposite of what is was" (*these new discoveries turn the accepted paradigms on their head*).

The research I and my team have been pursuing over the last few years[4] has been designed to establish in a more principled way the important conceptual metaphors or metaphor themes for English, and to compare these with Chinese metaphors. The website 'Metalude' (<u>Met</u>aphor <u>A</u>t <u>L</u>ingnan <u>U</u>niversity <u>D</u>epartment of <u>E</u>nglish) is the result of these endeavours[5]. I would recommend consultation of Metalude, which has a map of metaphor themes as well as a database. As apparent corroboration of the experiential hypothesis, the vehicles of these metaphor themes can be largely classified into Space and Orientation, the (Human) Body and the Senses, Movement and Action. However, the database also includes metaphor themes which, unlike the metaphor themes in conceptual metaphor theory, do not concretise abstract concepts, but systematically compare one physical thing/substance with another, for example HUMAN IS FOOD, or BUILDING IS BODY. *Metalude* will provide important evidence for Donne's reliance on, and manipulation of conceptual metaphors in the poems we analyse.

8.2.5   *More than Cool Reason* and conceptual metaphor as 'code'

One of the more interesting developments of conceptual metaphor theory relevant to stylistics is represented in Lakoff and Turner's (1989) *More than Cool Reason: a field-guide to poetic metaphor*. If one accepts that metaphor is indispensable for abstract thought, then one would expect any poetry which deals with abstract topics such as emotions would be bound to use metaphorical vocabulary. A stronger claim would be that, unless this metaphorical lexis somehow plugs into the conceptual metaphorical patterns through which we think, they may be incomprehensible, not *lisible*. Lakoff and Turner's book presents a good deal of evidence for this claim. Metaphors which might, at first blush, appear original, in many cases can be related back to quite conventional conceptual metaphors already manifest in the lexicon of English (see *Metalude*). For example, 'the algebra was **glue** they were stuck in' appears to be introducing a novel metaphor, but, although the lexical item realising it may be unusual, it depends upon the conceptual metaphor SUCCESSFUL ACTIVITY IS MOVEMENT FORWARDS, as the more conventional lexis for expressing this metaphor, 'stuck', makes clear. Schleiner (1970: 140) in discussing SIN IS SICKNESS in Donne's sermons, puts it thus: 'once a field of imagery that has as its centre an important metaphor is taken over, it will "by itself," as it were, generate new and similar images'. If this strong claim were true, and these 'new' images cannot be so new after all, then scope for originality in metaphor would be confined to the metaphorical description of concrete objects rather than of abstract concepts.

In the introduction to this book (chapter 1) I suggested that structuralist stylistics saw the surface structures and meaning or narrative patterns of a literary text as the realisation of an underlying code or 'syntax', for example the various particular texts of Russian folktales would be the realisation of the 'syntactical rules' for the possible alternatives of the interactions of characters in plots, as characterised by Vladimir Propp in *The Morphology of the Russian Folktale*. We can perhaps locate conceptual metaphor stylistics within this 'structuralist' tradition, by which the particular poetic metaphor for a thought or emotion is the realisation of an underlying pattern, a syntax or grammar of metaphor, for which I have attempted to give details in *Metalude*.

What I attempt to explore in this chapter is how John Donne's poems especially his Songs and Sonnets, but also some of his Holy Sonnets, depend upon, realise, play with and challenge these underlying metaphorical patterns. Because we have to do with play and paradox the chapter will be an exemplification not only of structuralist stylistics, but also 'deconstructionist' stylistics.

Donne may be a particularly interesting poet in which to investigate metaphor themes or conceptual metaphors, because of the influence on him of Ramist writings, where invention relies on *argument*, meaning "the relatableness of a word or thing; that aspect by which we conceive of it as relatable to another word or thing" (Tuve 1961: 344, and chapter 12 passim). 'One may go *almost* so far as to state that Donne believed a proposition was established if it could be proved by means of similitudes' (Sloan 1963: 34), an argument by analogy. These analogies, this relatability is much enhanced by the concrete visible image.

> In Donne's poetry a proposition is frequently established by starkly visual means: vision brings an image of the proposition within the light of reason with sharp clarity, and reason agrees not only that the proposition implies the image but also that the image demonstrates the existence of those things stated in the proposition. (Sloan 1963: 36)

It is also interesting to note that, back in 1970, before Lakoff and Johnson's apparently groundbreaking *Metaphors We Live By* (1980), and building on work already done by Weinreich (1958, 1963, 1966), Schleiner investigated conceptual metaphors or metaphor themes, which she called 'fields of imagery', in the sermons of John Donne (1970: 67–8 and chapter 3 passim). However, I have discovered no systematic treatment of such metaphor themes in Donne's poetry.

8.3   Metaphor in Donne's poetry

8.3.1   Donne's 'platonic love' and the mind/body relationship

A strong element of Lakoff's theory is that bodily experience provides the metaphorical source for abstract conceptualisation, and that thereby mind and body are intimately linked. It is therefore interesting to explore what Donne has to say about the Mind-Body relationship, especially in relation to love.

> But since my soul, whose child love is,
> Takes limbs of flesh, and else could nothing do,
> More subtle than the parent is,
> Love must not be, but take a body too.
> And therefore what thou wert and who,
> I bid Love ask, and now
> That it assume thy body, I allow,
> And fix it self in thy lip, eye and brow. ('Air and Angels')

In 'The Blossom', too, Donne seems to be stressing the necessity of the body for a relationship, at least for women. 'A naked thinking heart that makes no show,/Is to a woman but a kind of ghost' and real relationships are found with those 'as glad to have my body as my mind'.

In 'The Extasie' Donne explores this theme at length. He and his lover sit together holding hands (even their sweat mixes) looking fixedly into each other's eyes to see each other's reflection. Simultaneously their two souls hang between them outside their bodies, where they mix and unite, showing that their love is not a matter of sex, while their bodies remain the whole day like motionless corpses. But the end of the poem recognises the importance of the body: it is the means through which the lovers meet, sense and develop affection for each other and so indispensable to any later union of souls; it is also the means for revealing the wonder of spiritual love to ordinary 'weak' men. Moreover, as Grierson points out in his notes 'spirit is a subtle kind of matter … the thin and active part of the blood' whose role is to 'unite and apply the faculties of the soul to the organs of the body' (Empson 1993: 100). Particularly interesting is the idea that if confined to spiritual union one is imprisoned and powerless:

> So must pure lovers' souls descend
> T'affections, and to faculties,
> Which sense may reach and apprehend,
> Else a great Prince in prison lies.

8.3.2   Relationship and Proximity/Cohesion

The theme that spiritual unity without bodily expression is a form of imprisonment leads us to consider the first set of clashing metaphor themes in Donne, namely RELATIONSHIP IS PROXIMITY/COHESION and its sub-themes, which, as a group, conflict with FREEDOM IS SPACE TO MOVE, EMOTION IS MOVEMENT and TIME IS TRAVEL.

Good relationships are metaphorically conceptualised as being close physically, or being physically attached, or forming one indivisible unit. Undoubtedly these have metonymic connections grounded in our physical bodily experience as Lakoff's theory predicts. At the outset of our infant bodily experience we are part of our mother before birth, and after birth often cry to demand closer bodily contact, becoming physically attached in the process of breast-feeding. Slightly later infants are satisfied if their mother is sufficiently near, visible and audible, although they remain quite close to their mothers in strange environments. Personal space for infants increases from about 0.2 metres nose-to-nose indoors at 2½ years to 0.5 metres at twenty (Hayduk 1983, quoted in Argyle 1988: 172). We continue to need the security of being close to our parents until our teenage years, and then, even though we may not wish to be seen with them, will nevertheless live in the same house. Our adult bodily experience takes us in the opposite direction, as we establish our own relationships as adolescents. Morris (1971) suggests that in western culture couples normally go through twelve stages of intimacy, always in the same order: from (1) eye to body, via (6) arm to waist, and (7) mouth to mouth, to (12) genitals to genitals (Argyle 1988: 102).

We note the increasing proximity or attempt to combine and share surface areas and attachment in a striving for cohesion. At stage 12, teenagers or adults, in most cases, become attached in sexual intercourse, attempting as best we can to achieve a physical union of our bodies, which may or may not symbolise the intellectual and emotional union we feel.

Physical proximity therefore becomes symbolic of emotional attitude and relationship, and this proximity can be divided into four zones:

1   *Intimate*, from contact to 6–18 ins., for people in intimate relationships they can touch, smell, feel heat, can talk in a whisper, but cannot see very well.

2   *Personal* distances, from 1 ½ – 4 ft; this corresponds to 'personal space', closer than which discomfort is commonly experienced; it is possible to touch the other by reaching, and they can now be seen clearly, but not smelt.

3   *Social* distances are from 4 –12 ft. and are used for formal business purposes, e.g. across a desk. Interactors use a higher level of gaze and need to speak louder; body movements are visible.

4   *Public* distance is over 12 ft and up to 25ft or more and is the distance kept from important public figures. Facial expression is more difficult to see, a louder voice is needed, and bodily movements need to be exaggerated. (Hall 1966, quoted in Argyle 1988: 169–70)

Metalude shows that the metonymies and symbols of relationship as proximity and contact are elaborated into metaphors in the lexicon, which we might label as RELATIONSHIP IS PROXIMITY/COHESION. Proximity is an indication of a good relationship. **Close** means "intimate" and **close circle** "an intimate group", and the relatives with whom you have the most strong or intimate relationship are ***next* of kin.** Affection towards friends or family is **togetherness,** and if two people are **together** or **go together** they are "intimately related romantically or sexually".

Having physical contact or attachment is a metaphor, as well as an index or symbol, of affection and love. In general **be attached to** means "love, have affection for", and business relationships are **connections** or **contacts.** This attachment may be based on bodily contact, such as **cling to** "love possessively" (*she clung to him in her despair and he had no freedom*). Quite often the metaphorical vehicle schema is one of tying with rope or string: **bind** "make people feel they belong together" (*the English language binds the UK and the US together and encourages political alliances*), **ties** "friendly feelings or relationships", **tie the knot, get spliced, get hitched,** "get married" (*when are you going to tie the knot?*), **knit** "unite people closely", **close-knit** "united" and the more pejorative **entangled** "personally involved with" (*he became romantically entangled with a student*). Less easily detachable physical contact, which may make you **inseparable** "very good friends", is associated with **glue** or **cement** "means of strengthening a relationship within a social group" (*poverty used to be the glue that preserved the extended family–till the advent of the Welfare State*) used to **cement** "make a relationship stronger" (*their friendship was cemented by a mutual interest in aerobics*), or to, even more strongly, **weld** "make people into a united organisation" (*he had the personality to weld the party together*). The result is a **bond** "close relationship" (*the bond between mother and child is enhanced by breast-feeding*), as in **male bonding** "close friendship between men".

The converse of these metaphors is that lack of relationship is distance, not having or breaking of an attachment, and division. **Remote** and **distant** mean "unfriendly, unemotional", and **distance** is "lack of an intimate relationship". If you deliberately avoid intimate relationships you **keep your/at a distance** do "not become very involved with" (*Grant always tended to keep his girlfriends at a distance*) or **keep at arm's length** "avoid becoming too friendly or involved with" (*I keep my students at arm's length so they show me respect*), with the result that you may get the reputation of being **unapproachable** "unfriendly and intimidating in manner" (*she was quite a bitch, an unapproachable character, and everyone at school was scared of her*) or **aloof** "not very friendly or sociable". Moving apart becomes the vehicle for the weakening, ending or failure of a relationship: **part/go their separate ways** "end a relationship", **separate** "end the relationship of marriage", **grow apart/drift apart** "fail or become estranged in a relationship" (*over the years Paul and his wife grew/drifted apart*).

Otherwise the end of a relationship is seen as a break or division: **break-up, breach** "ending of a relationship", **break off/split up** "end a relationship" (*I decided to break off/split up with Sam last night because I'm more interested in Bob*), **rupture** "damage or end a relationship between people", **sever** "end a relationship between" (*I severed my relationship with him as soon as I knew he was on heroin*).

8.3.3   RELATIONSHIP IS COHESION/PROXIMITY versus FREEDOM IS SPACE TO MOVE

There is however an intrinsic ambiguity in our evaluation of the metaphorical meanings of proximity and touch. It could also be related to the ambiguity of physical touch, which is seen as an indication of both 'warmth' and dominance. It has been experimentally shown, for example, that subjects who see couples in silhouette where one member of the pair touched the other gave higher ratings for status, assertiveness and warmth to the toucher compared with the touched (Argyle 1988: 226). Some kinds of bodily contact are, of course, aggressive, which may underlie these findings. This tension could be seen as a manifestation of the approach-avoidance conflict which underlies degrees of proximity – the need for company versus the need for privacy, personal territory and individual freedom, in short, negative face (Argyle 1988: 184).

Partly as a result of this ambiguity, these generally positive metaphors for friendship, affection, solidarity and belonging conflict with another important set of positively evaluated metaphors, which might be collectively labelled FREEDOM IS SPACE TO MOVE. **Room, latitude, space,** means "freedom or opportunity for action" and the narrower space of **elbow-room** and **leeway** mean "freedom to act within certain limits" (*he gave me a certain amount of leeway in the application of the examination mark scheme*), while **loose** means "sexually free or immoral". There are a number of adjectives with the negative suffix *un-* to do with freedom: **unrestricted** "free to do something in the way you want", **unfettered** "free to act without being limited by rules or influence" (*pubs are now unfettered by limits on their opening times*), **unbridled** "not controlled or limited" (*we need to campaign against the unbridled use of cars*), which may also apply to the freedom to express emotion like, **unrestrained** (*there was unrestrained joy on the faces of the mothers*). Continuing the idea here that the removal of a physical restraint to movement confers freedom we have **give a free rein to** "allow the freedom to act" (*the young film-makers were given free rein to experiment*), **let loose** "have complete freedom in a place or situation" (*she has all the excitement of a little girl let loose in a candy store*).

It follows that lack of freedom is being bound, tied or otherwise physically restrained. **Bind** means "force by rule, agreement or restriction" (*authorities will* *be legally bound to arrest any suspects*), while **bondage** means "being under the control of" (*Marxism was supposed to free people from the bondage of superstition*). If you are **tied/tied down** you are "forced to accept limitations to your freedom" (*he didn't have a family as he didn't want to be tied down*), and if one's **hands are tied** one is "prevented from taking action" (*her hands were tied by the US constitution*). The metaphor theme includes items such as **chained to** "unhappy with because of lack of freedom to avoid" (*he felt chained to a boring badly paid job*), **fettered/shackled** "prevented from acting or behaving freely" (*a private trust would not be so fettered/shackled by bureaucracy*). The topics of rules, controls, limits and oppression have as their vehicles various means of physical restraint: **restraint** "rules or conditions", **chains** "oppression or lack of freedom" (*the colonies suffered for years from the chains of economic exploitation*), **straitjacket** "severe limit to development or activity" (*the national curriculum must be a guide, not a straitjacket*). And control is associated with reins: **rein in** "control", **keep on a tight rein** "have a lot of control over" (*her parents had kept her on a tight rein*), though one may **kick over the traces** "show no respect for authority by breaking rules" (*on their day off the football team would kick over the traces*).

Another converse of the analogy FREEDOM IS SPACE TO MOVE is NO FREEDOM IS ENCLOSURE. If you are in a **prison** you feel that you are in "a situation that it is impossible to change" (*he felt his marriage had become a prison*) and a **trap** is "a dangerous or unpleasant situation you cannot escape" (*young and friendless people are prone to falling into the trap of strange cults*), while a **prisoner** is "someone who has no freedom to avoid a situation" (*he's a prisoner of his own addictions*). If you restrict someone's freedom of action they feel **hemmed in** or **hedged about** with rules and conditions. And if they are **besieged** they are too busy to do what they want because they are "receiving, or subjected to, and with no chance of avoiding" something negative (*the TV company was besieged with phone calls after the sex education programme*). If it is an emotional state that you cannot avoid you may be **locked** in it "dominated (by negative emotions)" (*survivors of disasters often remain locked in a state of guilt for years*).

The conclusion is that we have two basic metaphorical patterns here, which are at odds with each other. On the one hand there is the idea that bonding, being attached is a positive thing, a way by which we establish meaningful relationships within society. On the other we have a set of metaphors which suggests that bonding could be bondage, and being tied to a family or entangled in a relationship should be avoided.

8.3.4   RELATIONSHIP IS COHESION/PROXIMITY and its paradoxes in Donne

In Donne, who might be seen as obsessed with the metaphysics of unity (Kawasaki 1971), the symbols and metaphors of physical unity are common enough. In 'The Extasie' firstly the two bodies are as attached as they can be:

> Our hands were firmly cemented
> With a fast balm, which thence did spring,
> Our eye-beams twisted, and did thread
> Our eyes upon one double string;
> So t'intergraft our hands, as yet
> Was all the means to make us one,
> And pictures in our eyes to get
> Was all our propagation.

But their souls become united, too.

> But as all several souls contain
> Mixture of things, they know not what,
> Love, these mixed souls, doth mix again,
> And makes both one, each this and that.
> …
> When love, with one another so
> Interinanimates two souls,
> The abler soul, which thence doth flow,
> Defects of loneliness controls.

Lying behind this idea is probably the theory of the four elements, which if mixed equally admit no decay or change, as made more explicit in 'The Dissolution':

> And we were mutual elements to us,
> And made of one another.
> My body then doth hers involve,
> And those things whereof I consist, hereby
> In me abundant grow, and burdenous,
> And nourish not, but smother.

The same symbolism of mixture of uncountable substances, which, conceptually, unlike countable things, have no boundaries, and are therefore more easily mixed, is evident in 'The Flea'. This poem is, however, rather more humorous in tone, and may be a parody of the sacrament of the Eucharist, as elsewhere the poem parodies the marriage sacrament:

> It sucked me first, and now sucks thee,
> And in this flea, our two bloods mingled be…
> Ye this enjoys before it woo,
> And pampered swells with one blood made of two,
> And this, alas, is more than we would do.

In 'Song', there is the same tendency to metaphorise unity in terms of substances: liquids or gases, tears/blood or breath/soul:

> When thou sighest, thou sighest not wind
> But sighest my soul away
> When thou weepst, unkindly kind,
> My life's blood doth decay…
> They who one another keep
> Alive, ne'er parted be.

The second major metaphor sees relationship as a binding, rather than unity or mixture. Given this metaphor, concrete objects which bind are commonly thought of, through literalisation, as symbols of a relationship. For example in 'Sonnet: The Token' Donne rejects such symbols in favour of the reality of the mental recognition of his love:

> I beg no riband wrought with thine own hands
> To knit our loves in the fantastic strain
> Of new-touched youth; nor ring to show the stands
> Of our affection, that as that's round and plain
> So should our loves meet in simplicity.
> No, nor the corals which thy wrist enfold
> Laced up together in congruity
> To show our thoughts should rest in the same hold.

In 'The Funeral' Donne elaborates on the ambiguity of the binding metaphor, suggesting the negativity of loss of freedom.

> Who ever comes to shroud me, do not harm
> Nor question much
> That subtle wreath of hair, which crowns my arm;
> The mystery, the sign you must not touch
> For 'tis my outward soul,
> Viceroy to that, which then to heaven being gone,
> Will leave this to control
> And keep these limbs, her provinces from dissolution.

When he is buried he asks the undertaker not to remove the hair of his mistress that he has bound around his upper arm, as it symbolises his soul, a viceroy which (according to the BODY IS A CITY) controls his limbs/provinces. Since they are 'her' provinces, we already have the suggestion that this symbolises the relationship between him and his lover, that she is, in some sense, his soul, controlling him by this binding, this relationship which is the sole means of keeping him from dissolution (decay or disunity). The binding more clearly becomes an image of imprisonment later in the poem:

> Except she meant that I
> By this should know my pain,
> As prisoners then are manacled, when they are condemned to die.

The conflict between freedom and relationship is clearly found in 'Confined Love', whose very title suggests the negative metaphors of imprisonment and restricted movement that we listed above. Here the persona, if not Donne, seems to be questioning the law of fidelity in love. He uses the images of movement to suggest the freedom to choose new lovers:

> Are birds divorced or are they chidden
> If they leave their mate, or lie abroad a-night.
>
> …
>
> Who e'er rigged fair ship to lie in harbors,
> And not to seek new lands, or not to deal withal?

The conflict between these two metaphor themes of relationship and freedom can also be found in religion. Within Christianity there is this paradox that God's 'service is perfect freedom'. And this paradox is most forcefully expressed in the Holy Sonnet 'Batter my heart three-person'd God'. In lines 8 and 11, Donne uses the familiar metaphor of lack of freedom being captivity or tying, when the persona of the poem complains that the viceroy, reason, who should govern and defend him (the usurped town), is not free to do so because he has been taken captive; and when he talks of his betrothal to God's enemy, the devil, as a knot that needs to be untied. But the paradox comes in lines 13 and 14: "I will never be free unless you make me a prisoner, and will never be sexually pure unless you rape me".

> BATTER my heart, three person'd God; for, you
> As yet but knock, breathe, shine, and seek to mend;
> That I may rise, and stand, o'erthrow me, and bend
> Your force, to break, blow, burn and make me new.
> I, like an usurped town, to another due,   5

> Labour to admit you, but Oh, to no end,
> Reason, your viceroy in me, me should defend,
> But is captived, and proves weak or untrue.
> Yet dearly I love you, and would be loved fain,
> But am betrothed unto your enemy: 10
> Divorce me, untie, or break that knot again;
> Take me to you, imprison me, for I
> Except you enthral me, never shall be free,
> Nor ever chaste, except you ravish me.

There is another paradoxical escape which Donne hints at in a passage we have already quoted from 'The Extasie' (8.3.1): the state where a spiritual or Platonic relationship has no bodily expression is a kind of prison. Here lack of physical relationship is seen as a lack of freedom.

8.3.5   Parting as symbolic through literalisation

In 'A Valediction: forbidding mourning', we have a symbolic interplay between the literal and metaphorical levels of separation. Since LACK OF RELATIONSHIP IS DISTANCE then any literal movement away from the beloved, a literalisation of the vehicle, symbolically threatens the relationship. Donne argues that this physical presence is not of the greatest importance, since their love has been refined into something Platonic.

> Dull sublunary lovers' love
> (Whose soul is sense) cannot admit
> Absence, because it doth remove
> Those things that elemented it.
>
> But we by a love, so much refined,
> That our selves know not what it is,
> Inter-assured of the mind,
> Care less, eyes, lips and hands to miss.

Nevertheless, despite his denial of the need for literal contact, Donne still strives for metaphors of cohesion and contact. Since the refined gold of their love is ductile it simply expands to cover the distance between them, maybe becoming more important by this expansion (IMPORTANT IS BIG).

> Our two souls therefore, that are one,
> Though I must go, endure not yet
> A breach, but an expansion,
> Like gold to airy thinness beat.

He goes on to use the pair of compasses metaphor: though the feet of the compasses are separated they are joined at the top, and the fixed foot leans after the moving foot. This reflects the metaphor theme DESIRE IS ATTRACTION/ BENDING: **Attract**, **pull** and **draw** (literally meaning "cause to move towards") all mean metaphorically to "stimulate interest pleasure or desire in" (*it was her sense of humour that first attracted me*). As more specifically in the Donne poem, desire and interest can also be conveyed by bending: from the perpendicular – **inclined to** "tending towards, preferring" (*I'm inclined to stay at home during the holiday*), **lean towards** "tend to be interested in" (*he's always leaned towards Socialism*), **leanings** "interests, desires" (*I think his paedophile leanings disqualify him*); or from a straight line – **bias** "preference for" (*hiring practice shows a bias towards whites*), and **bent** "attachment to particular beliefs or activities" (*government advisers are all economists of a socialist bent*).

'A Valediction: forbidding mourning' exemplifies a major theme of Donne's poetry, to do with parting, not only in his valedictory poems but also those which lament the need to leave his beloved's bed because of pressure of work. One's daily job takes one away from the beloved, a further tension against the desire for physical unity as a symbol of spiritual union. In 'Break of Day' Donne expostulates:

> Why should we rise, because 'tis light?
> Did we lie down, because 'twas night?
>
> …
>
> Must business thee from hence remove?
> Oh, that's the worst disease of love,
> The poor, the foul, the false, love can
> Admit, but not the busied man.
> He which hath business, and makes love, doth do
> Such wrong, as when a married man doth woo.

There are several defences against the metaphorical logic that physical separation means emotional distancing: the annihilation of space, the phenomenon of reflection, and the portability of pictures. The first idea is that space can expand or contract to make distance meaningless: 'For love, all love of other sights controls/And makes one little room an everywhere' ('The Good Morrow'); or in 'The Sun Rising':

> Look, and tomorrow late, tell me
> Whether both the Indias of spice and mine
> Be where thou left them, or lie here with me.
> Ask for those kings whom thou sawest yesterday,
> And thou shalt hear, 'all here I one bed lay.'

> …
> Thou, sun, art half as happy as we
> In that the world's contracted thus;
> Thine age asks ease, and since thy duties be
> To warm the world, that's done in warming us.
> Shine here to us and thou art everywhere;
> This bed thy centre is, these walls thy sphere.

This shrinking of space might be seen as a symptom of the seventeenth century's valuing of the microcosm over the macrocosm (Kawasaki 1971: 25–6).

In 'A Valediction: of my name in the window' his name is engraved in the glass so:

> 'Tis much that glass should be
> As all confessing, and through-shine as I,
> 'Tis more, that it shows thee to thee,
> And clear reflects thee to thine eye,
> But all such rules, love's magic can undo
> Here you see me, and I am you.

Or there is the related conceit of seeing oneself in one's lover's eyes 'My face in thine eye, thine in mine appears' ('The Good Morrow') or in 'Witchcraft by a Picture':

> I fix mine eye on thine, and there
> Pity my picture burning in thine eye
> My picture drowned in a transparent tear
> When I look lower, I espy.
> Had'st thou the wicked skill
> By pictures made and marred, to kill,
> How many ways mightst thou perform thy will?

These two strategies for overcoming symbolic distance or separation, the annihilation of space and reflection come together in 'The Canonisation':

> You …
> Who did the whole world's soul contract, and drove,
> Into the glasses of your eyes
> So made such mirrors and such spies,
> That they did all to you epitomise
> Countries, Towns, Courts.

The confluence of these strategies for overcoming separation and the nothing-ness that distance implies (Empson 1993: 71) is also a starting point for 'A Valediction of Weeping'. Here the lovers' tears both reflect their images, like a stamp on a coin, and can be compared to a previously empty globe which now represents all the world's continents, the world of the two lovers.

> Let me pour forth
> My tears before thy face, whilst I stay here,
> For thy face coins them, and thy stamp they bear
> And by this mintage they are something worth,
> For thus they be
> Pregnant of thee;
> Fruits of much grief they are, emblems of more
> When a tear falls, that thou falls which it bore,
> So thou and I are nothing then, when on a diverse shore.
>
> On a round ball
> A workman that hath copies by, can lay
> An Europe, Afrique, and an Asia,
> And quickly make that, which was nothing, *All*,
> So doth each tear,
> Which thee doth wear,
> A globe, yea world by that impression grow,
> Till thy tears mixed with mine do overflow
> This world, by waters sent from thee, my heaven dissolved so.

However, the purpose of the poem is to stop the lady (and the protagonist) crying too much:

> The roundness of the teardrop will be disfigured by too much water, and
> the reflected image of the lover will be blurred and destroyed. Excessive
> weeping will symbolize destruction of the man, or of the man and the
> lady together (the microcosm), and will subsequently allude to the
> macrocosmic cataclysm, the Flood. (Kawasaki 1971: 30)

8.3.6   Overcoming separation through RELATIONSHIP IS TRANSACTION

Another important metaphorical way of attempting to overcome physical part-ing and the threat to unity and cohesion is through the metaphor of exchange, in which the love relationship is seen as a transaction. This in fact depends upon the premise that the lovers are metaphorically separated. If they are a unity giving and taking make no sense.

We should remind ourselves that Donne was writing at the beginning of the capitalist era, and this might produce the emphasis on relationship as transaction. Schleiner has claimed, in respect of Donne's sermons, that SALVATION IS PURCHASE has a pedigree in the Fathers and liturgical texts (1970: 122). However, Freer (1996) has shown the extent to which Donne was involved in business, commerce, and even economic speculation, and how he deliberately used commercial imagery, for instance in his 1626 funeral sermon for Sir William Cockayne, one of the wealthiest merchants and former Lord Mayor, where the congregation included many financiers and merchants. As I demonstrated elsewhere (Goatly 2007 chapter 8), just as quality can be reduced to quantity through classification and mathematics, so money can be the common denominator which enables the capitalist enterprise to succeed by equating anything with anything else through the mechanism of the market. Humans themselves also become valued in terms of money, as their value is dependent upon the monetary value of the goods they produce or accumulate, and their credit consists on the probability of their working hard enough to repay their debts. Heidegger warns that

> the humanness of man and the thingness of things dissolve into the
> calculated market value of a market which … trades in the nature of Being
> and thus subjects all beings to the trade of a calculation that dominates
> most tenaciously in those areas where there is no need of numbers.
> (Heidegger 1971: 114–5)

As William Downes has shown, King Lear's opening question of the play implies an equation between money/goods and love, and thereby suggests that love can be quantified:

> Tell me, my daughters,
> (Since now we will divest us both of rule,
> Interest of territory, cares of state)
> Which of you shall we say doth love us most?
> That we our largest bounty may extend
> Where nature doth with merit challenge. (*King Lear* 1.i.)

Lear's assumption is that, as Downes points out:

> There is a quantitative hierarchy of love and it must be possible to truly
> calculate from a verbal response … a person's relative position in this
> hierarchy. But within Lear's sentence this hierarchy does not stand alone.
> The final adverbial clause … explicitly relates this scale to two others,
> a quantitative hierarchy of bounty, and also one of merit. And all three
> scales are interlocked. The most love merits the extension of the largest

> bounty. Thus degree of love is calculable. This linkage establishes the motif
> of calculation as an interpretative norm within the text. It recurs ... in the
> rational calculation of their self-interest by Goneril, Regan and Edmund,
> the individualist 'new men' of the play. (Downes 1989: 235)

As an example of this, the lexis in RELATIONSHIP/AFFECTION IS MONEY/
WEALTH can be seen in terms of Reciprocation: **indebted to**, "grateful for help
given", **debt**, "appreciation, gratitude" (*I can never repay the debt I owe him*),
with the result that you **owe**, "feel gratitude and the need to reciprocate" (*I owe
him for babysitting so often*) and will need to **repay**, "do something good to
somebody in return for past favours" (*how can I ever repay you for your kind-
ness*) or, more contractually **pay your dues**, "do your duty" (*I've paid my dues
by looking after the children for four years – now it's your turn!*). And if acting
according to morality will be careful not to **short-change**, "give inferior or
inadequate service or treatment to" (*on taking the job I was promised promotion
at the first opportunity – I think I've been short-changed in the present personnel
actions*). Or moral accounting might take the form of Retribution: **pay back**,
"take revenge on someone who has treated you badly"; **settle accounts/old
scores**, "take revenge by repaying an insult or harm" (*I've finally settled accounts
with her for refusing me a job*).

If one behaves well one builds up **credit**, "honour, pride, reputation" (*his
credit is high with the President*) so that people **appreciate** "feel gratitude for"
you or your actions. If you are lucky, when you behave badly people may **make
allowances**, "refrain from criticism or judgement" (*we should make allowances
for him – he's just lost his wife*) (Lakoff 1996: chapter 4).

Donne's poems often suggest that parts of the human body are exchanged or
given to the beloved, most commonly the heart and the eyes as in 'The Message'
'Send home my long-strayed eyes to me .../Send home my harmless heart again',
but also sighs, tears, or breath and blood as in 'The Prohibition': 'my unthrifty
waste/Of breath and blood upon thy sighs and tears'.

In 'Love's Exchange' Donne talks of his rejection in terms of receiving
nothing in return for his soul:

> Love, any devil else but you
> Would for a given soul give something too...

While courtiers receive more than they deserve,

> Only I have nothing which gave more.

He therefore asks Love to give him his weakness, that is to make him blind so
that he will not know how childish Love (Cupid) is, or know that others know
that she realises his suffering. Or otherwise he asks Love to give him nothing.

In 'The Will' Donne elaborates relationship as a transaction by suggesting various ways in which he might bequeath his body parts and the attributes of his character. He gives his eyes to Argus, or if they are blind to Love, his ears to ambassadors, his tongue to fame, his tears to women or the sea, all such gifts being unnecessary as the recipients already have what he gives in abundant quantities:

> Thou Love, has taught me heretofore
> By making me serve her who had twenty more
> That I should give to none, but such as had too much before.

He gives his constancy to the planets, truth to courtiers, ingenuity and openness to Jesuits, pensiveness to buffoons, silence to people coming back from their travels, and money to Capuchin monks, since all these recipients are incapable of using what he gives:

> Thou, love, taught'st me, by appointing me
> To love there, where no love received can be,
> Only to give to such as have an incapacity.

He gives his faith to Roman Catholics, his good works to Protestants, his politeness and courtesy to universities, his modesty to soldiers, his patience to gamblers, since these recipients would undervalue his gifts:

> Thou Love, taught'st me, by making me
> Love her that holds my love disparity,
> Only to give to those that count my gifts indignity.

He will give back what he received from others: his reputation to his former friends; his industry to his enemies with whom he was competing; his doubts to schoolmen; his sickness to physicians or to the excess which caused it; his poetry to nature; and his wit to his companions.

> Thou Love, by making me adore
> Her, who begot this love in me before,
> Taught me to make, as though I gave, when I did but restore.

He will bequeath his books on medicine to dead men, his rules of moral advice to the insane, his medals to the starving, his English to those travelling abroad, gifts which do not match the recipients' needs:

> Thou, Love, by making me love one
> Who thinks her friendship a fair portion
> For younger lovers, dost my gifts thus disproportion.

In the end he decides to give no more. He will die, and thereby annihilate both himself, her and Love. Then:

> All your beauties will be no more worth
> Than gold in mines, where none doth draw it forth;
> And all your graces no more use shall have
> Than a sundial in a grave.

'Lovers' Infinitenesse' is the most interesting of the Songs and Sonnets in its development of the metaphor of love as a transaction, as it explores the distortions brought about by the metaphor, finally rejecting it by resorting to the alternative metaphor of unity. In the first stanza Donne talks of spending all his treasure 'sighs, tears, oaths, letters' to purchase his beloved and her love completely, so that if he does not yet have it all, he never will. Moreover, she may, in the original bargain, have only agreed to give some of her love to him, reserving the remainder for others:

> If then thy gift of love were partial
> That some to me, some should to others fall,
> Dear, I shall never have Thee All.

An additional problem might be that in the original bargain she only agreed to give the love that she had at the time. If she now has new love created in her heart by other men who have used all their sighs, tears, oaths and letters to 'outbid' him, she is not breaking her bargain, because she only vowed to repay him with the original amount of love.

This metaphor of love as something to be bought in a transaction is, however, radically undermined by Donne, as he recognises that it distorts the nature of love. First he attempts to modify the transaction with the image of growth on agricultural land. If she gave him all her heart in exchange for his expressions of love, and this heart is equivalent to the land on which her love grows, then he is entitled to whatever grows there, so that he should be given all her love, and not allow it to be shared around with others. However, finally he has to abandon the transaction metaphor altogether. Once all her love, or her heart, has been given, then she cannot give it any more. But since his love for her increases day by day he would expect her to give him more each day. Finally he realises the riddles or paradoxes which make the transaction metaphor break down: though your heart departs (is given) it still remains with you, and by losing it you save it, so, presumably you can give it again. The solution to this is to give up the whole metaphor of exchanging hearts/loves, and to talk about uniting hearts.

> But we will have a way more liberal
> Than changing hearts, to join them, so we shall
> Be one, and one another's All.

The metaphor of agricultural growth is pursued in 'Love's Growth', but this time not as an alternative to transactional metaphors. For the logic would be that if love grows in the spring, then it declines or dies in the winter. So, to avoid this logic he says that although his love seems to increase just as growth does in the spring, the love was in fact there all the time, it was simply less obvious.

> And yet no greater, but more eminent;
> Love by the Spring is grown;
> As in the firmament
> Stars by the sun are not enlarged but shown.
> Gentle love deeds, as blossoms on a bough,
> From love's awakened root, do bud out now....

In fact he manages to modify the monetary metaphor to account for the increase in love:

> As princes do in times of action get
> New taxes, and remit them not in peace,
> No winter shall abate the spring's increase.

The RELATIONSHIP IS TRANSACTION metaphor not only applies to human relationships, but to the relationship between man and God. In Holy Sonnets XV and XVI he uses the legacy metaphor for this relationship. In XVI Donne talks of Jesus' 'double interest' in his father's kingdom. He has two wills, one which he inherits from his Father, and the other that he bequeaths by his death. The first will, half of the bequest, 'his jointure in the knottie trinity', he keeps, and part he gives to Donne. Both of these wills could be invested in humanity, but no man can fulfil the statutes governing the first will, from his father. Donne therefore pleads that the second will, the will of Christ's sacrificial love, should be the one that remains valid, not the first which requires keeping the Old Testament law.

> ...but all-healing grace and spirit
> Revive again what law and letter kill.
> Thy law's abridgment, and thy last command
> Is all but love; Oh let this last will stand.

In Holy Sonnet XV the legacy metaphor is repeated, but also revives the traditional biblical metaphor of redemption, or ransom, buying back what was, in any case, rightfully His.

> The Father having begot a Son most blest
>
> …
>
> Hath deigned to choose thee by adoption
> Coheir to his glory, and Sabbath's endless rest.
> And as a robbed man, which by search doth find
> His stolen stuff sold, must lose or buy it again:
> The Son of glory came down and was slain
> Us whom he had made, and Satan stolen, to unbind.

However, unlike the metaphor of earthly love as transaction, in both these poems there is no reciprocity: the giving is all on Christ's side; 'the wages of sin is death, but the gift of God is eternal life' (Romans ch. 6 v. 23). In Holy Sonnet XI, for example, Donne contrasts the pecuniary motives of Jacob, who cheated in getting the blessing and inheritance of his blind father Isaac by covering his arms with goatskin and impersonating Esau, with the unconditional generosity of God.

> And Jacob came clothed in vile harsh attire
> But to supplant, and with gainful intent:
> God clothed himself in vile man's flesh that so
> He might be weak enough to suffer woe.

In his sermons, too, according to the metaphor theme SALVATION IS PURCHASE, the transactional metaphor breaks down: 'This is a circumstance, nay, an essential difference peculiar to our debts to God, that we do not pay them, except we contract more; we grow best out of debt, by growing further in debt' (quoted in Schleiner 1970: 134).

8.3.7   EXISTENCE IS PROXIMITY and death as separation

We have seen that relationship as transaction metaphors are an attempt, if a distorting one, to overcome the impossibility of cohesion or physical unity. Donne frequently stresses the impossibility of a lasting physical unity, for example in 'The Anniversary':

> Two graves must hide thine and mine corpse
> If one might, death were no divorce.

The metaphorical logic seems to go as follows: RELATIONSHIP IS PROXIMITY, but DEATH IS SEPARATION so END OF RELATIONSHIP = DEATH. This logic seems to lie behind the metaphorical structure of 'The Expiration':

> So, so, break off this last lamenting kiss,
> Which sucks two souls, and vapours both away,
> Turn thou ghost that way, and let me turn this,
> And let ourselves benight our happiest day,
> We asked none leave to love; nor will we owe
> Any, so cheap a death, as saying, go;
>
> Go; and if that word have not quite killed thee,
> Ease me with death, by bidding me go too.
> Oh, if it have, let my word work on me,
> And a just office on a murderer do.
> Except it be too late to kill me so,
> Being double dead, going and bidding, go.

This logic is bolstered by the metaphor theme EXISTENCE IS PROXIMITY and DEATH IS DEPARTURE. In Metalude we see that reality is presence, **real and present danger,** while unreality is distance as in **remote possibility** "slight likelihood". Beginning of existence (or birth) is arrival or movement towards: **come into existence** "begin to exist" (*before plastic came into existence littering was not a problem*), **come about** "become" (*how did this awful situation come about?*), **bring into existence** "cause to exist" (*before you bring any more children into existence you must decide how you are going to support them*), **usher in** "mark the beginning of or cause to exist" (*the oil shortage ushered in a number of alternative energy technologies*), **arrival** "birth" (*Edgar and Eileen are pleased to announce the arrival of Philip, born on August 8*).

It follows that DEATH IS DEPARTURE. Death is conveyed by metaphors of leaving: **pass away, depart this life** "die" (*in loving memory of my husband, who departed this life/passed away on May 31st 2000*), **the departed** "people who have died", **leave** "die and have surviving relatives" (*he leaves two young daughters and a 23 year-old wife*) and "a person certain to die" is a **goner**. Otherwise death or end of existence is associated with movement away: **die out, go out of existence, die away** "diminish" (*the sound died away in the distance*). Moving something away is therefore abolishing it, **do away with** (*Bush is planning to do away with the FBI*) destroying it, **remove** (*your mission is to remove as many of the opposition infantry as possible*) or killing it, **blow away** (*I'm gonna blow him away when I find him*), **take out** (*he hired a gunman to have the rival politician taken out*).

Donne exploits this metaphor theme in 'Song':

> Sweetest love, I do not go,
> For weariness of thee
> Nor in hope the world can show

> A fitter love for me;
> But since that I
> Must die at last, 'tis best,
> To use myself in jest
> Thus by feigned deaths to die.
>
> …
>
> But think that we
> Are but turned aside to sleep
> They whom one another keep
> Alive, ne'er parted be.

'The Legacy' combines the idea of love as transaction with death as parting into an extended metaphor.

> When I died last, and dear, I die
> As often as from thee I go
> Though it be but an hour ago
> And lovers' hours be full eternity,
> I can remember yet, that I
> Something did say, and something did bestow;
> Though I be dead, which sent me, I should be
> Mine own executor and legacy.

In 'A Nocturnal upon St. Lucy's Day' we see that her death or lack of existence implies his own death or lack of existence, so lack of relationship is death. Or, to put it another way, because he and she were everything, her death makes him nothing, once the relationship is gone.

> But I am by her death (which word wrongs her)
> Of the first nothing the elixir grown;
> Were I a man, that I were one,
> I needs must know; I should prefer
> If I were any beast,
> Some ends, some means; yea plants and stones detest,
> And love; all all some properties invest;
> If I an ordinary nothing were,
> As shadow, a light, and body must be there.

We have a similar idea in 'The Computation'. However, in the latter poem, Donne exploits the idea that, if the end of a love relationship is death/separation, then the converse is that love, symbolised by proximity, itself must be life. Yet, since time seems to drag when separated from the beloved, one appears to be experiencing a longer life during separation, a conclusion which Donne is at pains to deny: 'Yet call not this long life; but think that I/Am, by being dead, immortal; can ghosts die?'

'The Paradox' takes up this theme by suggesting that, although love is life, there is an inevitability about its end, which is death, so that even while it is being enjoyed it is associated with death (maybe reinforced by the sexual pun on *die* 'lose an erection').

> I cannot say I loved, for who can say
> He was killed yesterday?
> Love with excess of heat, more young than old,
> Death kills with too much cold;
> We die but once, and who loved last did die,
> He that saith twice doth lie.

In 'Farewell to Love' Donne seems to go even further. He toys with the idea that (sexual) love is life, before undermining it metonymically. At the outset he would seem to be hinting that Love may be a deity, a force of life beyond death, whom men, even if they are atheists, long for on their deathbeds.

> Whilst yet to prove
> I thought there was some Deity in love
> So did I reverence and gave
> Worship; as atheists at their dying hour
> Call, what they cannot name, an unknown power,
> As ignorantly did I crave.

However, this argument appears a little two-edged, since we are not sure whether the ignorance lies in his lack of knowledge of the true name of Love or in his being deceived about Love's being an eternal deity. And as the poem progresses, Donne indicates that sexual love is painfully transient and leads to post-coital depression:

> Being had, enjoying it decays:
> And thence
> What before pleases them all, takes but one sense,
> And that so lamely, as it leaves behind
> A kind of sorrowing numbness to the mind.

Indeed he suggests that the act of sex, though creating new life, diminishes the metaphorical length of our lives, as well as, one supposes, diminishing the length of the penis:

> Unless wise
> Nature decreed (since each such act, they say,

Diminisheth the length of life a day)
This, as she would man should despise
The sport
Because that other curse of being short,
And only for a minute made to be
Eager desires, to raise posterity.

8.4   CERTAINTY/RELIABILTY IS STABILITY versus love as change and destruction

In this last poem, 'Farewell to Love', sexual passion, and love or emotion more generally, are conceived of as a threat to life and as potentially destructive of enduring relationships. This is reflected in the opposed metaphor themes CERTAINTY/RELIABILTY IS STABILITY v. EMOTION/TIME/CHANGE IS MOVEMENT.

The concept of reliability can be applied to people, especially in their relationships with others, and Metalude provides plenty of evidence that physical stability is used to speak metaphorically of lasting and trusting relationships. So we have the adjectives **solid** "loyal and dependable" (*he has been a solid friend to me for many years*), **steady** "reliable, constant" (*they have a steady relationship*), **stable** "unchangeable, dependable" (*we had a stable six-year relationship together*) and **indissoluble** (literally "unable to be dissolved) "impossible to change or end" (*their marriage was indissoluble*). And we have nouns which apply literally to solid objects, **brick** "trustworthy person" (*my aunt was a real brick*), or means of providing stability/solidity: **footing** "basis for a relationship" (*we have to know on what footing you intend staying with us–lodger or guest?*), **ballast** "qualities that make a relationship or person's character stable" (*his faith in God has always been a kind of emotional ballast*), and **sheet anchor** "source of stability or confidence" (*complete honesty is the sheet anchor of marriage*).

It is quite obvious that the above metaphor theme CERTAINTY/RELIABILITY IS SOLIDITY/FIRMNESS is related to the already discussed RELATIONSHIP IS PROXIMITY/COHESION. Their lexical data shows that relationships can be seen as depending on stability. This puts it in contrast with emotions, which are conceptualised, at least in English-speaking cultures as movement: EMOTION IS MOVEMENT.

Emotion and Time are Movement

According to most of the lexical evidence, the experience of emotion is metaphorically movement caused by some external force. **Move/moving** means "cause/causing strong feelings" (*the generosity of the villagers moved me intensely/*

was very moving). A force which causes you to go or travel somewhere causes you to have emotion: **send/transport** "cause delight/extreme happiness in" (*I was transported by the playing of the orchestra*), **get/be carried away** "become very excited and lose control" (*the crowd of students was carried away by his violent speech*). All the above involve change of location from one place to another.

But emotion may be a slighter movement, or one which does not necessarily permanently change location: **unsettle, disturb, perturb** "cause anxiety to" (*the prospect of war is unsettling/disturbing/perturbing investors in the stock market*), **excite** (literally "cause to make frequent small movements") "make feel happy, eager, or enthusiastic" (*he was excited by the prospect of visiting Thailand*). Emotions may be more violent movements such as shaking **shake** "make upset or troubled" (*the news of Wilson's resignation shook the whole country*), **rattle** "worry or make nervous" (*I was really rattled by the man following me home through the fog*), and a shake of the wings is a **flap** "state of anxious excitement" (*I'm in a great flap because I haven't prepared tomorrow's lecture yet*). Revolving also indicates emotion: a **whirl** is "excitement and confusion" (*my head was in a whirl and I lost control of the car*), **flip** "become very angry" (*my father flipped when he discovered me smoking*), and **turn … upside down** "change completely making people too confused or upset to act" (*when Hamlet realises his uncle killed his father his world is turned upside down*), suggesting that change causes emotions, a metonymic link with CHANGE IS MOVEMENT; and **throw … into a spin** "make anxious and emotional" (*the bad news threw them into a spin*).

As in this last example, emotion can be throwing too: **throw** "confuse" (*I wasn't expecting any visitors, and I was really thrown*), **throw … into** "cause to experience an emotion" (*the last song threw the crowd into a frenzy*), and a **fling** is "a short period of enjoyment and excitement" (*he's out having his last fling before he gets married tomorrow*).

Forces causing an emotion can also move you by their impact: **hit** "have a strong emotional effect on" (*I was hit by the poverty in which most Rwandans have to struggle to survive*), **hit/knock for six** "make extremely surprised or upset and unable to speak or act" (*the diagnosis of cancer knocked him for six*), **shock,** "surprise or emotional upset", and **jolt** "cause a lesser shock" (*failing the exam jolted him out of his complacency*), while **jar** means "cause unpleasant feelings" (*her rather supercilious comments jar after a while*). **Repel** (literally, "push away") means "cause disgust" (*US foreign policy repels me*), **stagger,** the transitive verb meaning "cause to walk unsteadily" means metaphorically "cause shock or surprise in someone" (*the news that they were going to marry staggered him*). This category overlaps slightly with the metaphor theme EMOTION IS TOUCH/IMPACT.[6]

The main contrast in the metaphorical conceptualisation of relationships and emotions is between the passivity of humans when affected by emotions, compared with the active rationality of humans in dealing with relationships. Emotional forces tend to produce movement which threatens the stability of structures (Kövecses 2000: 113). Indeed, more generally, CHANGE IS MOVEMENT (see 8.2.4) and in combination with EMOTION IS MOVEMENT, this suggests that emotions are inherently changeable. Just like the tension between freedom and belonging (8.3.4), we also seem to have an intrinsic tension between the need for stable lasting relationships, and the changeable emotions which we experience as part of these relationships. Fortune – change of power through the revolving of a wheel over time – is a whore. Relationships should be stable, but TIME IS TRAVEL or movement, and therefore unstable.

Time can **pass, go by**, meaning "elapse" (time passes/goes by slowly when your boyfriend is away), or **go on**, **roll by** "continue to elapse" (*as time goes on/rolls by the memories of that far-off summer begin to fade*), **move on** "bring changes by elapsing" (*time moves on and we need to change our operating system*), **drag** "elapse slowly so that it seems long and boring" (*the time dragged while we waited for the results*) and so on. So we talk of **times gone by,** "in the past" (*in times gone by speech was always face to face*), and **in the long run,** means "eventually, after a period of time" (*in the long run you'll be pleased you went to university*).

This tension between stability and change is apparent in 'The Anniversary', where, despite Donne's protestations that his love will not decay, it is hard to deny the metaphoric logic:

> All kings, and all their favourites,
> All glory of honours, beauties, wits,
> The sun itself, which makes times, as they pass,
> Is elder by a year, now, than it was
> When thou and I first one another saw:
> All other things to their destruction draw,
> Only our love hath no decay;
> This no tomorrow hath, nor yesterday,
> Running it never runs from us away,
> But truly keeps his first, last, everlasting day.

The metaphorical source/vehicle of movement – of times changing 'as they pass', of destruction over time, 'to their destruction draw'– is paradoxically also applied to their love: 'running it never runs from us away'. The love is active 'up and running' but this does not imply change, he protests, countering its opposed metaphor themes EMOTION/CHANGE IS MOVEMENT and TIME IS TRAVEL.

'The Broken Heart', by contrast, admits the transitoriness of love, and it is worth considering the opening, as it introduces a number of other metaphor themes which relate love to destructiveness:

> He is stark mad, who ever says,
> That he hath been in love an hour,
> Yet not that love so soon decays,
> But that it can ten in less space devour;
> Who will believe me, if I swear   5
> That I have had the plague a year?
> Who would not laugh at me, if I should say,
> 'I saw a flask of powder burn a day'?
>
> Ah, what a trifle is a heart,
> If once into love's hands it come!   10
> All other griefs allow a part
> To other griefs, and ask themselves but some;
> They come to us, but us Love draws
> He swallows us, and never chaws
> By him as by chained shot, whole ranks do die,   15
> He is the tyrant pike, our hearts the fry.

The destructiveness of love is expressed through diverse conventional metaphor themes to be found in Metalude: SEX IS VIOLENCE (line 15), FEELING/EMOTION IS BEING EATEN (lines 4, 14, 16), LOVE/PASSION IS HEAT (line 8) EMOTION IS EXPLOSION (line 8), EMOTION IS DISEASE (line 6). The first three of these metaphor themes of love observed in 'The Broken Heart' are found repeatedly exploited and played with in the Songs and Sonnets.

Love as war and violence

Love as war or violence is exemplified in 'Love's Exchange':

> Small towns which stand stiff, till great shot
> Enforce them, by war's law condition not.
> Such in love's warfare is my case,
> I may not article for grace,
> Having put Love at last to show his face.

This reflects the theme SEX IS VIOLENCE. Much of the lexis in this metaphor theme is quite recent in origin, though the association can be traced back at least as far as classical times, where **phallus** meant "sword", **vagina** meant "sheath or scabbard", an association still preserved in **sheath** meaning "condom". As in these examples, the male is usually constructed as the aggressor, so that the penis is a **chopper, weapon,** or, by collocation a gun with which a man can **shoot his load** "ejaculate semen", or **fire blanks** "produce semen without any sperm in it". The weapon might be a sword as in **make a pass at,** literally "attempt to stab with a rapier" and metaphorically "speak to or touch to show sexual attraction", or an arrow so **shaft** means "have penetrative sexual intercourse with" (*he claims he's been shafting 3 different women a week for the last six months*). Even the traditional symbol for male seems to incorporate an arrow: ♂. By this violence men may achieve their **conquests** "women they have had sexual intercourse with" and be **lady-killers** "seducers", though notice that women too can be **dressed to kill** "wearing clothes that attract sexual attention". Less violently, sex is associated with hitting. Some of this lexis is associated with men as the hitters, too, as in **wham-bang-thank-you-mam** "a very quick act of sex", **knock up** "make pregnant", **knock off** "have sex with a woman", **gang bang** "group rape of a woman". Verb lexis that can take either sex as agent includes **hit on** "indicate your sexual attraction for", or **bang/bonk** "have sex with". A sexually attractive person of either sex is a **knockout** and, more gently, playful sex is **slap and tickle.**

Love as eating and being eaten

In 'The Broken Heart' love is not only violent but it eats or devours those experiencing it. This reflects two themes in Metalude: DESIRE IS APPETITE, HUMAN IS FOOD and EMOTION IS FOOD/EATING (HUNTING). Love or sexual desire can, like other emotions, be a **hunger** or something for which you have an **appetite** or are **hungry** for, especially if you have been **starved** "deprived" of it or your desire is **insatiable.** The object of desire may be as attractive as food **mouth-watering, delicious, succulent, tasty** or **luscious** "sexually attractive" (*he'd make a tasty boyfriend; who was that luscious blonde I saw you with?*), or simply **sweet** "charming or attractive". The effect of a love relationship may be like the effect of food or drink: **intoxicating,** "exciting and producing strong emotions" (*the production of Macbeth was intoxicating*), something which you **savour** "enjoy" and may provide emotional **sustenance,** "emotional support" (*Claudia provided me with emotional sustenance in this recent family crisis*). However sometimes love might **go/turn sour,** "become unpleasant" (*things went sour in their marriage when the kids were born*). Or the loved one, especially if a woman, may be the food itself in HUMAN IS FOOD: **cheesecake** "half-naked, female, photographic models", **crackling** and **crumpet** both meaning "sexually attractive woman", **tart** "sexually immoral/attractive woman", **mutton dressed as lamb** "older woman trying to look young" and **lollipop** "attractive young girl". The next group, though sometimes referring to men, more often apply to women: **peach** "good, attractive person or girl", **arm-candy** "attractive companion at social events", **honey** "pleasant person", **sugar** "person you are fond of", **sweetie** "pleasant, kind person" and **past their sell-by-date** "no longer attractive". This compares with relatively few used more of men than women: **dish, dishy** "sexually attractive (person)". Only two in my list – **beefcake** "man or male models with a muscular body which is attractive to women", and **stud-muffin** "sexually attractive young man" – are used exclusively for men.

We see this metaphor theme realised in 'Community' where Donne talks of women as fruit:

> But they are ours as fruits are ours,
> He that but tastes, he that devours,
> And he that leaves all, doth as well:
> Changed loves are but changed sorts of meat,
> And when he hath the kernel eat,
> Who doth not fling away the shell?

Conversely, as we have seen in the 'Broken Heart' you may find the experience of love is like being eaten: **eat up, consume,** "cause to experience strongly" (*she was eaten up/consumed with love for Ringo*), **devour** "obsess and control completely" (*he has a devouring passion for Julia*). You may become hunted by love or passion or other strong emotions, **prey to** "feeling unhappy because of" them (*he was prey to unrequited passion*).

Modifying this metaphor theme Donne in 'Love's Diet' has a personified Love growing according to the experiences and expressions of love which feed it.

> To what a cumbersome unwieldiness
> And burdensome corpulence my love had grown
> But that I did, to make it less,
> And keep it in proportion,
> Give it a diet, made it feed upon
> That which love worst endures, *discretion*.
>
> Above one sigh a day I allowed him not,
> Of which my fortune, and my faults had part;
> And if sometimes by stealth he got
> A she sigh from my mistress' heart,
> And thought to feast on that, I let him see
> 'Twas neither very sound, nor meant to me.

> If he wrung from me a tear, I brined it so
> With scorn or shame, that him it nourished not;
> If he sucked hers, I let him know
> 'Twas not a tear, which he had got,
> His drink was counterfeit, as was his meat;
> For eyes, which roll towards all, weep not, but sweat.
>
> Whatever he would dictate, I writ that,
> But burnt my letters; when she writ to me,
> And that that favour made him fat.
> I said, 'If any title be
> Convey'd by this. Ah, what doth it avail
> To be the fortieth name in an entail?'
>
> Thus I reclaimed my buzzard love, to fly
> At what, and when, and how, and where I choose;
> Now negligent of sport I lie,
> And now, as other falconers use,
> I spring a mistress, swear, write, sigh and weep:
> And the game killed, or lost, go talk and sleep.

In the last stanza a different schema emerges in which one of the lovers is the dominant hunter who feeds/preys on the other. Possibly employing the same falconry image ('stoop'), in 'Negative Love' Donne talks of Platonic Love as higher than physical sex, which he metaphorises as preying on the loved one's flesh:

> I never stooped so low, as they
> Which on an eye, cheek, lip, can prey,
> Seldom to them, which soar no higher
> Than virtue or the mind to admire
> For sense and understanding may
> Know, what give fuel to their fire.

In 'The Baite' the LOVE IS FISHING metaphor manages to combine LOVE IS HUNTING with DESIRE IS ATTRACTION and RELATIONSHIP IS PROXIMITY/COHESION (lexical details of which appear in 8.3.2). Just as loving can be either like eating or being eaten, there is some confusion between who is hunting whom, since the fishes wish to be caught, and the woman apparently doing the catching is not so much the fisherman as the bait –

> And there the enamored fish will stay
> Begging themselves they may betray.
>
> When thou wilt swim in that live bath,
> Each fish, which every channel hath,
> Will amorously to thee swim
> Gladder to catch thee, than thou him.
> …
> For thee, thou need'st no such deceit,
> For thou thyself art thine own bait;
> That fish that is not catched thereby,
> Alas, is wiser far than I.

This particular metaphor has a long genealogy, which, within the classical Greek and Roman tradition stresses that flesh or sexuality is bait, often the bait of sin. But within Christianity the bait is ambiguously evaluated, since Christ is a fisher of men, and became incarnated in the flesh to catch men's souls. Similarly in the Middle Ages Dante sees Beatrice as 'the divine lure to his revelation in contrast to the devil's hook baited with the pleasures of the world' (Cunnar 1989: 83). Cunnar claims that the love depicted in the poem 'involves the union of the sacred and the sexual. The speaker's initial perception that the sexual relationship is structured and dominated by the male as fisher is subverted as male and female roles are reversed through the woman's atoning role' (Cunnar 1989: 92). By alluding to the genealogy of the LOVE IS FISHING metaphor, and through its relation to the other conceptual metaphors DESIRE IS ATTRACTION, RELATIONSHIP IS PROXIMITY/COHESION, the poem touches on themes we have already explored in this chapter: the necessity for the manifestation of love by a physical union which at once abolishes distance and matches or creates a spiritual/Platonic union.

Love as fire

Another potentially destructive metaphor complex is LOVE/PASSION IS HEAT/FIRE. General heat metaphors include **hot-blooded** "very quick to express or feel emotion or passion" (*he was a hot-blooded young man, but too tactless to keep his girlfriends for long*), **white heat** "very strong feelings" (*she succumbed to the white heat of his passion*). Burning and fire are the typical manifestations of extreme heat: **the fires of** "the very strong emotions associated with" (*her letters simply fuelled the fires of his desire*), **flame** "strong feelings" (*flames of passion surged through Paul's veins*), **burning** "strong and persistent" emotions (*he had a burning desire to grab her around the waist*), which may be expressed as in **blaze** "express a strong emotion" (*Pauline's eyes blazed with passion*), or difficult to get rid of as in **inextinguishable** "impossible to stop feeling"(*her inextinguishable love for her daughter will never disappear*). In this script for fire, causing or encouraging the emotion is lighting, fanning and fuelling it: **kindle** "start an emotion or feeling" (*her phone call kindled his desire to see her again*), **rekindle** "renew positive feelings or friendship" (*his poems and letters rekindled my love for him*), **fan** "encourage or enhance an emotion" (*Powell's love songs fanned the flames of her passion for him*).

Besides the more general lexis given above, which applies heat both to other emotions as well as love, we have more particular heat metaphors referring to passion. Again we have heat in general: **have the hots for** "be sexually attracted to" (*as soon as I saw him I had the hots for him*), which by a transferred epithet gives us **hot stuff** "exciting or sexually attractive" (*I think Maria is really hot stuff*). Fire is also found here in **smoulder** "have a sexually passionate nature" (*Alan Rickman seems to smoulder intensely in this latest movie*), **aflame** "sexually excited" (*her appearance in a swim suit set his desires aflame*) and similarly with another transferred epithet **old flame** "former lover or sexual partner" (*he had several old flames from Loughton High School*). Hot liquids also figure as sources – **sizzling** "exciting" (often sexually) (*she was a blonde girl with a sizzling figure*), **steamy** "erotic or passionate" (*we saw a steamy film and then went back to Paul's flat*) as does hot climate – **torrid** "showing strong (sexual) feelings" (*the movie ends with a torrid love scene*).

In 'The Canonization' love as fire and hunting with birds ('eagle and dove'), are jointly sublimated into the symbol of eternal renewal by the image of the phoenix who rises from its own ashes.

> Call her one, me another fly,
> We are tapers too, and at our own cost die,
> And we in us find the eagle and the dove.
> The phoenix riddle hath more wit
> By us, we two being one are it.
> We can die by it, if not live by love…

In a religious context Donne exploits the mutivalency of the fire vehicle: it is a fire of passionate lust, but also the fire of holy zeal, as in Holy Sonnet V:

> But, oh, it [my body, the little world] must be burnt! Alas the fire
> Of lust and envy have burnt it heretofore,
> And made it fouler; let their flames retire,
> And burn me, O Lord, with a fiery zeal
> Of thee and thy house, which doth in eating heal.

And if this metaphorical fire in turn metaphorically consumes or eats up its fuel, the metaphor has to be resolved in a paradox which denies the metaphorical logic: this eating and burning is a healing process rather than a destructive one.

Donne is more successful in avoiding metaphorical contradictions when he finds another target/topic for the multivalent source/vehicle fire, taken from the biblical notion of God's anger as a refiner's fire. Fire, then, becomes a symbol of purification. In Holy Sonnet XIV, God becomes a goldsmith refashioning sinful humanity:

> Batter my heart, three-personed God; for you
> As yet but knock, breath, shine, and seek to mend;
> That I may rise, and stand, o'er throw me and bend
> Your force to break, blow, burn and make me new.

The metaphor of fire as purification dovetails with the metaphor theme CHARACTER IS METAL. The most prized human characters are compared with gold: **golden-hearted** or with a **heart of gold,** "very generous and kind". Iron and steel often convey admiration too: **iron, steel** "strength and determination" (*Indira was a woman of iron/steel*), **iron man,** "very strong man capable of great endurance" (*it's blazing hot for the marathon, but he's an iron man and is bound to finish*), **nerves of iron/steel** "extreme courage or lack of fear" (*to climb the north face of the mountain you have to have nerves of steel*). However **mercurial,** "changeable and unpredictable" (*what will she do next? she's so mercurial*) and **brass** "shameless confidence, courage" (*how did these chief executives have the brass to award themselves such pay increases?*), **brazen** "bold and unashamed" (*it was a brazen attempt at bribery*) are less then complimentary, while tin conveys low importance or value: **tin-pot** "unimportant of little value (*Chile used to be one of those tin-pot South American military dictatorships*), **tin god** "person considered more important than they really are" (*Catholic priests in Ireland are often tin gods*).

The refining process has left its mark on the lexis of English too: **unrefined** "rough, impolite" (*we don't like loutish unrefined behaviour here*), **dross,** "something useless or worthless" (*most TV programmes are just dross*), **temper,** literally "the right consistency of alloy in steel", metaphorically "state of feelings that make you calm or angry" (*Miriam has a very bad temper and is always shouting at the kids*). Genuineness of character or identity can be tested or guaranteed as with gold or silver by an **acid test** or a **hallmark.**

This theme is common enough in Donne's religious poems. In 'Good Friday, 1613, Riding Westward', Donne pleads with his Saviour:

> Oh think me worth thine anger, punish me
> Burn off my rust and my deformity
> Restore thine image, so much, by thy grace,
> That thou mayest know me, and I'll turn my face.

The metaphor theme ANGER IS FIRE is apparent here, as well as the underlying metaphor that the metal which has been marred is the coin bearing God's image, like the seal of the heavenly monarch, since man was made in the image of God.[7]

The Christ in 'Resurrection Imperfect' is compared to gold when dead for three days, and to gold tincture when he rose from the dead, a tincture which can turn baser metals to gold:

> He was all gold when he lay down, but rose
> All tincture, and doth not alone dispose
> Leaden and iron wills to good, but is
> Of power to make even sinful flesh like his.

8.5   Summary and conclusion

I hope I have shown in this chapter

- how reliant Donne is upon prevalent (if not universal) metaphor themes, bearing out the contentions of Lakoff and Turner in *More than Cool Reason*, whether or not these themes were made culturally and historically more prominent by the ideology of early capitalism, as with RELATIONSHIP/AFFECTION IS MONEY/WEALTH.

- how Donne wrestles with metaphorical paradoxes of conflicting metaphors such as RELIABILITY IS STABILITY versus EMOTION IS MOVEMENT, RELATIONSHIP IS PROXIMITY/COHESION versus FREEDOM IS SPACE TO MOVE and the symbolic threat to relationship/proximity in the literalised symbol of separation.

- that he recognises the distortions of the metaphorical logic and is forced to abandon the metaphors, as when he gives up RELATIONSHIP IS TRANSACTION for RELATIONSHIP IS COHESION (unity), or insists on the symmetry of love denied by the metaphor LOVE IS HUNTING or LOVE IS EATING and BEING EATEN or manages to transform the destructiveness of LOVE IS FIRE through the myth of the Phoenix and the image of refining metals.

In any case, Donne's poetry, especially his *Songs and Sonets* does not depend for its success upon metaphorical consistency, but dramatic insistence: metaphorical logic is abandoned in the demands to go on talking, thinking aloud and spinning new conceits.

Notes

1   'Apply' covers various pragmatic and semantic relations such as reference, modification, predication and complementation of prepositions

2   http://cogsci.berkeley.edu/lakoff/home/html

3   http://www.collinswordbanks.co.uk/

4   The research was funded by the Research Grants Council of the Hong Kong SAR, project reference LC3001/99H.

5   http://www.ln.edu.hk/lle/cwd03/lnproject_chi/home/html (userid <user>; password <edumet6>).

6   Kövecses 2000a discusses these metaphor themes comprehensively in terms of the idea that EMOTION IS STATE (PLACE), CAUSES ARE FORCES, CHANGES ARE MOVEMENTS, so that BECOMING EMOTIONAL IS MOTION INTO A STATE (PLACE), CAUSING EMOTION IS CAUSING MOTION INTO A STATE (PLACE).

7   The importance in Donne's sermons of the seal and coin image for the incarnation is interestingly discussed by Schleiner (1970: 113–21).

References

Alderson, J.C. and Short, M. (1989) Reading literature. In M. Short (ed.) *Reading, Analysing and Teaching Literature* 72–119. Harlow: Longman.

Argyle, M. (1988) *Bodily Communication.* Madison Connecticut: International Universities Press.

Asker, B. (2003a) Ancestral memory: the cases of Kazuo Ishiguro and J. M. Coetzee. In M. Gomille and K. Stierstorfer (eds) *Xenophobic Memories: otherness in post-colonial constructions of the past* 51–76. Heidelberg: Heidelberg University Press.

Asker, B. (2003b) 'The next time I looked, Japan was gone.' Home is where the fiction is – Ishiguro and the sense of dis-place. In R. Ahrens, D. Parker, K. Stierstorfer and K-K.Tam (eds) *Anglophone Cultures in Southeast Asia* 295–309. Heidelberg: Heidelberg University Press.

Babb, H. S. (1970) *The Novels of William Golding.* Columbus: Ohio State University Press.

Bäcklund, I. (1990) Theme in English telephone conversation. Paper delivered at the 17th International Systemic Congress, Stirling, Scotland, June 1990.

Bakhtin, M./Volosinov (1984/1963) *Problems of Dostoevsky's Poetics.* (C. Emerson, trans.). Minneapolis: University Of Minneapolis Press.

Bakhtin, M./Volosinov (1984) *Rabelais and His World.* (H. Iswolsky trans.). Bloomington: Midland Books.

Bakhtin, M. (1981) *The Dialogic Imagination.* M. Holquist and C. Emerson (eds). Austin: University of Texas Press.

Barthes, R. (1984) *S/Z.* (R. Miller, trans.). New York: Hill and Wang.

Berry, M. (1987) The functions of place-names. In I. Turville-Petre and M. Gelling (eds) *Leeds Studies in English New Series.* XVIII: 71–88.

Black, E. (1993) Metaphor, simile and cognition in Golding's 'The Inheritors'. *Language and Literature* vol.2. no.1: 37–48.

Black, M. (1962) *Models and Metaphors.* Ithaca New York: Cornell University Press.

Bohm, D. (1980) *Wholeness and the Implicate Order.* London: Routledge.

Boyd, S. J. (1988) *The Novels of William Golding.* Sussex: The Harvester Press.

Brown, P. and Levinson, S. C. (1987) *Politeness: some universals in language use* Cambridge: Cambridge University Press.

Chilton, P. (1996) *Security Metaphors: cold war discourse from containment to common house.* New York: Peter Lang.

Cunnar, E. R. (1989) Donne's witty theory of atonement in 'The Baite'. *Studies in English Literature, 1500-1900: the English Renaissance* vol. 29.1: 77–98.

Davidse, K. (1992) Transitivity/ergativity: the Janus-headed grammar of actions and events. In M. Davies and L. Ravelli (eds) *Advances in Systemic Linguistics* 105–166. London: Pinter.

Dawkins, R. (1989) *The Selfish Gene* (2nd edition). Oxford: Oxford University Press.

Derrida, J. (1973) *Speech and Phenomena*. Evanston, Illinois: Northwestern University Press.

Derrida, J. (1978) *Writing and Difference*. (A. Bass, trans.). Chicago: University of Chicago Press.

Dick, B. F. (1967) *William Golding*. New York: Twayne.

Dickson, L. L. (1990) *The Modern Allegories of William Golding*. Tampa: University of South Florida Press.

Donne, J. (1929) *Complete Poetry and Selected Prose*. J. Hayward (ed.). London: Nonesuch Press.

Downes, W. (1989) Discourse and drama. King Lear's 'question' to his daughters. In W. Van Peer (ed.) *The Taming of the Text* 225–258. London: Routledge.

Eggins, S., Wignell, P. and Martin, J. R. (1993a) The discourse of history: distancing the recoverable past. In M. Ghadessy (ed.) *Register Analysis: theory and practice* 75–109. London: Pinter.

Eggins S., Wignell, P. and Martin, J. R. (1993b) The discourse of geography: ordering and explaining the experiential world. In M. A. K. Halliday and J. R. Martin (eds) *Writing Science: literacy and discursive power* 136–165. London: Falmer Press.

Empson, W. (1993) *Essays on Renaissance Literature, volume 1: Donne and the new philosophy*. J. Haffenden (ed.). Cambridge: Cambridge University Press.

Esslin, M. (1980) *The Theatre of the Absurd* (3rd edition). Harmondsworth: Penguin.

Fairclough, N. (1989) *Language and Power*. Harlow: Longman.

Fairclough, N. (1992) *Critical Language Awareness*. Harlow: Longman.

Fairclough, N. (1995) *Media Discourse*. London: Arnold.

Firbas, J. (1992) On some basic problems of functional sentence perspective. In M. Davies and L. Ravelli (eds) *Advances in Systemic Linguistics* 167–88. London: Pinter.

Fish, S. (1980) *Is There a Text in this Class?* Cambridge Mass.: Harvard University Press.

Fowler, R. (1996) *Linguistic Criticism* (2nd edition). Oxford: Oxford University Press.

Fowler, R. (1991) *Language in the News*. London: Routledge.

Fowler, R., Hodge, R., Kress, G. and Trew, T. (1979) *Language and Control*. London: Routledge.

Francis, G. (1990) Theme in the daily press. *Occasional Papers in Systemic Linguistics* 4: 81–87.

Freer, C. (1996) John Donne and Elizabethan economic theory. *Criticism* Fall 1996: 1–15. Retrieved on 13 April 2007 from http://findarticles.com/p/articles/ mi_m2220/is n4 v38/ ai_ 18981382.

Fries, P. (1983) On the status of Theme in English: arguments from discourse. In J. S. Petöfi and E. Sozer (eds) *Papers in Textlinguistics* 48: 116–182.

Fries, P. (1991) The structuring of information in written English text. Paper delivered at the 18th International Systemic Functional Congress, Tokyo, Japan.

Fries, P. (1992) Themes, methods of development and texts. Unpublished manuscript.

Frye, N. (1957) *The Anatomy of Criticism*. Princeton, NJ: Princeton University Press.

Frye, N. (1967) *Fools of Time*. Toronto: University of Toronto Press.

Gardner, E. (1992) *A. E. Housman: the critical heritage*. London: Routledge.

Genette, G. (1966) Structuralisme et critique litteraire. *Figures II*: 145–170. Paris: Seuil.

Ghadessy, M. (1993) Thematic development and its relationship to registers and genres. *Occasional Papers in Systemic Linguistics* 7: 1–25.

Gibbs, R. (1994) *The Poetics of Mind: figurative thought, language and understanding*. Cambridge: Cambridge University Press.

Goatly, A. (1987) Interrelations of metaphors in Golding's novels: a framework for the study of metaphoric interplay. *Language and Style* vol.20. no.2: 125–144.

Goatly, A. (1994) Register and the redemption of relevance theory. *Pragmatics* vol.3 no.2: 139–82.

Goatly, A. (1995a) Congruence and ideology. *Social Semiotics* vol.5 no.1: 23–64.

Goatly, A. (1995b) A stylistic analysis of A.E. Housman's 'On Wenlock Edge'. *Language and Style* vol.23 no.4: 383–408.

Goatly, A. (1997) *The Language of Metaphors*. London: Routledge.

Goatly, A. (2000) *Critical Reading and Writing*. London: Routledge.

Goatly, A. (2002) The representation of nature on the BBC World Service. *Text* vol.22 no.1: 1–27

Goatly, A. (2007) *Washing the Brain: metaphor and hidden ideology*. Amsterdam: Benjamins.

Goffman, E. (1981) *Forms of Talk*. Oxford: Blackwell.

Golding, W. (1956) *Pincher Martin*. London: Faber.

Golding, W. (1961) *The Inheritors*. London: Faber.

Goodman, N. (1968) *Languages of Art: an approach to a theory of symbols*. Indianapolis: Bobbs-Merrill.

Greimas, A. J. (1966) *Sémantique structurale*. Paris: Larousse.

Grice, H. P. (1975) Logic and conversation. In P. Cole and J. L. Morgan (eds) *Syntax and Semantics 3: speech acts* 41–58. New York: Academic Press.

Guralnick, E. S. (1996) *Sight Unseen*. Athens, Ohio: Ohio University Press.

Hall, E. T. (1966) *The Hidden Dimension*. New York: Doubleday.

Hall, P. (2001) Directing the plays of Harold Pinter. In P. Raby (ed.) *The Cambridge Companion to Harold Pinter* 145–154. Cambridge: Cambridge University Press.

Halliday, M. A. K. (1967) Notes on transitivity and Theme in English. *Journal of linguistics* vol.3 no.2: 199–244.

Halliday, M. A. K. (1973) Linguistic function and literary style: an inquiry into William Golding's *The Inheritors*. In M. A. K. Halliday *Explorations in the Function of Language* 103–138. London: Arnold.

Halliday, M. A. K. (1985a) *An Introduction to Functional Grammar.* London: Arnold.

Halliday, M. A. K. (1985b) *Spoken and Written Language.* Oxford: Oxford University Press.

Halliday, M. A. K. (1994) *An Introduction to Functional Grammar* (2nd edition). London: Arnold.

Hasan, R. (1989) *Linguistics, Language and Verbal Art.* Oxford: Oxford University Press.

Hawkes, T. (1977) *Structuralism and Semiotics.* London: Methuen.

Heidegger, M. (1971) *Poetry, Language, Thought.* New York: Harper and Row.

Housman, A. E. (1967) *The Collected Poems.* London: Cape.

Hayduk, L.A. (1983) The permeability of personal space: where we stand now. *Psychological Bulletin* 94: 293–335.

Ishiguro, K. (1989) *An Artist of the Floating World.* New York: Vintage/Random House.

Ishiguro, K. (1993) *The Remains of the Day.* New York: Vintage/Random House.

Jacobson, N. P. (1966) *Buddhism: the religion of analysis.* London: Allen and Unwin.

Jacobson, N. P. (1988) *The Heart of Buddhist Philosophy.* Carbondale and Edwardsville: Southern Illinois University Press.

Jakobson, R. (1960) Closing statement. In T. E. Sebeok (ed.) *Style in Language* 351–377. Cambridge Mass: MIT Press.

Jefferson, A. and Robey, D. (eds) (1982) *Modern Literary Theory.* London: Batsford.

Jennings, E. (2002) *New Collected Poems.* Manchester: Caracanet Press.

Johnson, M. (1987) *The Body in the Mind.* Chicago: University of Chicago Press.

Kashyap, J. (1954) *The Abidhamma Philosophy.* Nalanda Pali Institute.

Kawasaki, T. (1971) Donne's microcosm. In E. Miner (ed.) *Seventeenth Century Imagery* 25–44. London: University of California Press.

Kinkead-Weekes, M. and Gregor, I. (1967) *William Golding: a critical study.* London: Faber.

Kinkead-Weekes, M. and Gregor, I. (2002) *William Golding: a critical study of the novels* (3rd edition). London: Faber.

Knowles, R. (2001) Pinter and twentieth century drama. In P. Raby (ed.) *The Cambridge Companion to Harold Pinter* 73–86. Cambridge: Cambridge University Press.

Kövecses, Z. (2000) *Metaphor and Emotion.* Cambridge: Cambridge University Press.

Kulkarni, I. (2003) *The Novels of Golding.* New Delhi: Atlantic Publishers.

Lakoff, G. (1987) *Women, Fire and Dangerous Things.* Chicago: University of Chicago Press.

Lakoff G. and Johnson, M. (1980) *Metaphors We Live By.* Chicago: University of Chicago Press.

Lakoff, G. and Turner, M. (1989) *More than Cool Reason: a field guide to poetic metaphor.* Chicago: University of Chicago Press.

Laver, J. (1975) Communicative functions of phatic communion. In A. Kendon, R. M. Harrris and M. R. Keys (eds) *Organization of Behaviour in Face to Face Interaction* 215–240. Harmondsworth: Penguin.

Leech, G. N. (1969) *A Linguistic Guide to English Poetry.* London: Longman.

Leech, G. N. (1983) *Principles of Pragmatics.* Harlow: Longman.

Leech, G. N. (1987) Stylistics and functionalism. In N. Fabb, D. Attridge, A. Durant and C. McCabe (eds) *The Linguistics of Writing* 76–88. Manchester: Manchester University Press.

Leech, G. N. and Short, M. (1981) *Style in Fiction.* Harlow: Longman.

Leggett, B. J. (1978) *The Poetic Art of A. E. Housman.* Lincoln: University of Nebraska Press.

Levinson, S. C. (1983) *Pragmatics.* Cambridge: Cambridge University Press.

Levinson, S. C. (2002) *Presumptive Meanings: the theory of generalized conversational implicature.* Cambridge Mass.: MIT Press.

Lim, L. (1992) *Resolving Clashes of Maxims of the Co-operative and Politeness Principles in Singapore.* Unpublished final year project. Department of English, National University of Singapore.

Lodge, D. (1992) *The Art of Fiction.* New York: Viking.

Long, Nie (1991) An analysis of texts of different genres in terms of thematic selections and process types. Unpublished manuscript.

Lovelock, J. (1988) *The Ages of Gaia.* Oxford: Oxford University Press.

Lucy, J. A. (1992) *Language Diversity and Thought: a reformulation of the linguistic relativity hypothesis.* New York: Cambridge University Press.

Malalasekera, G. P. (1951) Some aspects of reality as taught by Theravada Buddhism. In C. A. Moore (ed.) *Essays in East–West Philosophy* 185–223. Honolulu: University of Hawaii Press.

Marlow, N. (1958) *A. E. Housman: Scholar and Poet.* London: Routledge.

Martin, J. R. (1985) *Factual Writing: exploring and challenging social reality.* Geelong: Deakin University Press.

Martin, J. R. (1986) Intervening in the process of writing development. *ALAA Occasional Papers* 11–43.

Martin, J. R. (1992) *English Text: system and structure.* Amsterdam: Benjamins.

Martin, J. R. and Matthiessen, C. (1990) Systemic typology and topology. In F. Christie (ed.) *Literacy in Social Processes* 345–383. Darwin: Northern Territories University.

Matthiessen, C. (1992) Interpreting the textual metafunction. In M. Davies and L. Ravelli (eds) *Advances in Systemic Linguistics* 37–81. London: Pinter.

Metalude (Metaphor at Lingnan University Department of English) http://www. ln. edu.hk/lle/cwd03/lnproject_chi/home.html user id <user,>, password <edumet6>

Mills, S. (1995) *Feminist Stylistics*. London: Routledge.

Morris, D. (1971) *Intimate Behaviour*. London: Cape.

Neill, A, S. (1968) *Summerhill*. Harmondsworth: Penguin.

O'Brien, S. (1996) Serving a new world–order: postcolonial politics in Kazuo Ishiguro's *The Remains of the Day*. *Modern Fiction Studies* vol.42 no.4: 787–806.

O'Halloran, K. (2003) *Critical Discourse Analysis and Language Cognition*. Edinburgh: Edinburgh University Press.

Page, N. (1983) *A. E. Housman: a critical biography*. London: Macmillan.

Paprotte, W. and Dirven, R. (eds) 1985. *The Ubiquity of Metaphor*. Amsterdam: Benjamins.

Peacock, D. K. (1997) *Harold Pinter and the New British Theatre*. London, Westport Connecticut: Greenwood Press.

Pinter, H. (1968) *The Birthday Party and The Room*. New York: Grove Press.

Pratt, M. L. (1981) The ideology of speech act theory. *Centrum* (*New Series*) 1: 5–18.

Pratt, M. L. (1989) Conventions of representation: where discourse and ideology meet. In W. Van Peer (ed.) *The Taming of the Text* 15–34. London: Routledge.

Prigogine, I. and Stengers, I. (1985) *Order out of Chaos*. London: Flamingo.

Propp, V. (1968) *The Morphology of the Folk–tale*. Austin, Texas: University of Texas Press.

Quirk, R. and Greenbaum, S. (1973) *A University Grammar of English*. Harlow: Longman.

Raby, P. (ed.) (2001) *The Cambridge Companion to Harold Pinter*. Cambridge: Cambridge University Press.

Redpath, P. (1986) *William Golding: a structural reading of his fiction*. London: Barnes and Noble.

Ridley, M. (1997) *The Origins of Virtue*. Harmondsworth: Penguin.

Rifatterre, M. (1966) Describing poetic structures: two approaches to Baudelaire's « Les chats ». *Yale French Studies* 36/37: 200–242.

Ross, R.H. (1965) *The Georgian Revolt*. Carbondale: Southern Illinois University Press.

Rowling, J. K. (1997) *Harry Potter and the Philosopher's Stone*. London: Bloomsbury.

Sacks, H., Schegloff, E. A. and Jefferson, G. (1974) A simplest systematics for the organization of turn–taking in conversation. *Language* vol.50. no.4: 696–735.

Said, E. (1978) *Orientalism*. London and New York: Routledge.

Sarangi, S. and Slembrouck, S. (1992) Non–co–operation in communication: a re–assessment of Gricean pragmatics. *Journal of Pragmatics* 17: 117–153.

Schleiner, W. (1970) *The Imagery of John Donne's Sermons*. Providence: Brown University Press.

Searle, J. (1969) *Speech Acts*. Cambridge: Cambridge University Press.

Sell, R. (1991) *Literary Pragmatics*. London: Routledge.

Sherburne, D. W. (ed.) (1981) *A Key to Whitehead's Process and Reality*. Chicago: University of Chicago Press.

Short, M. (1996) *Exploring the Language of Poems Plays and Prose*. Harlow: Longman.

Short, M. (ed.) (1989) *Reading, Analysing and Teaching Literature*. Harlow: Longman.

Short, M. and Van Peer, W. (1989) Accident! Stylisticians evaluate: aims and methods of stylistic analysis. In M. Short (ed.) *Reading, Analysing and Teaching Literature* 22–71. Harlow: Longman.

Simpson, P. (1989) Phatic communion and fictional dialogue. In R. Carter and P. Simpson (eds) *Language, Discourse and Literature* 43–60. London: Unwin.

Simpson, P. (1993) *Language, Ideology and Point of View*. London: Routledge.

Sinclair, J. M. (1966) Taking a poem to pieces. In R. Fowler (ed.) *Essays on Style and Language* 68–81. London: Routledge.

Sinclair, J. M. (1989) Poetic discourse: a sample exercise. In W. Van Peer (ed.) *The Taming of the Text* 258–279. London: Routledge.

Skinner, B. F. (1971) *Beyond Freedom and Dignity*. Harmondsworth: Penguin.

Sloan, T. O. (1963) The rhetoric in the poetry of John Donne. *Studies in English Literature, 1500–1900, The English Renaissance* vol.3. no.1: 31–44.

Sperber, D. and Wilson, D. (1995) *Relevance: communication and cognition* (2nd edition). Oxford: Blackwell.

Spitzer, L. (1948) *Linguistics and Literary History*. Princeton, NJ: Princeton University Press.

Steiner, G. (1975) *After Babel*. Oxford: Oxford University Press.

Stubbs, M. (2001) Texts, corpora and problems of interpretation. *Applied Linguistics* vol.22 no.2: 149–172.

Talib, I. S. (2002) *The Language of Postcolonial Literatures*. London: Routledge.

Thomas, J. (1995) *Meaning in Interaction*. Harlow: Longman.

Tiger, V. (1974) *William Golding: the dark fields of discovery*. London: Caldar and Boyars.

Tiger, V. (2003) *William Golding: the unmoved target*. New York, London: Marion Boyars.

Toolan, M. (2001) *Narrative: a critical linguistic introduction* (2nd edition). London: Routledge.

Tuve, R. (1961) *Elizabethan and Metaphysical Imagery*. Chicago and London: University of Chicago Press.

Vendler, Z. (1968) *Adjectives and Nominalizations*. The Hague: Mouton.

Verdonk, P. (1991) Poems as text and discourse: the poetics of Philip Larkin. In R. Sell (ed.) *Literary Pragmatics* 94–109. London: Routledge.

Vickers, B. (1970) *Classical Rhetoric in English Poetry*. London: Macmillan.

Wall, K. (1994) 'The Remains of the Day' and its challenges to theories of unreliable narration. *Journal of Narrative Technique* vol.24: 18–42.

Wang, Ling (1991) Analysis of thematic variations in 'Buried Child'. Paper delivered at the 1st Biennial Conference on Discourse. Hangzhou, Peoples' Republic of China.

Wardle, I. (1958) Comedy of menace. *Encore* 15.5.3: 28–33.

Weinreich, H. (1958) Münze und Wort: Untersuchungen an einem Bildfeld. In H. Lausberg and H. Weinreich (eds) *Romanica: Festschrift für Gerhard Rohlfs*. Halle: M. Niemeyer.

Weinreich, H. (1963) Semantik der kühnen Metaphor. *Deutsche Viertlesjahrschrift für Literaturwissenschaft und Geistergeschichte* 37: 325–344.

Weinreich, H. (1966) *Linguistik der Lüge*. Heidelberg: L. Schneider.

Whitehead, L. M. (1988) The moment out of time: William Golding's 'Pincher Martin'. In J. R. Baker (ed.) *Critical Essays on William Golding* 41–60. Boston Massachusetts: G. K. Hall.

Whorf, B. L. (1956) *Language, Thought and Reality*. J. B. Carroll (ed.). Cambridge Mass.: MIT Press.

Widdowson, H. G. (1998) The theory and practice of critical discourse analysis. *Applied Linguistics* vol.19 no.1: 136–151.

Widdowson, H. G. (2000) On the limitations of linguistics applied. *Applied Linguistics* vol.21 no.1: 3–25.

Winner, E. (1988) *The Point of Words: children's understanding of metaphor and irony*. Cambridge, Mass.: Harvard University Press.

Winter, E. (1977) A clause–relational approach to English texts: a study of some predictive lexical items in written discourse. *Instructional Science* vol.6. no.1: 1–91.

Wolfson, N. (1988) The bulge: a theory of speech behaviour and social distance. In J. Fine (ed.) *Second Language Discourse: a textbook of current research* 21–38. Norwood, N.J.: Ablex.

Wong, C. (2005) *Kazuo Ishiguro* (2nd edition). Tavistock: Northcote House Publishers.

Xiao, Qun (1991) Toward thematic selection in different genres: fables and recipes. Unpublished manuscript.

Index

Index of metaphor themes

CPSIA information can be obtained
at www.ICGtesting.com
Printed in the USA
BVHW082153220219
540989BV00004B/47/P